LABOURING WOMEN

Labouring Women

Issues and Challenges in Contemporary India

Edited by

Praveen Jha
Avinash Kumar
Yamini Mishra

Orient BlackSwan

LABOURING WOMEN: ISSUES AND CHALLENGES IN CONTEMPORARY INDIA

ORIENT BLACKSWAN PRIVATE LIMITED

Registered Office
3-6-752 Himayatnagar, Hyderabad 500 029, Telangana, India
e-mail: centraloffice@orientblackswan.com

Other Offices
Bengaluru, Bhopal, Chennai, Guwahati,
Hyderabad, Jaipur, Kolkata, Lucknow, Mumbai,
New Delhi, Noida, Patna, Visakhapatnam

First published by Orient Blackswan Private Limited 2020

ISBN 978-93-90122-07-3

Typeset in
Adobe Jenson Pro 11/13
by Shine Graphics, Delhi 110 094

032401

Printed in India at
Akash Press, Delhi

Published by
Orient Blackswan Private Limited
3-6-752 Himayatnagar, Hyderabad 500 029, Telangana, India
e-mail: info@orientblackswan.com

Contents

Abbreviations

AIDWA	All-India Democratic Women's Association
ANM	Auxiliary nurse and midwife
ASHA	Accredited Social Health Activist
ASSOCHAM	Associated Chambers of Commerce and Industry of India
AWC	Anganwadi Centre
AWH	Anganwadi Helper
AWW	Anganwadi Worker
BE	Budget estimate
BRICS	Brazil, Russia, India, China and South Africa
BRICSAM	Brazil, Russia, India, China, South Africa and Mexico
CBGA	Centre of Budget Governance and Accountability
CGE	Computable general equilibrium
CISLS	Centre for Informal Sector and Labour Studies
CPR	Common property resources
CSO	Central Statistical Organisation
CSS	Centrally Sponsored Scheme
CWDS	Centre for Women's Development Studies
DAC	Department of Agriculture and Cooperation
DDS	Deccan Development Society
ESI	Employees' State Insurance
ETR	Effective taxation rate
FCA	Forest Conservation Act
FICCI	Federation of Indian Chambers of Commerce and Industry

FLFPR	Female labour force participation rate
FWPR	Female work participation rate
GBS	Gender Budget Statement
GDP	Gross domestic product
GI	Geographical Indication
GRB	Gender-responsive budgeting
HHMPCE	Household monthly per capita consumption expenditure
HUF	Hindu Undivided Family
ICAR	Indian Council of Agricultural Research
ICDS	Integrated Child Development Scheme
ICLS	International Conference of Labour Statisticians
ICT	Information and communication technologies
IETF	Internet Engineering Task Force
ILO	International Labour Organisation
IMF	International Monetary Fund
IPR	Intellectual Property Rights
ISNA	Indian System of National Accounts
ISOPOM	Integrated Scheme of Oilseeds, Pulses, Maize and Oilpalm
ISRO	Indian Space Research Organisation
ISST	Institute for Social Studies Trust
IT	Information technology
JFM	Joint Forest Management
JMS	Janwadi Mahila Samiti
JNU	Jawaharlal Nehru University
LAA	Land Acquisition Act
LFPR	Labour force participation rate
MGNREGA	Mahatma Gandhi National Rural Employment Guarantee Act
MIS	Management information system
MLFPR	Male labour force participation rate
MNC	Multinational corporation
MPCE	Monthly per capita expenditure
MRTP	Monopolies and Restrictive Trade Practices
NCR	National Capital Region

NGRCA	National Gender Resource Centre for Agriculture
NGO	Non-government organisation
NHM	National Health Mission
NMOOP	National Mission on Oilseeds and Oil Palm
NREGA	National Rural Employment Guarantee Act
NRHM	National Rural Health Mission
NRLM	National Rural Livelihood Mission
NSS	National Sample Survey
NSSO	National Sample Survey Office
NTFP	Non-timber forest products
OAW	Own-account workers
OBC	Other Backward Classes
OECD	Organisation for Economic Cooperation and Development
OOP	Out-of-pocket
PESAA	Panchayats (Extension to the Scheduled Areas) Act
PLFS	Periodic Labour Force Survey
R&D	Research and development
RCH	Reproductive and child health
SAP	Structural adjustment programme
SC	Scheduled Caste
SDG	Sustainable Development Goals
SEZ	Special Economic Zone
SHG	Self-help Group
SEWA	Self-employed Women's Association
SMSC	Stree Mukti Sangharsh Chalwal
SNA	System of National Accounts
SS	Usual Subsidiary Status
SSA	Sarva Shiksha Abhiyan
ST	Scheduled Tribe
TUS	Time-use survey
UN	United Nations
UNDP	United Nations Development Programme
UNRISD	United Nations Research Institute for Social Development

UN SNA	United Nations System of National Accounts
UPS	Usual Principal Status
UPSS	Usual Principal and Subsidiary Status
W3C	World Wide Web Consortium
WEF	World Economic Forum
WLPA	Wildlife Protection Act
WPR	Workforce participation rate
WTO	World Trade Organisation

Figures and Tables

Figures

Tables

Introduction

Praveen Jha, Avinash Kumar and *Yamini Mishra*

Contemporary debates on the place of women in the world of work in all developing countries, including India, confront serious academic challenges. Though the scholarly work of the last few decades has thrown some light on the relevant basic theoretical, conceptual and empirical issues, the overall terrain remains slippery and contentious. For instance, as was noted at the conclusion of what the United Nations had adopted as the Decade for Women during the Nairobi Conference in 1985, even though the importance of women's work in the overall world of labour was duly acknowledged, adequate enumeration of women workers in the national labour force statistics across the globe (particularly in developing countries) still remained a distant dream. Three decades down the road, in this respect, academics working on women workers in India would have a strong sense of *déjà vu*.

Seen in the context of larger macroeconomic and social trends, it appears that these adverse trends are part of a larger context characterised by a scenario where growth trends have little relationship with the wellbeing of the mass of the working population. For women, the disassociation between growth and growing informalisation of work is perhaps even more adverse as distress conditions produce longer working hours and a higher reliance on unpaid work. This is evident in the recent trends which show that the gender gaps in paid work have only narrowed slightly in the developed countries, whereas these have increased in 'emerging economies' like India; in developing countries in general, there are no signs of the gaps, in part due to the concentration of women in 'distress' employment. As per the International Labour Organisation's (ILO 2018) recent estimates, the proportion of women likely to be in vulnerable employment tends to be higher. This obviously implies that both women's burden and drudgery are increasing in this neo-liberal world, not least because of the strengthening of conservative patriarchal institutions.

The increasing vulnerable situation of India's women, particularly of its women workers, is confirmed by the Global Gender Gap Report published by the World Economic Forum (WEF) in 2017. The report looks at four components—economic participation, educational attainment, health status and political empowerment. In three of these four indicators, India ranks in the bottom half of the table. For example, in terms of economic empowerment for women, India ranked 139 out of 144 countries, and in terms of health and survival, it ranked 141 out of 144 countries. Even in educational attainment, a factor hyped by the government as a major achievement, the country only ranked 112 out of 144 countries. The only indicator where it ranked in the top-20 was political empowerment. Because of this, the overall position of India improved slightly, but the country still ranked a poor 108 amongst 144 nations as far as gender gap was concerned (World Economic Forum 2017: 11).

The macro-trends hinted at here have been interpreted by scholars and activists in multiple ways and through diverse theoretical perspectives. But there are common themes of discussion, some of which are briefly stated here. The first major focus of research and debate has been the relationship between capitalism and patriarchy, with particular reference to the transformations within the class structure and production relations in the macroeconomic context. Impact of technological changes on labour processes and the impact of changing methods of appropriation of surplus value constitute important aspects in the contemporary debates. Second, there are methodological issues which concern the 'value of women's unpaid labour' and its relationship with respect to processes of social reproduction and the political economy of care. Here the role and status of the family in the capitalist order is of utmost importance. The third important theme dwells on the impact of persistent informality and the participation of women in the labour market with focus on the question of the feminisation of the labour force and poverty in a neo-liberal world. A fourth overarching theme concerns the relationship between custom, law and the division of labour. The impact of the State-aided corporate acquisition of private and common property resources affects the position of women adversely, especially since families are dispossessed and rely more on the unpaid labour of women for their subsistence. Fifth, a large strand of scholarship deals with the important issue of the transformation of the State and public policy, especially with significant compression in the share of social sector spending. This is not an exhaustive list; it only indicates some important aspects of the contemporary concerns of scholars and activists with respect to women's work, and also constitutes important elements of the contemporary women's movement across the world.

The present volume addresses some aspects of the issues and challenges just outlined. It is the outcome of an engagement with the issues of women, work and resources at an international conference organised by the Centre for Informal Sector and Labour Studies (CISLS) in the School of Social Sciences, Jawaharlal Nehru University (JNU), in association with United Nations (UN) Women. The volume makes an attempt to understand the methodological and conceptual issues regarding women's work, and enquire and assess their position and condition of work at the contemporary juncture. It argues that despite policy reforms and rhetoric of equality, experiences show that challenges faced by labouring women have hardly diminished both at work and at home. The volume contextualises these themes within the contemporary debates, including debates on land use and rights over nature, the links between paid and unpaid labour, and concepts of free and unfree labour, etc. The 12 essays in this book, which also represent diverse perspectives on these themes, may be broadly categorised as speaking to the following broad areas.

Women's Question and the Labour Question

One of the major concerns of this volume revolves around the different facets of the interface between the women's question and the labour question. Traditionally speaking, liberal feminists have treated the problem in terms of the 'emancipation of women' from political and social discrimination that manifests itself in the patriarchal structures in different institutional and communitarian forms. In such liberal discourses, a primacy was given to achieving political and social equality (Donner 1993), and there was little emphasis on redistribution of material resources as a way of addressing the concerns of women's emancipation. In other words, such a liberal view did not focus on the links between the reorganisation of the labour process and women's emancipation till the Second World War. However, after this there was a broadening of the terrain with the advent of the Welfare State, which was supposed to recognise the value of women's work. But feminists of the time argued that the impact of social policies and welfare remained limited because the distribution of benefits was influenced and mediated by patriarchal social institutions and cultural values (MacKinnon 1989; Nussbaum 1997). Like its predecessor, this analysis also gave more importance to social institutions and placed lesser emphasis on the material reality. Some elements of these arguments are captured in different essays in this volume. Mary John (Chapter 1) raises the question whether the labour theory of value applies at all, or is it 'the stigma theory' of work that should be used as a theoretical framework. Vinoj Abraham (Chapter 3) attributes the declining participation of women in the labour market to patriarchal norms, thus privileging cultural factors more than other macroeconomic factors.

However, as is well known, Russian and German socialist feminists like Alexandra Kollontai (Kollontai and Menon 2017) and Clara Zetkin (1934) framed their discourses very differently as compared to the 'liberal feminists', and focused on the issue of the 'value' in women's work in terms of its reproductive labour and social reproduction of labour power. For them, the relationship between an existing mode of production and the position of women was central to the understanding of the processes of exploitation. In other words, patriarchal oppression was linked to the class structure that formed the core of the labour process in capitalist systems. In this sense, the women's question could not be disassociated from the labour question under capitalism. Hence, the emancipatory project of the women's movement had to be linked to struggles for freedom from capitalist exploitation. Such perspectives apply the labour theory of value to women's work in a more classical sense. Jayati Ghosh's essay (Chapter 2) shows that value is extracted from the woman in terms of the extraction of social time. Thus, 'time poverty' is in fact crucial to the understanding of the extraction of absolute surplus value through the extension of the working day of all women. This analysis is very much in line with the work of Peter Custers and Silvia Federici on the nature of capitalist accumulation from women's paid (Custers 2014) and reproductive labour (Federici 2004).

Despite the disagreements between the aforementioned different ideological strands of women's scholarship, it is now well accepted that the concepts of 'work' and 'value' have expanded to assess the full significance of women's labour in the processes of reproduction of capitalism (both in terms of the generation of surplus value and social reproduction) (Vogel 2013). It is also well acknowledged that forms of social reproduction are diverse in nature and are not identical; rather, they are impacted by the influence of social institutions, norms and cultural cognition (Bhattacharya 2017).

Methodological Issues in Measuring Women's Work

These diverse perspectives on the relationship between the cultural and the material terrains in discussing the place of women in the world of work also have a bearing on the way in which women's labour is accounted for and what parameters are used to assess its value. It is well acknowledged that the prevalent notions of work and employment in our official data systems continue to undermine women's work. There are troubling conceptual and empirical challenges with respect to recognition and measurement of a great deal of women's invisible work and typical distinctions such as those between work and leisure, economic and non-economic activities, market and non-market labour, paid and unpaid work, productive and unproductive labour (Antonopoulos and Hiraway 2010). It is obvious that conventional economic frameworks, which use market standards to assess work and build up large data systems, have ignored the question of unpaid household work in the datasets of the early post-Independence years. As shown by Ghosh (Chapter 2), the pre-1993–94 datasets defined work as 'gainful' activity and therefore included only paid work. The change from this definition to that of work as an 'economic activity' opened up the space for considering at least some of the diverse forms of unpaid work. Abraham (Chapter 3) shows that even the current classification (code 93) does not take the variety of care activities into account and only covers a negligible portion of the range of tasks performed by women. This argument is further extended by Neetha N. (Chapter 5), who contends that the invisibility of women's work is often subsumed in the category of 'self-employed', where both paid and unpaid work are lumped together. In terms of interpretation, this often leads to overestimating paid work and underestimating unpaid work. The category of the 'self employed' is also unpacked by Nisha Srivastava and Anjor Bhaskar (Chapter 8), where they explore the diverse aspects of rural women's unpaid work.

Methodological issues in the study of the world of women's work are, however, not confined to the critiques of large-scale datasets. Scholars also point out that the process of research can provide women with a platform to represent themselves and therefore give women 'a voice'. The merits of the 'subjective' factor and method have been well debated in the scholarship within this interdisciplinary field of study (Kannabiran and Swaminathan 2017). The preference for methods such as life histories, case studies and ethnographies has also been justified as a political act of providing an opportunity to women to self-represent themselves and thereby unpack the 'intersectionality' between different factors like caste, class and ethnicity. However, the larger question of the relationship between the objective material reality and the subjective consciousness remains a valid and an open question even now. This volume makes some progress towards showing the ways of tackling this problem, particularly in the essays by Mary John (Chapter 1) and Ritu Dewan (Chapter 7). The contextualisation of the 'peasant woman's experience' within the larger picture of materialist transformation is also done by Sumi Krishna (Chapter 10) in her discussion on common property resources. The methods employed by these essays highlight the need for further research that makes more complex relations between experience and the objective material reality, that is capitalism in the present context.

Interlinkages between Paid and Unpaid Work

The problems of method discussed here have highlighted the need to explore the links between 'paid' and 'unpaid' work which have, in the past, attracted the work of several scholars. The consideration of these interlinks also raises issues of what type of social reproduction is required to sustain capitalism. Contemporary theory has made some advances in this direction by highlighting the relationship between the reproduction of labour power and the accumulation process (Bhattacharya 2017; Vogel 2013). This volume also addresses several aspects of the concerns arising out of such scholarship. The theoretical problematic of 'domesticity' clearly emerges as a common theme in this volume (Federici 2004; Ray and Qayum 2009). For example, Abraham (Chapter 3) clearly outlines the hierarchy and power relations within the family as his main analytical framework. At the same time, Neetha (Chapter 5), and Archana Prasad and S. Krithi (Chapter 6) explore the different aspects associated with the embeddedness of the household within the larger economy and within the processes of accumulation. Within this framework, the household is clearly a site for the penetration of capital and is integrated into the labour markets through paid domestic work.

The need to develop this linkage highlights the importance of studying the way paid and unpaid work is organised, both socially and through the production process (Basu 2005). The institutional aspects of this organisation related to the way in which customs are codified (for example, the taxation system and its links with the Hindu Undivided Family) are noted by Chirashree Das Gupta, Isha Ralli and Mohit Gupta (Chapter 4). Such institutionalisation structures the process of the recognition of work and workers. Neetha (Chapter 5) also discusses how macroeconomic factors influence forms of patriarchy and cultural attitudes. This process of structuring the link between paid and unpaid work clearly shows that the household and its socio-cultural forms are not 'autonomous' and are impacted by structural and macroeconomic transformations (Ghosh 2009).

Private Property, the Commons and Structural Changes

The power relations that influence the relationship between paid and unpaid work are deeply structured by rules of property ownership and inheritance. The transformations that occur as a result of the changes in ownership and control over land can influence the power relations within the family, as well as the status of women in the society. It is therefore argued by some that land titles for women will play an important role in their emancipation (Agarwal 1994) as rights over inheritance structure the character of patriarchal oppression (see Chapter 4). However, this proposition has come under the critical scrutiny of both scholars and activists who contend that land is a crucial factor for a particular class of women farmers (Basu 2005) and land titles will not have a universal impact on the 'empowerment of women' (Agnihotri 1996). This proposition is confirmed by some of the essays in this volume which argue that livelihoods and land rights have to be seen in a more holistic fashion. It is argued by both Krishna (Chapter 10) and Smita Gupta (Chapter 11) that the land question needs to be broadened to include common property resources. As Krishna states, since the 1970s women have been at the centre of the discourse on rights over common property resources and therefore any consideration of sustainable livelihoods for them has to rethink the whole concept of the 'agrarian' and of 'development' itself. On the other hand, Gupta contends that the women's movement has to redefine the relationship of women with land by taking the 'commons' into account.

However, the 'commons' is not only relevant for rural India as new forms of ownership and property has been created under contemporary capitalism. These include ownership of technology, access to knowledge and its privatisation, and the use of these by corporations for making super profits. The privatisation of 'digital commons' and the structural changes within the service sector through the use of information technology have had a transformational impact on the daily life of workers, particularly for women. The emergence of 'digital taylorism' has been studied by scholars like Christian Fuchs (2014) and Ursula Huws (2014). In line with this scholarship,

Anita Gurumurthy (Chapter 12) highlights the question of women's 'autonomy and agency' in the context of the ongoing changes in the 'digital commons'. The author concludes that the rebuilding of 'digital commons' is an essential part of the emancipatory project of the women's movement. This contribution helps to widen the debate on the new forms of resistance that the women's movement needs to evolve if it is to combat the acquisition of both physical as well as digital commons, a process which results in the dispossession of women and impacts their status in the world of work.

Employment Trends and the Feminisation Debate

The factors detailed in this discussion reveal themselves in declining trends in female labour force participation rates (FLFPR) since the 1980s due to the changes in the overall macroeconomic policy regime from the *dirigiste* to the neo-liberal era. The structural changes brought about in the latter era have led to a significant decline in the formal employment, and contributed to the already overwhelming informality which may have impacted the world of women's work even more adversely. As is well known, apart from a host of critical concerns with respect to the informal, even the elementary issue of enumeration trends, women continue to be overrepresented in casual work and self-employment in the National Sample Survey (NSS) data (Papola 2013). Not only are their wages lower than their male counterparts, but their conditions of work are also relatively more vulnerable in nature. Thus, even basic minimum needs such as availability of maternity leave and childcare benefits are out of their purview. This disincentivises women to seek work outside the home. Subsequently, it has been witnessed (from the analysis of NSS data) that in the total share of home-based workers, which constitute a significant share (15.2 per cent) of the total non-agricultural workforce in India, the share of women is one third (31.7 per cent) of all females employed in non-agricultural work in 2011–12, compared to 11 per cent of males (Dasgupta and Verick 2016; Raveendran et al. 2013).

Women are concentrated in sectors such as *beedi* work, apparel and crafts industries, assembling or packaging of electronics, automobile parts and pharmaceutical products, which are remunerated on a piece-rate basis. With the rise of the service sector and global value chains, studies have shown that women's growing participation is low wage with unacceptable conditions of work, especially in the growing market for care work (Ghosh 2009; Mazumdar 2007). With gender-biased definition and methods (as mentioned earlier), it is not surprising that studies based on official data have identified a declining trend in FLFPR in paid 'work' as one of the distinguishing features of the Indian labour market (Mazumdar and Neetha 2011). The FLFPR had declined from 23.7 per cent in 1993–94 to 18.1 per cent in 2011–12 for the rural areas and it had been stagnant at around 13–14 per cent in the urban areas during the same period. With the secular official decline in FLFPR, it is becoming more evident that the most dominant activity that females are now engaged in is either in unpaid self-employed or domestic duties (Ghosh 2009). Among those employed, the data suggests that women are highly concentrated and overrepresented in casual work and unpaid self-employment (Papola 2013). The marginal improvement of share of women in regular employment (from 6.4 per cent in 1993–94 to 11 per cent in 2009–10) in the official dataset is largely in domestic low-paid work (Mazumdar and Neetha 2011). Thus, despite the recognition of gender equality in law, the progress towards gender equality in outcomes in the labour market remains quite insignificant. There exists a whole range of dense, diverse and often overlapping categories of exclusion of women, particularly from the marginalised groups, from just conditions of work in socially devalued, stigmatised and hazardous occupations (Anon 2015).

These conditions of work are in stark contradiction with the international norms which are set for equal rights at the workplace. The ILO as early as in 1951 adopted the Equal Remuneration Convention [popularly known as ILO Convention 100 (C100)] with regard to the principle of equal remuneration for men and women workers for work of equal value. Similarly, Convention 111 (C111) laid out principles for covering both equality of opportunity, in terms of access to labour markets and labour market-related enhancements such as training and social protection, and equality of treatment, in terms of non-discriminatory remuneration and conditions of work. All this finally led to the adoption of the 1998 Declaration of Fundamental Principles and the Right to Work with four core labour standards by the ILO. India, despite being a staunch supporter of this process, however, allows the practice of several forms of discrimination and vulnerability in work conditions in general and as it regards women workforce in particular (Srivastava 2016).

In this context, the feminisation of work has to be seen in a holistic manner as pointed out by several essays in this volume. The first obvious trend is the lack of paid employment in the labour market as pointed out by Srivastava and Bhaskar (Chapter 8) which influences the increase in unpaid women's work in agriculture. This trend is also evident in the essay by Neetha which shows that unpaid work in self-employment is largely done by women and that there is no decline in women's labour force participation if unpaid and paid work are counted together. Hence as Ghosh discusses (Chapter 2), the drudgery of women's work has to be considered in that context. Second, the persistent informality with respect to women's work ensures that most women are concentrated in low-paid work which is invisible in large datasets. Hence even though code 93 exists, the number of workers, as Abraham suggests (Chapter 3) is highly underestimated. Further, the question of informality cannot be merely confined to the question of visibility, but must denote a certain set of labour relations that structures the deteriorating position of women. This form of labour has undergone worthwhile changes and temporal shifts for women workers while locating these in the larger trajectory of occupational transformation in India as pointed out by Das Gupta, Ralli and Gupta (Chapter 4), among others.

From the foregoing discussion it is quite evident that the question of the feminisation of work is a complex one, and can only be grasped within the complex framework of the interplay between different forms of paid and unpaid labour on the one hand, and the policy and institutional frameworks that regulate this work on the other. That women form a bulk of the workforce that contributes to the economy is well established by the essays in this volume; but it is also acknowledged that the macroeconomic large-scale datasets which have been considered by the authors do not show this because they only consider paid work in the calculation of labour force participation rates (LFPR). The essays here demystify this and take a considered view of the feminisation debate.

Need for Universal Social Protection

Public interventions and policies towards facilitating decent work, social security provisions, etc., have seen marked shifts, in general, in the neo-liberal era. It would be helpful to unpack the story for India's women workers in a comparative framework in the context of questions of market discrimination in recruitment and patriarchal norms and authority that structure the division of labour within and outside the home. Apart from the disparity between men and women's ability to bargain for their choice of work outside home, women, due to the complex relationship between patriarchy, caste and class, are usually found working in unjust conditions. For example, in India, about 93 per cent of the women workers work under conditions of informality without any social protection. The ILO flagship report on World Social Protection (2017) illustrates that only 29 per cent of the world's population receives social protection. One of the reasons for such under-protection is the inadequate investment in social protection policies, especially in countries of Asia, Africa and the Arab States. The standard for social protection is set by a series of social security conventions which provide maternity benefits, benefits for children, unemployment allowances, old age pension and other provisions under Conventions 103, 118 and 130. Of these, India has only ratified Convention 118 for providing maternity benefits, where about 41 per cent of the mothers are said to be covered by maternity benefits. But in overall terms, only 19 per cent of the population of the country is covered by at least one scheme of social protection (ibid.: 235, 244). Along with this, the share of public expenditure on social security remained a meager 0.53 per cent of the total expenditure and 0.07 per cent of the gross domestic product (Centre of Budget Governance and Accountability 2018).

This declining trend in social security expenditure is also accompanied by reforms that will limit social security coverage. Recent analysis suggests that the current proposed code on social security will truncate the infrastructure needed to provide universal social security.

The essay by Kanika Kaul and Saumya Shrivastava (Chapter 9) has to be seen in this context, where the design and nature of social security schemes is itself problematic. The authors make a forceful case for gender-responsive budgeting in the context of overall fiscal policy and highlight the challenges that arise with the informalisation of government services.

The Challenges before Women's Movement

Overall, this volume has to be seen in the context of the rising demands for decent work and the recognition of women as 'workers'. The lack of focus of public policy on this aspect has given birth to a range of trade union and women's organisations, which are pushing the concept of 'emancipation' beyond the limited statist notion of 'empowerment'. The concept of 'empowerment' is critiqued by the women's movement because it assumes that someone gives women the power to change. However, struggles have demonstrated that the organisation of women is essential for a change in consciousness to recognise multiple forms of oppression and deprivation. This self-recognition is the first step towards a meaningful struggle against multiple forms of discrimination faced by women, not least because of caste, class and patriarchy. The complex interplay of these factors influences and is essential for understanding the diverse nature of women's struggles against their collective subordination and exploitation.

Some common challenges and trends within the diverse women's movement must be noted in this context and also within this volume. First, the reversal of the 'social reform' project of the dirigiste era has only intensified the process of discrimination. Therefore, the advocates of women's rights are compelled to be strong critics of neo-liberalism also. The essays in this volume also have this common ideological thread. Second, the contributors of this volume support the demand by women's and workers organisations for universal social security for informal sector workers. This ongoing struggle has to be seen in the context of the changing nature of the State and the acceleration of uneven development that has a differential impact on women according to their social groups and class positions. Several essays in this volume show that growing informality poses a grave threat to the future of building a strong movement of women workers. Third, one of the main demands of the women's movement is recognition of land rights over private and common property to break the patriarchal stranglehold over productive resources. Corporate acquisition of both private and common property and its use significantly impacts the status and wellbeing of women, especially with respect to their unpaid work. However, as this volume shows, the question of property cannot merely be confined to rural areas. Rather, sustainable livelihoods and decent work demand that the women's movement adapts itself to the changing forms of capital and assess its impact on women at the current conjuncture.

References

Agarwal, B. 1994. *A Field of One's Own: Gender and Land Rights in South Asia*. Cambridge: Cambridge University Press.

Agnihotri, I. 1996. 'Bringing Land Rights Centrestage'. *Economic and Political Weekly* 31 (9): 526–28.

Anon. 2015. *India Exclusion Report*. Delhi: Yoda Press.

Antonopoulos, R., and I. Hiraway. 2010. *Unpaid Work and the Economy: Gender, Time Use and Poverty in Developing Countries*. New York: Palgrave Macmillan.

Basu, S. 2005. *Dowry and Inheritance*. Delhi: Women Unlimited.

Bhattacharya, T. 2017. *Social Reproduction Theory: Remapping Class, Recentring Oppression*. London: Pluto Press.

Centre of Budget Governance and Accountability. 2018. *Of Hits and Misses: An Analysis of the Budget 2018–19*. Delhi: CBGA.

Custers, P. 2014 [1995]. *Capital Accumulation and Women's Labour in Asian Economies*. Delhi: Aakar Books.

Dasgupta, S., and S. Verick. 2016. *Transformation of Women's Work in Asia: An Unfinished Agenda*. Delhi: Sage Publications and International Labour Organisation.

Donner, W. 1993. 'John Stuart Mill's Liberal Feminism'. *Philosophical Studies* 69: 155–66.

Federici, S. 2004. *Caliban and the Witch: Women, The Body and Primitive Accumulation*. New York: Autonomedia.

Fuchs, C. 2014. *Digital Labour and Karl Marx*. New York: Routledge.

Ghosh, J. 2009. *Never Done and Poorly Paid: Women's Work in Globalising India*. Delhi: Women Unlimited.

Huws, U. 2014. *Labor in Digital Economy: The Cybertariat Comes of Age.* New York: Monthly Review Press.

International Labour Organisation. 2017. *World Social Protection Report.* Geneva: ILO.

———. 2018. *World Employment and Social Outlook: Trends for Women, 2018.* Geneva: ILO.

Kannabiran, K., and P. Swaminathan, eds. 2017. *Re-presenting Feminist Methodologies: Interdisciplinary Explorations.* London: Routledge.

Kollontai, A., and P. Menon. 2017. *The Soviet Woman and Other Essays.* Delhi: Leftword.

MacKinnon, C. 1989. *Towards a Feminist Theory of the State.* Cambridge: Harvard University Press.

Mazumdar, I. 2007. *Women Workers and Globalisation: Emergent Contradictions in India.* Delhi: Stree and Samya Books.

Mazumdar, I., and Neetha N. 2011. 'Gender Dimensions: Employment Trends in India'. *Economic and Political Weekly* 46 (43): 1949–65.

Nussbaum, M. 1997. *The Feminist Critique of Liberalism: The Lindsay Lecture.* Kansas: Kansas University Press.

Papola, T. 2013. *Role of Labour Regulation and Reforms in India: Case Study of Labour Market Segmentation. Working Paper No. 147.* Geneva: ILO Employment.

Raveendran, G., R. Sudarshan and J. Vanek. 2013. *Home-based Workers in India: Statistics and Trends.* WEIGO.

Ray, R., and S. Qayum. 2009. *Cultures of Servitude: Domesticity and Class in India.* Stanford: Stanford University Press.

Srivastava, R. 2016. *Structural Change and Non-standard Forms of Employment in India.* Geneva: ILO.

Vogel, L. 2013. *Marxism and the Oppression of Women: Towards a Unitary Theory.* London: Brill.

World Economic Forum. 2017. *The Global Gender Gap Report.* Geneva: WEF.

Zetkin, C. 1934. *Lenin on the Women Question.* New York: International Publishers.

1

Women's Labour through Life Narratives

*Mary E. John**

What makes all the work that women do in a country like India elude worth and value? Why has more than a century of struggle yielded so little on this front? With the help of a small selection of pioneering autobiographies written by women from the late nineteenth century into the first decade of the twenty-first, I hope to shed some light on the theoretical and political challenge of women's labour in our context, which is as persistent as it is confounding.

The problem is not one of absence or loss; women's labour has by no means fallen off the agendas of activists and academics. However, even though they are expanding, current interests suffer from a remarkable degree of ideological, disciplinary and thematic compartmentalisation. Thus, we have a wide range of well-established and emerging fields such as labour history and its engendering; the macro-analysis of women's labour participation rates in different sectors of the economy; women's role in subsistence economies;

* An earlier and longer version of this essay appeared in 2013 as 'The Problem of Women's Labour: Some Autobiographical Perspectives', *Indian Journal of Gender Studies* 20 (2): 177–212. I thank the organisers of the conference at Jawaharlal Nehru University, Praveen Jha, Avinash Kumar and Yamini Mishra for inviting me to present a version of this essay and including it in this volume.

transnational studies around the care economy examining women's paid and unpaid care work; domestic workers and their struggles; sex work and debates around prostitution and trafficking; anthropologies of marriage and kinship; recent caste-based approaches to discrimination and exclusion in labour markets; Dalit women's movements; and queer critiques of sexuality and marriage. And yet, despite the significance of this enormous body of work, the interconnected yet conflicting characteristics of women's labour—unpaid and paid, domestic and public, structured as much by caste and sexuality as by class—are not sufficiently highlighted.

Given such a situation of multiple yet disconnected investigations into women's labour, it is surely odd to be bringing in the lens of life stories. After all, what could be more singular than writing a woman's life?[1] My strategy in these preliminary explorations is twofold. The first part of the essay will attempt to identify some of the sources of the problem and why a more multivalent analysis has proved so elusive in the Indian context in particular. As we shall see, contradictions abound once an effort is made to bring a range of interpretations to bear on the labouring bodies of women. Second, I am interested in exploring what we can learn about the place and value of labour imposed upon very different women, from the kinds of conflicts and problems they articulate and find worth telling. It is precisely the disparate ways in which women in changing historical and social contexts have reflected on labour in the course of writing more generally about themselves, their experiences and their worlds that interests me here. To guard against misunderstanding, I am certainly not interested in privileging women's voices as necessarily more authentic in comparison to all the historical investigations, ethnographic accounts and statistical analyses available. Rather, it is simply to see what questions are asked or not asked, and what answers are offered in the retelling of life itself, and how such a perspective might complement existing concerns. The texts I have chosen are Rashsundari Debi's *Amar Jiban* (*My Life*, partially translated in the volume *Words to Win* by Tanika Sarkar), Binodini Dasi's *Amar Katha* (*My Story and My Life as an Actress*, translated by Rimli Bhattacharya), Baby Kamble's *Jina Amucha* (translated as *The Prisons We Broke* by Maya Pandit), Baby Haldar's *Aalo Andhari* (translated as *A Life Less Ordinary* by Urvashi Butalia), and Nalini Jameela's *Njan Laingikatozhilali* (translated as *the Autobiography of a Sex Worker* by J. Devika).

These texts, in a sense, chose themselves because they spanned the period of the late-nineteenth century to the end of the twentieth century and could all be called the first of their kind. Rashsundari Debi's *Amar Jiban* is the first known autobiography of a woman and has been celebrated as such, even if subsequent scholarship might in fact yield new and earlier names such as Savitribai Phule. Binodini Dasi's autobiographical texts are the first of a woman who lived the life of a professional actress in the early twentieth century. Baby Kamble's belatedly discovered testimonial is the first known writing by a Dalit woman. Baby Haldar is the first domestic worker to write her story and Nalini Jameela is another first to put down her life as a self-described sex worker. Between them they span the regions of Bengal, Maharashtra, Delhi and Kerala—so there can be no question that this is in any way representative regionally. How much can be generalised based on such a sample? I would not venture to say, but given their range in place and time, they certainly deserve to be taken seriously.

Some Theoretical Considerations

Let me outline the problem as I see it, beginning with the findings of those who have analysed women's work within the Indian economy as a whole and so provided an effective framework for contemporary and historical analysis. One of the early shocking discoveries that went into *Towards Equality: Report of the Committee on the Status of Women in India* of 1974 (Sharma and Sujaya 2012) was the long-term decline in women's participation revealed over successive censuses from the beginning of the twentieth century, a decline that could not be put down to colonial policies alone but even continued after Independence. A couple of decades later, in the wake of the famous 'feminisation' thesis put forward by Guy Standing (1989), which looked at global data from across the world to claim that the flexible workplace after structural adjustment now preferred women to men, most feminists examining Indian trends refuted such processes here.[2] The only signs of feminisation during the 1990s till 2005 seemed to be in agriculture, a sector where the largest proportion of women workers (mainly unpaid family cultivators and wage workers) were already to be found, and therefore hardly the site from which an argument about the positive effects of the new global economy could be made. Moreover, following 2005, statistical sources have pointed to disturbing declines in women's work participation rates, most markedly in manufacturing. As Nirmala Banerjee (1997) pointed out, the whole question of 'feminisation' needs a much more nuanced analysis, especially in countries like India, where it is necessary to contextualise the initial position of women in relation to their possible entry into the labour market, both in relation to larger economic trends as well as micro-level experiences in select sectors.[3]

Since the 1970s, the burden of many scholars and activists in India has been to show that our data sets are fundamentally misleading—women are indeed engaged in productive economic work of all kinds, but our accounting systems are unable to capture and measure this. Efforts to improve the situation led to important changes, for instance in Census enumeration after 1991, as well as in expanding definitions of women's unpaid work in the NSSs after the 1980s.[4] But this does not take away from the huge gap that is recorded between men and women in our workforces, especially in urban areas. After all is said and done, not to put too fine a point on it, we have one of the lowest female work participation rates in the world. When it comes to recent trends, some speak of an overall stagnation in women's work, others notice levels of volatility, oscillating nonetheless around a very low average. Indrani Mazumdar and Neetha N. have recently made an important intervention in current debates by distinguishing between trends in women's paid and unpaid work. The figure they put out, based on analysis of NSS data (64th Round 2007–08) for women's overall paid work is as low as 15 per cent (Mazumdar and Neetha 2011). By way of clarification, what this means is that only 15 per cent of all women in India receive a direct payment as self-employed, through a wage or salary, whether in the so-called formal sector or the informal sector, whether working as home workers in a putting-out system, in factories, in fields, as domestic workers or in the service sector. In other words, no one beyond this figure receives remuneration for the work that they do. Notice that the period of their analysis coincides with a time when India has witnessed the highest growth rates in its economy, and where a certain commonsense would have us believe that we live in a time of unprecedented job opportunities. But what the data in fact says is that the contemporary economic regime is one where 85 per cent of all women, however long and hard many of them may be working—at home, on family farms, in various artisanal or other productive contexts—are effectively living in relations of dependency, fundamentally attached to households, since they are engaging in some form or other of unpaid family labour. These relations of dependency, while initially those of a daughter, are subsequently invariably structured by marriage. And from what we know about the lack of any effective implementation of property rights for those with land, assets or other forms of capital (implying, in other words, the negligible presence of women as employers), this means registering the enormity of such dependency and its wider ramifications for any discussion of women's work and chances for autonomy in India. This leads to my first point in an analytical account of women's labour in our context: the centrality of the household and of the family within it (which are by no means coterminus, as we shall see).

It is commonplace to list the range of work that is constitutive of the core of domestic labour—food preparation, cleaning, childcare, house maintenance. Notice that this list omits sexual services, a point I will come back to later. In a pioneering essay on the materiality and ideologies of domestic life, Kumkum Sangari (1993: 4–5) has drawn on the thesis of Colette Guillaumin that 'unpaid household labour is given the framework of lasting personal relationships which are not and cannot be measured in terms of time and money ... hence that patriarchies build personal relationships into exploitation, operate inside the spheres of relationships of love, nurture and sexuality, are indeed inseparable from them'. Sangari goes on to speculate whether this is the source of ideologies of selfless devotion in contexts like ours, which render this domain as non-alienated labour by daughters, wives, mothers, daughters-in-law. After considering the narratives in the next section we will have an occasion to re-examine this thesis in the light of women's own accounts from the nineteenth century to the present day.

Prominent analyses in India, when trying to conceptualise women's work, have drawn from both feminist and Marxist traditions of understanding labour, where labour represents value, and women's low status was seen to be a consequence of their lack of acknowledged economic participation. Considerable effort and much debate have gone into contesting conceptions of productive and non-productive labour. Given the low levels of women's presence in the workforce overall and the even lower proportions of those women who are paid for their labour, broadly two kinds of arguments have been forthcoming: the first, which I have already touched upon, involved making women's labour more visible, giving it value by attempts to measure it, especially domestic and family labour. The second consisted in demanding an increasing share for women in labour markets that were turning out to be increasingly masculinist. Contrasts have been drawn between north and south India, for instance, arguing that the lower work participation rates in the north made for more gender inequality, especially towards daughters.

However, this is where we already come up against a problem. A feminist analysis, even of a Marxist-feminist kind that only looks at the gendered division of labour within the domestic sphere and women's chances for paid work in the labour market beyond it, is flawed. Even when differences of caste and class are acknowledged, these become secondary to the main effort of highlighting the working of patriarchal biases. Over and over again, in a range of studies, the main focus is to question the perception of women as non-workers, at best supplementary or contingent, whether they be poor or educationally highly qualified.[5]

Borrowing the concept of intersectionality may be helpful here. Though the explicit use of the term comes from the work of Kimberle Crenshaw, the idea it draws from goes back to the first Black feminist organisations of the 1970s, such as the Combahee River Collective. Their statement described the simultaneity of oppressions experienced by black women in American capitalism, and the need for an 'identity politics' precisely because of ways in which those at the 'bottom' or at the 'intersections' of gender, class, race and sexuality were getting lost (Combahee River Collective 1979). 'All the women are white, all the blacks are men, but some of us are brave' was the title of a Black women's studies text of that time, which nicely captures the problem of intersectionality (Hull et al. 1982). In other words, if we go back to the conceptual underpinnings of identity politics, its purpose was never to prioritise a particular identity (such as Black women) against other structures (such as capitalism), but rather to recognise what constitutive mechanisms (such as race) were disappearing at the intersections. In the context of my discussions here, it is the determinations of caste, class and sexuality sustaining the domestic sphere which are in danger of getting lost. This is not to diminish the gender dimensions of domestic relations, given the ongoing naturalisation of the sexual division of labour, but only to say that feminists need to do more than to render this dimension more visible. To put it differently, those at the margins or 'bottom' of hierarchies of caste and sexuality, inhabit extremely fragile domestic spaces and are invariably rendered invisible in the reproduction of the domestic spheres of those in positions of relative privilege.

Labour as Stigma

Bringing in questions of caste raises some fundamental questions for a Marxist-feminist approach to theorising women's labour.[6] To put it at its sharpest, a labour theory of value stands in conflict with a caste-structured society wherein public labour represents stigma and humiliation. In her suggestive discussion of the problems B. R. Ambedkar and the Dalit theorists have encountered in relating caste to class, Anupama Rao (2012) argues that the experience of labour as degradation and not just exploitation has profound implications since stigma cannot be valorised like value-producing labour. This is because stigma cannot be abstracted from the body. I would want to add that this is also because the body is always 'sexed'. If there is a distinctive quality to the degradations of (male) Dalit labour, this quality attains a new register when the labouring body is that of a Dalit woman. In the course of a wide-ranging review of the relations across caste, gender, sexuality and labour, dwelling on the social status of the work that lower-caste and Dalit women undertake, Meena Gopal (2012: 6) has pointed out how it is precisely the nature of the work she has to perform that signifies her as low, inferior and stigmatised.

While her labour in other households for the women of those households marks her as clearly inferior but provides a modicum of respectability, those forms of paid labour associated with public manual work most definitely do not, and are precisely the signs of her lack of social status, from the rural agricultural labourer to the urban construction worker. Notice that all these are forms of paid work. This is why it is not enough to offer a gender or class analysis of women's paid and unpaid work in our context. As V. Meera (1979) argued several decades ago, the overwhelming proportion of women's paid work has been subject to the stigma of being lower caste; apart from its onerous and vulnerable nature, it also marks the lower-caste working body as sexually available to men of all castes. This is how a contrast comes to be drawn with the dependent unpaid labour of other women, who nonetheless hope to avoid such sexual and caste stigmatisation, by their withdrawal from the public domain of paid work and protection within the institution of marriage.

Maitreyi Das (2012) has looked at patterns of women's labour participation by education and caste in contemporary India. In the statistical picture she provides, Dalit and Adivasi women predominate both among those with no education and who labour 'out of necessity'; the middle and upper castes with education up to primary levels of schooling and employed husbands 'opt out of the work force'; only with further education (where predominantly the upper castes are to be found) is there a small if positive correlation with work. The so-called lower castes or backward castes (including, I may add, Muslims) are among the most invisible of India's working women, folded into households and family labour. If one were to plot women's labour participation in relation to education and income in a graphic form, the Indian case therefore takes on an overall U-pattern, namely high labour participation among the poorest as well as among the relatively well-to-do at the other end of the spectrum, with very low levels for large sections of women in between (unlike most other parts of the world where women's labour participation increases with education and income). This is a harsh empirical reminder of the combined normative and structural effects of caste and class in India's economy today, when the dominant view is that the hold of caste is weakening, especially in the link with work and occupations.

Even more significant is that this pattern does not appear to have altered to any appreciable extent with the promises of globalisation and 'inclusive growth'. Against the contours of a field unwilling to think beyond economic criteria, Ashwini Deshpande (2011) has unveiled what she calls 'the grammar of caste' in the discriminatory and exclusionary workings of India's labour markets (see also Thorat and Newman 2010). But this also means that the actual struggles of working women, especially those who are most marginalised, will require a correspondingly nuanced analysis as they negotiate simultaneously with stigma, poverty and family oppressions. The effects of access to education also need much more careful analysis than the equivocal comment Das (2012: 153) herself provides—'women with education may stay out of the labour force because of an income effect, but this conclusion is muddied by the lack of jobs that women would want to do'. This is why one must underscore that only a tiny segment of overwhelmingly urban upper-caste women have gained entry into a workforce with no connection to a labouring body, who may therefore work without social stigma (including in the ever-shrinking formal sector, and the more globalised enclaves such as the financial, media and entertainment industries), though this by no means precludes other gendered and sexual forms of harassment. This picture clearly calls for more detailed analysis than I can offer here.

How then do we square a labour theory of value with a stigma theory of labour, the very negation of value, whose fullest contradiction is embodied by Dalit women?

Domestic Work

There is a further flaw in most theorisations of the domestic sphere, whose common assumption is that the sexual/gender division of labour within it can be analysed outside the market and its logic. Here it becomes necessary to pause and recognise that the domestic sphere is both a familial sphere and a household; that the domestic sphere is not outside the market but rather is co-constructed by it. Let us revisit the list of activities mentioned earlier—cooking, cleaning, childcare. One cannot but notice that these labours are as much structured by lasting personal relationships (within the family) as they are by paid domestic work, albeit to varying degrees and in historically changing forms. Or, to put this differently, the reproduction of class hierarchies through the family requires the differentiation of women's domestic labour into those who can lay claim to the assistance of paid domestic work and those who cannot do so. Rajni Palriwala and Neetha N. (2011) have called this social structure 'stratified familialism'.[7] Cooks, housemaids, babysitters or child carers—these are all clear occupational categories for which wages are paid. Notice further that over the last decade, paid domestic work has risen the most in urban India, whose only other competitor in salaried work is (school) teaching. In rural contexts especially, the boundaries of the domestic economy extend well beyond the 'home', including a range of subsistence labour, the collection of water and fuel, and here, too, both unpaid and paid labour are involved.

Thus, the normative household extends well beyond the domain of the familial, and indeed makes the normative family possible. While the history of various forms of servitude was a well-known aspect of pre-modern households the world over, it is interesting that with the rise of the women's movement and feminism, one of whose breakthroughs was to expose the oppressions of the home through housework and the sexual division of labour, servants were conspicuous by their absence. (This situation has changed post-globalisation following major international migration patterns of domestic workers from Third World locations to First World homes and workplaces, leading to the formulation of the care economy.) One might even want to speculate on the seeming disappearance of the Black 'help' from White middle-class households in post-Second World War United States, including the extent to which Betty Friedan's conceptualisation of the 'problem with no name' suffered by the American suburban housewife was not simply a crisis of marriage and family ideology, but equally due to the loss of the Black women who did everything from cooking multi-course dinners, cleaning the house, to taking care of young children.

Having earlier highlighted the contradictory realm of women's public labour outside the home through the conflicted lens of stigma and value, I am now trying to get at the peculiar nature of the normative domestic realm—where wives render their labour 'lovingly', seemingly outside the circuits of exchange value, but actually not. For there is a market wage for housework already in place, whose bottom end is amongst the most exploited imaginable. When we keep asking ourselves about the persistent non-recognition of women's work in the home ('my wife does not work, my mother does not work', say patriarchal husbands and children to this very day), we are simultaneously forgetting the labours of those that are even deeper in the shadows, whose devaluation, in my view, is part of the overall problem of valuing domestic labour itself. An essential aspect of this overall devaluation, of course, is that 'their' domestic spaces need not count for anything in comparison to 'ours'. This is the humiliation and failure every domestic worker knows, as she combines poorly paid domestic work in the households of others together with unpaid labour in her own.[8]

It is my further submission here that this complex domestic relation of power and exploitation, that results in making the unpaid oppressed housewife 'the employer' of the paid servant, requires structures of non-economic forms of discrimination under modern capitalism—race and ethnicity elsewhere, caste in India. The question of what kinds of paid domestic work are done by what castes in whose households and at what wages deserves detailed analysis. But I can probably risk the provisional generalisation that the most ubiquitous and basic work of cleaning other people's homes is a lower-caste if not Dalit occupation. I would further venture to say that the very decades of globalisation which have witnessed some mobility for the dominant middle castes, and much more for sections of urban upper castes, along with a significant reduction in fertility patterns, have led to a marked increase in the individualisation and intensification of personal relationships between husband and wife, and increasingly in the bringing up of children as women devote themselves to 'child craft'.[9] All this is placing unprecedented and enormous demands on such women, to the extent of pushing even the tiny segment of those with 'good jobs' to consider giving them up (in interesting contrast to an earlier generation and familial patterns). Further reinforcements can be found in contemporary capitalist workplaces, the media and right-wing ideologies. At the same time, the sustainability of the new family requires an increase in paid domestic services. Consider the growing market for provisioning Adivasi women as live-in maids in north Indian cities; or again the rise in various level's of 'nursing' care for the elderly, especially in the demographically aging southern states.

Let me now return to the list of household tasks mentioned earlier on in this essay and the missing item: sexual services and the relationships of love and intimacy that are becoming part of an evolving new norm. While the women's movement in India has been at the forefront of exposing marriage and family as sites of violence, discrimination and exploitation, questions of love and sex, and their fundamental underpinning of these institutions, has received at least some sustained critique from queer perspectives.[10] What makes these aspects of the domestic domain so intractable and difficult to discuss? One radical answer could be that this is because they belong within the realm of the pure relationship, carried by *eros* and affect, thus not work at all. It would be nice to think that we inherit something of the libertarian strand from Alexandra Kollontai to Herbert Marcuse on this score. Perhaps. But there are signs that today's companionate couple might be closer to inhabiting the world so hilariously and yet starkly described by Laura Kipnis (2000) as 'surplus monogamy'. Surplus monogamy refers to all the surplus labour that has to go into the creation and sustenance of sexual intimacy, the extra hours, the renunciations, the sheer labour of it all. No other aspect of lasting personal relationships has been more romanticised, or subjected to silence, while perhaps sharing considerably more with Marx's discussions of the onerous production of surplus value in Volume I of *Capital,* than has been allowed for! While this may well be part of the intractability of this domain, I would also like to suggest that a fundamentally related aspect is due to the enormous distance that today separates the normative domestic sphere from the world of sex work. This is in some contrast to earlier times, where the historical record amply attests to the open yoking of procreative and non-procreative sexualities, 'good' and 'bad' women, including the high social status that certain women could achieve as in the *devadasi*[11] tradition of southern India, and the greater visibility of prostitutes in social life, which lasted well into the early decades of twentieth-century colonial India. Also consider the Marxist feminist Kollontai, for one, who could not imagine liberation without socialising household labour, as well as critiquing both marriage and prostitution as part of the same system of control, so much so that no genuine change was possible without addressing both these institutions in the same frame. There are few contexts or struggles today where such sexual relations, even if hierarchised, are nonetheless brought together. Contemporary debates over prostitution and sex work, and especially trafficking, rarely feel the need to bring the institution of marriage into their analytical and political grid to begin with. The telling exceptions concern those marriages that are debased and suspect precisely because the wives may have been bought or ostensibly trafficked.[12]

While the paid domestic worker is part of the reproduction of the household but her exploitation rendered invisible within it, prostitution is sought to be segregated from the rest of society, under constant threat of abolition. Knotty questions surround comparative levels of earnings, and whether higher earnings 'compensate' for the enormous levels of stigma associated with sex work, and the extreme abjections of family life.

I have been trying to theorise women's labour in the Indian context by indicating the extent to which it is shot through with contradictions. There are the contradictions of caste which render paid labour as stigma and vulnerability rather than value and autonomy; the contradictions of class whereby the ubiquity of the caring domestic sphere must include its co-construction through the market of paid domestic work; and finally, the 'abjected'[13] sphere of sex work. Where, then are the signs such that these contradictions of caste, class, gender and sexuality, and the deep dependencies on marriage and family, could be questioned if not subjected to transformation?

Women's Life Stories

This brings me to the texts (autobiographies/life narratives) and the women who wrote them. Scholars commenting on the emergence of the autobiographical form, beginning in the latter part of the nineteenth century in colonial Bengal, invariably focus on the term 'new'—the new woman, the new voices, the new writing. In her pioneering study of Bengali women's writings from this period, Malavika Karlekar (1991: 195) proposed that a 'new femininity' emerged from the *antahpur* (the inner quarters), dismissed by many as a realm of foolishness, mindless ritual and idle gossip. Instead she argued for subtle forms of resistance, even if the evidence came from but a few women and could not be called a movement. Partha Chatterjee (1994: 137) reformulated this very question of the new as the question of modernity—under the specific conditions of colonial society, this modernity was 'to be found less in the external domain of political conflict and more in the "inner" space of the middle class home', and the principle archive for his thesis were women's autobiographies. The main constraining force for this new woman came from her own complicity in the cultural project of nationalism. He further claimed that the very first autobiography of them all, *Amar Jiban* (*My Life*) by Rashsundari Debi—who struggled as a housewife to read in secret for fear of what would befall her if she were discovered—did not qualify as modern. Her text was too structured by the belief that her achievements were not hers but shaped by the inscrutable fancies of a divine power, and was hence more beholden to the devotional literature of an earlier era (ibid.: 142). This reading has been directly contested by Tanika Sarkar (1999: 222) who argues that her writing is a 'modern articulation about the inwardness of an individuated self'; Rashsundari certainly refers to her life 'as entirely of God's designing, but she does, nonetheless, have a clear sense of the social making of it' (ibid.: 121).

My own interests in the five disparate texts I have chosen are much more limited and strategic, given the theme of this essay. Questions of modernity and the 'new' are undoubtedly at work in all the texts we will be looking at, and are surely never 'resolved' when change is as ongoing in the context of a globalising nation in the twenty-first century as it was in colonial times.

Rashsundari Debi was born into a Hindu upper-caste zamindari family in what is now Bangladesh, and wrote about a life that spanned the nineteenth century. Binodini Dasi (born in 1863) was to become the most celebrated actress on the Calcutta stage but had to endure the chasm of being debarred from the very society that delighted in her performances. Baby Kamble (born 1929) takes us to the Mahar community in Maharashtra and the impact that Babasaheb Ambedkar and his movement were to have on their lives. Both Baby Haldar and Nalini Jameela are our contemporaries, living, working and writing in Delhi and Kerala respectively. Where Baby Haldar reveals the twists and turns that bring her to domestic work, Nalini Jameela reflects on the equally complex terrain of becoming a sex worker.

Given the variety of texts and their span—the first version of Rashsundari's Bengali autobiography was finished in 1868 and a final version published in 1897, while Nalini Jameela wrote hers in Malayalam in 2005—I cannot even begin to provide the requisite account of their respective times and places, the discourses that made them possible or their subsequent impact. Each of these women has been granted a pioneering status as a writer by virtue of her social location in diverse ways—housewife, actress, Dalit leader, domestic worker, sex worker—so that each of them is understood to have cleared a space without precedent. By reflecting on what these women wanted to say about their labouring lives I hope to open up the concerns raised in the first part of this essay to further discussion.

We discover, to begin with, that all their childhoods are broken and effectively ended by entering lives of labour, whether within a home or beyond. This is significant in itself, in spite of Nalini Jameela's casual remark that child labour was not an issue in 'those days', which in her case would have been as recent as the 1960s, when she began working in a tile factory. Furthermore, each one of them not only identifies women's labour as a problem, but turns it into an experience that enables their critique. Almost all of them discuss the sphere of the home, the ones they were born into or those they acquired upon marriage, as places where work has to be performed. (The only exception is Binodini Dasi, who resolutely articulated her work in relation to her life as an actress on the stage, and whose 'home' is never explicitly alluded to after the first pages of her autobiography.) Let us recall Kumkum Sangari's arguments regarding the ideologies underpinning domestic life, such that women's lasting personal relationships render their labour as unalienated, as selfless devotion. This is not what we hear in the texts before us. Already with Rashsundari Debi, a transitional figure who desired and came to claim a modern sense of self, the very endlessness of household tasks provokes a double-voiced stance, inwardly critical and only apparently compliant. 'Newly wedded girls had to be especially hard-working and quiet. This was how young married women were supposed to work', she wrote (Sarkar 1999: 160). In the case of the others, the critiques are sharper but also multivocal, as questions of caste, class and sexuality become visible.

As it turns out, the contradictions identified in the first part of this essay find several echoes in these texts, but there are also new ones. Baby Kamble's style reveals the cross-hatchings of caste and gender in the lives of Mahar women—their degraded labour as untouchables in the fields and for the prosperity of upper-caste households is sought to be overcome through codes of 'honour' in those Mahar households that can somehow create an *antahpur*—inner quarters—of their own, including the capacity to make slaves out of daughters-in-law. Baby Haldar's descriptions of her life as a domestic worker demonstrate the workings of her lower-caste identity through her very labour, including the full recognition of the special dynamic that gets set in motion between a *memsahib*[14] and her maid, as the time and effort that must be given in serving one household has to be at the expense of the servant's own. Sexuality is by no means absent in these two texts—its legibility, however, is largely confined to jealous and violent husbands and neighbourhood gossip. Where Binodini Dasi rails against the injustice of not being allowed to forget being born in the prostitutes' quarters, Nalini Jameela, a century later, politicises sex work. This politicisation is particularly complex when it comes to Nalini Jameela's family life—while she is able to walk out of bad marriages, oppose dominant norms of femininity and the labours of the housewife, protecting her own daughter includes trying more than once to find her a marriage that lasts.

These contradictions open up a further challenge that goes to the very heart of conceptions of gender hierarchy that foreground women's oppression by men. Women certainly struggle against men in all these narratives. Nor do I wish to diminish case after case of men who fail in their normative roles as providers and protectors. Some readily compound their failure with violence, as when Baby Kamble becomes politically active, and Baby Haldar goes out to work (when both face the wrath of their husbands), or Nalini Jameela is thrown out of the house by her father when she goes looking for work. Binodini experiences failure at the hands of all the men in her life, both professionally and personally, and the worst betrayals are from those who present themselves as her mentors and benefactors. Towards the end of her book, Rashsundari makes rather perfunctory mention of her husband, referring to him in her text as her *karta*, that is, the head of the household, acknowledging that not having said anything about him made her story incomplete. He was a kind man, she allows. But her real purpose was to show that she could effectively handle a case of land litigation when he was away and she was left in charge. The one man who appears in a different mould is 'Tatush', Baby Haldar's final employer, whose plea to be considered as her 'father, mother, brother, friend, anything'—in other words, as anything but an exploiting master—appears consumed by a desire to transcend their working relationship into remaking her as a writer.

But where men occupy identifiably patriarchal positions in these authors' respective journeys, whether tragic or triumphant, my argument is that modernity's visible production of the 'new woman' masks the more complex and elusive fracturing of 'women' in the world of labour. Indeed, it is unclear whether they share a collective identity as women to begin with. Within the family domain itself we have heard about relations of power between daughters, mothers and mothers-in-law (and that, too, in hugely disparate upper-caste, Mahar, and lower-caste homes); then there is Dalit women's waged labour for Brahmin households; the relations between memsahib and servant; finally, the politicisation of sex work, abjected from society. These texts demonstrate my further argument that these class-, caste- and sexuality-inflected antagonisms are constitutive of the everyday devaluation of women's lives of labour. The reproduction of labour in households from the late-nineteenth century into the present requires, therefore, much more exploration of the familial, sexual, caste and class hierarchies that distribute and relegate work to different women. Perhaps this is why Baby Kamble has so much to say about mothers-in-law in Mahar households rather than her own violent husband. Rashsundari complained that even though she had nine servants, they all worked outside, leaving her to do all the housework alone—'in those days we did not have Brahmin cooks', she adds ruefully (Sarkar 1999: 207–08).

In her introduction to Nalini Jameela's autobiography, J. Devika draws attention to the dominant feminine ideal in Kerala, 'procreative, disciplined, family-centric', that was given shape 'through wave after wave of social and community reformism in the twentieth century ... [T]he Veshya—the prostitute figure—was marginally present in the early twentieth century ... as its abhorrent Other. However, the labouring woman's presence was even more marginal. Jameela's text actually made this voice audible' (Jameela 2007: *viii*). Nalini Jameela is very evidently engaged in writing back to Kerala's elites and progressives, and on more than one occasion she remarks on the growing social distance between the world of sex work and mainstream society. However, her text also demonstrates conflicted relations among the very margins Devika alludes to, when she mentions being equally unwelcome in the poor and Dalit parts of town. For her part, she placed sex workers somewhere above construction labourers and scavengers, remarking further that 'no one' expected such workers to enjoy the fruits of their labour or be considered for rehabilitation. Here she appears blind to movements such as the struggle for the abolition of scavenging as an untouchable profession, coming from these castes themselves, however limited their support from those 'above'. The grading of those abjected by caste, class and sexuality thus exacerbates conflict, and hardens differences among those striving for lives of labour beyond oppression, stigma and alienation.

Beyond Labour Oppression?

This essay began by asking why women's labour eludes worth and value, and I have tried to be faithful to the insights provided by a few pioneering women's life narratives, as they created certain alternatives out of the conditions imposed upon them. By way of a conclusion, I am therefore tempted to press further and ask whether these texts offer a view beyond labour oppression. As we will discover, we are left with more questions, whether those of the women themselves or our own. Rashsundari repeatedly connected a life confined to domestic chores with the absence of education, and she noted with great satisfaction that girls are now educated. *But for what, we have to ask, and how does it transform a life of labour?* We are not told. Her own life moves from the mute young bride to gradually enjoying the authority that comes with sons and grandsons, the ability to converse more freely with other members and servants, even use her secretly acquired literate skills to settle a court case. Thus, Rashsundari's affirmation of the value of education goes hand in hand with the firming up of a new upper-caste and upper-class feminine subjectivity, replete with son preference, and a clear aversion towards the onerousness of domestic labour, to be delegated to others, preferably servants. This is late-nineteenth century rural Bengal. By this time Binodini had already become the most famous actress on the Calcutta stage, indeed was about to give it up. If anyone is clear about achieving happiness through work it is Binodini, whose capacity to reflect on and delight in her own talent for performance is only matched by her desire for a life without subordination. Her sense of injustice is total.

We then move to the world of the Mahars caught up in Ambedkar's movement from the 1930s as experienced by a woman who grew up near Pune. In her own life, Baby Kamble found some resolution to untouchable labour and household slavery in running her own little grocery shop. *Is this a way out then, from exploitation and stigma to the dignity of self-employment?* It was the women around her who stepped forward to break with humiliating if not hazardous food and labour practices in the wake of Ambedkar's call and who found in education the major path to liberation. But it is Baby Kamble herself who is moved to ask of a new generation of educated 'daughters and daughters-in-law' what they have forgotten as beneficiaries of this very movement, and the question remains unanswered. Baby Haldar and Nalini are living in the present time, and are therefore witness to the peculiar forms that the Indian economy has been taking, the former carrying out an individual struggle in the city of Delhi, the latter a collective one in contemporary Kerala.[15] Both live outside the institution of marriage, both took up their respective professions because of the children in their care, and both appear not to have stopped working after becoming authors. Baby Haldar, acutely conscious of the exploitative nature of paid domestic work, ends her story with all the excitement of seeing her book in print. *Does such work become less exploitative when the employer has helped make you a writer?* Nalini Jameela offers several arguments in favour of sex work. Probably the most startling of them all is her suggestion that the negative and unwanted experience of sexual violence (certainly ubiquitous in her early working life) be turned into earning a living as a sex worker. She offers descriptions of clients and their varying needs, some of which may not be explicitly sexual, and claims to have evolved a certain power in her relations to them. Sex for money 'now and then' is thus offered as a viable alternative, given the much worse conditions within which most women find themselves. *By turning sexual violation on its head, does sex work then offer an alternate path out of victimhood?*

Having begun with a set of questions, we have found some answers and more questions. Five disparate life stories cannot substitute for the process of collective thinking and struggle over the future of women's labour, nor can they in any way be taken as representative of women in the worlds of work. Thus, it would be wonderful if there were more life narratives, such as of the 'factory girl' (whether in the jute mills of yesteryear or in the export processing zones of today), of Adivasi women struggling to uphold subsistence economies against all odds, or of women in self-employment, including those made famous by the Self-employed Women's Association (SEWA) or the governmentalised self-help groups (SHGs), all of which require contextualisation within recent history and India's globalising economy. It should be obvious that there is nothing essential or transhistorical about the problems identified in this essay, given all that we know about the contingency of social processes, including, let us not forget, the working of economic regimes. In the face of the emergence of modernity under colonialism, followed by promises of development with independence and more especially after the onset of a neo-liberal regime devoted to economic growth with increasingly precarious conditions of life and work, these texts from the world of labour strive for recognition and change. They attest to failed patriarchies as much as to the intersecting conflicts that constitute women's relations in the realm of labour. They also force us to rethink the institutions of marriage and family, given the deep divisions of gender, class, caste and sexuality upon which the successful household so completely depends. It is for us to ponder over why all this is more true today than at any time in recent history.

Notes

1. Different modes of naming women's writings about themselves and their worlds have been debated in the Indian context in particular. Sharmila Rege (2006) has argued that Dalit women's writings should not be called autobiographies but rather *'testimonios'*, a term that she takes from South American women's writing. We will discover contrasting approaches in modes of writing when we come to the women's texts themselves, and so I leave the question open.
2. Among the first in-depth interrogations of the feminisation thesis in India, which focused very significantly on the different meanings of feminisation in labour markets (are women taking over men's jobs, are women entering new workspaces, and with what consequences?), see especially Shah et al. (1994).
3. For a recent overview, see Ghosh (2009) and John (2009) that discuss the range of positions and debates on globalisation among feminists.

   Even though there are clearly no overall trends that indicate the large-scale entry of women into the Indian labour force, and these may in fact have declined in recent years, it is nonetheless still relevant to identify specific sectors—both old and new—however small they may be, where significant numbers of women workers are to be found. This could range from India's tea plantations, which took full advantage of migrant women during and after the colonial era, to the garment workers in south Indian cities producing for international 'brands' in the newly globalised twenty-first century. What unites such disparate workers are the extraordinary levels of exploitation that they have been and continue to be subjected to, which requires the kind of larger frame of analysis that my essay attempts to outline. See Gothoskar (2012) and Neetha (2002) for examples of micro-studies.
4. For early discussions of women's work in the context of the NSS, see Sen and Sen (1985), and in the Census, see Krishnaraj (1990).
5. See, for instance, the articles brought together by Swaminathan (2012) and their framing. Indeed, in her concluding introductory remarks, Swaminathan herself refers explicitly to how 'research undertaken from a gender perspective seems to be concerned by gender perspectives alone, while lip service may be paid to structural factors' (that is capitalist

accumulation, paradigms of development) (ibid.: 14–15). I would only add that structural factors are not exhausted by questions relating to development or capitalism but must include caste and sexuality as well.

6. In a recent essay, 'The Woman Question: Reflections on Feminism and Marxism' (2017), I have revisited the long and complex terrain of feminism and Marxism and its repercussions for thinking about stigma, caste and sexuality in the Indian context.
7. As Palriwala and Neetha (2011) elaborate, 'stratified familialism' results in the production of class difference through the creation of a 'care deficit' on the part of all those women who labour and are then blamed for not being in a position to provide sufficient care in their households. Their study focuses on the abdication of care provisioning by the State as a matter of public responsibility rather than as a residual welfare measure, which in turn has a long history.
8. Given the overwhelming feminisation of paid domestic work over the course of the last century, Radhika Chopra (2006) has provided an interesting ethnographic glimpse into the crisis faced by male domestic workers as 'invisible men' in negotiating their labour, identity and domestic spaces.
9. I am grateful to J. Devika for suggesting this phrase.
10. As Rinchin (2008: 576) pointed out in the context of a panel discussion on marriage and family from feminist, Dalit, Marxist and queer perspectives, marriage is the ultimate form that the binary division of the sexual and non-sexual takes, such that 'sexual liaisons are valued above others and the one sexual relationship in which sex becomes secondary after a while and "love and care" take over is the culmination of our quest ... Therefore, friends, siblings and others sharing home and life together will always be seen as living in limbo'. Analyses such as Rinchin's, however, are quite rare and are in urgent need of further amplification and debate. For an early argument on the need to develop better critiques of the institution of marriage within debates on sexuality, see John (1998).
11. Devadasis are women who were dedicated to serve in Hindu temples in south India as artists, dancers and singers. In several instances, they enjoyed prestige and rights before being the subject of efforts of social reform in late colonial India as the practice came to be seen as outside the fold of sexual respectability as well as oppressive.
12. The classic feminist essay to have retheorised a universal system of the 'exchange of women' by bringing together Lévi-Strauss, Freud and

Marx is Gayle Rubin's 'The Traffic in Women' (1975). For a subtle critique of symptoms of unwitting hierarchisation within Rubin's sex-gender system, see Naifei Ding (2007). In the Indian context, the pioneering historical essay on the devadasi tradition and its relations to sex work has been by Janaki Nair (1993). See also the Sex Workers' Manifesto brought out by the Durbar Mahila Samanwaya Committee, reproduced in Kotiswaran (2011). Prabha Kotiswaran's introduction to existing scholarship on sex work is an excellent overview of the debates in India, and foregrounds especially the need to bring together analyses of labour, marriage and sex work.

13. The notion of abjection comes from the work of Judith Butler (1993), who has drawn attention to the processes whereby the heterosexual matrix 'abjects' the lesbian as its 'constitutive outside'. I am using the term here to indicate how the sex worker today occupies the constitutive outside of a newly evolving normative marriage and family more generally.
14. The term 'memsahib' has colonial origins and denotes the wife of the head of the household, a position of authority.
15. This is not to suggest that there are no collective organisations or struggles of domestic workers in the Indian context, though they do not find mention in Haldar's text (for some discussions, see Devika et al. 2011; Neetha 2003). Indeed it would be extremely instructive to compare the trajectories and forms that struggles of domestic workers and sex workers have taken in recent decades. While the international links in the case of the latter are obviously visible, so also are the solidarities from gay, lesbian and transgender groups in an effort to build a larger network for the articulation of non-normative sexualities, to which Nalini Jameela herself attests. For a suggestive set of reflections on attempts to bring sex workers within the ambit of a broader platform of workers' unions, see Sukhthankar (2012), and for the findings of a recent survey among sex workers, see Sahni and Shankar (2011).

References

Banerjee, Nirmala. 1997. 'How Real is the Bogey of Feminisation?'. *Indian Journal of Labour Economics* 40 (3): 427–38.

Butler, Judith. 1993. *Bodies That Matter: On the Discursive Limits of Sex.* New York and London: Routledge.

Chatterjee, Partha. 1994. *The Nation and Its Fragments: Colonial and Postcolonial Histories.* Delhi: Oxford University Press.

Chopra, Radhika. 2006. 'Invisible Men: Masculinity, Sexuality and the Male Division of Labour'. *Men and Masculinities* 9 (2): 152–67.

Combahee River Collective. 1979. 'A Black Feminist Statement'. In *Capitalist Patriarchy and the Case for Socialist Feminism*, ed. Zillah Eisenstein, 362–72. Boston: Beacon Press.

Das, Maitreyi. 2012. *Poverty and Social Exclusion in India*. Washington, DC: World Bank Group.

Dasi, Binodini. 1998. *Amar Katha*. Edited and Translated into *My Story and My Life as an Actress* by Rimli Bhattacharya. New Delhi: Kali for Women.

Debi, Rashsundari. 1999. *Amar Jibon*. Partially translated into *Words to Win: The Making of Amar Jiban, A Modern Autobiography* by Tanika Sarkar. New Delhi: Kali for Women.

Deshpande, Ashwini. 2011. *The Grammar of Caste: Economic Discrimination in Contemporary India*. Delhi: Oxford University Press.

Devika, J., P. R. Nisha and A. K. Rajasree. 2011. '"A Tactful Union": Domestic Workers' Unionism, Politics and Citizenship in Kerala, India'. *Indian Journal of Gender Studies* 18 (2), June: 185–215.

Ding, Naifei. 2007. 'Wife in Monogamy and the "Exaltation of Concubines"'. *Interventions: International Journal of Postcolonial Studies* 9 (2), special issue on Women and Feminisms in Asia, ed. Mary E. John: 219–57.

Durbar Mahila Samanwaya Committee. 1997/2011. 'Sex Workers' Manifesto: First National Conference of Sex Workers in India', Kolkata. Reproduced in *Sex Work*, ed. Prabha Kotiswaran. New Delhi: Women Unlimited.

Ghosh, Jayati. 2009. *Never Done and Poorly Paid: Women's Work in Globalising India*. New Delhi: Women Unlimited.

Gopal, Meena. 2012. 'Caste, Sexuality and Labour: The Troubled Connection'. *Current Sociology* 60 (2): 222–38.

Gothoskar, S. 2012. 'This *Chay* is Bitter: Exploitative Relations in the Tea Industry'. *Economic and Political Weekly* 47 (50): 33–40.

Haldar, Baby. 2006. *Aalo Andhari: A Life Less Ordinary*. Translated into *A Life Less Ordinary* by Urvashi Butalia. New Delhi: Zubaan and Penguin.

Hull, G. A., P. Scott and B. Smith, eds. 1982. *All the Women Are White, All the Blacks Are Men, But Some of Us Are Brave: Black Women's Studies*. Boston: Feminist Press.

Jameela, Nalini. 2007. *Njan Laingikatozhilali*. Translated into *The Autobiography of a Sex Worker* by J. Devika. Chennai: Westland Press.

John, Mary. E. 1998. 'Globalisation, Sexuality and the Visual Field: Issues and Non-issues for Cultural Critique'. In *A Question of Silence?: The Sexual Economies of Modern India*, ed. Mary E. John and J. Nair, 368–96. New Delhi: Kali for Women.

———. 2009. 'Reframing Globalisation: Perspectives from the Women's Movement'. *Economic and Political Weekly* 44 (9), 7 March: 46–49.

———. 2017. 'The Woman Question: Reflections on Feminism and Marxism'. *Economic and Political Weekly* 52 (50), 16 December: 71–79.

Kamble, Baby. 2008. *Jina Amucha*. Translated into *The Prisons We Broke* by Maya Pandit. Hyderabad: Orient BlackSwan.

Karlekar, Malavika. 1991. *Voices from Within: Early Personal Narratives of Bengali Women*. Delhi: Oxford University Press.

Kipnis, L. 2000. 'Adultery'. In *Intimacy*, ed. Lauren Berlant, 9–47. Chicago: Chicago University Press.

Kollontai, A. 1977. *Selected Writings*, translated with an introduction and commentaries by Alix Holt. Westport: Lawrence Hill and Company.

Kotiswaran, Prabha. 2011. 'Introduction'. In *Sex Work*. New Delhi: Women Unlimited.

Krishnaraj, M. 1990. 'Women's Work in the Indian Census: Beginnings of Change'. *Economic and Political Weekly* 25 (48–49), 1–8 December: 2663–72.

Mazumdar, I., and Neetha N. 2011. 'Gender Dimensions: Employment Trends in India, 1993–94 to 2009–10'. *Economic and Political Weekly* 46 (43), 22 October: 118–26.

Meera, V. 1979. 'Prisoners of Inequality: Sexual Abuse of Dalit Women'. *Race and Class* 20 (4): 417–21.

Nair, Janaki. 1993. 'From Devadasi Reform to SITA: Reforming Sex Work in Mysore State, 1892–1937'. *National Law School Journal* 1: 82–94.

Neetha N. 2002. 'Flexible Production, Feminisation and Disorganisation: Evidence from Tiruppur Knitwear Industry'. *Economic and Political Weekly* 37, 25 May: 2045–52.

———. 2003. 'Migration, Social Networking and Employment: A Study of Domestic Workers in Delhi'. *NLI Research Study Series* No. 37. Noida: V.V. Giri National Labour Institute.

Palriwala, Rajni and Neetha N. 2011. 'Stratified Familialism: The Care Regime in India Through the Lens of Child Care'. *Development and Change* 12 (4), July: 1–30.

Rao, Anupama. 2012. 'Stigma and Labour: Remembering Dalit Marxism'. *Seminar, Issue on Caste Matters*, 633, May: 23–27.

Rege, Sharmila. 2006. *Writing Caste, Writing Gender: Narrating Dalit Women's Testimonios*. New Delhi: Zubaan.

Rinchin. 2008. 'Querying Marriage and Family'. In *Women's Studies in India: A Reader*, ed. Mary E. John, 573–79. New Delhi: Penguin.

Rubin, Gayle. 1975. 'The Traffic in Women: Notes on the Political Economy of Sex'. In *Towards an Anthropology of Women*, ed. Rayna R. Reiter, 157–210. New York: Monthly Review Press.

Sahni, R., and V. K. Shankar. 2011. 'The First Pan-India Survey of Sex Workers: A Summary of Preliminary Findings'. Available at https://www.sangram.org/resources/Pan_India_Survey_of_Sex_workers.pdf

Sangari, Kumkum. 1993. 'The Amenities of Domestic Life: Questions on Labour'. *Social Scientist* 21 (9–11): 3–46.

Sen, G., and C. Sen. 1985. 'Women's Domestic Work and Employment Activity: Results from the National Sample Survey'. *Economic and Political Weekly* 20 (17), 27 April: WS 49–55.

Shah, N., S. Gothoskar, N. Gandhi and A. Chhachhi. 1994. 'Structural Adjustment, Feminisation of Labour and Organisational Strategies'. *Economic and Political Weekly* 29 (18), 25 April: WS 39–48.

Sharma, K., and C. P. Sujaya, eds. 2012. *Towards Equality: Report of the Committee of the Status of Women in India*. New Delhi: Pearson Education.

Standing, Guy. 1989. 'Global Feminisation Through Flexible Labour'. *World Development* 17 (7): 1077–95.

Sukhthankar, A. 2012. 'Queering Approaches to Sex, Gender and Labour in India: Examining Paths to Sex Worker Unionism'. In *South Asian Feminisms*, ed. Ania Loomba and Ritty A. Lukose, 306–60. Durham: Duke University Press.

Swaminathan, Padmini, ed. 2012. *Women and Work: Essays from the Economic and Political Weekly, Readings on the Economy, Polity and Society*. Hyderabad: Orient BlackSwan.

Thorat, S., and K. S. Newman, eds. 2010. *Blocked by Caste: Economic Discrimination in Modern India*. Delhi: Oxford University Press.

2

Time Poverty and Women's Work

*Jayati Ghosh**

Among the various aspects of deprivation related to poverty and inequality, one aspect which has seldom attracted the attention of scholars and policy-makers equally is that of time poverty. Ignoring this important dimension actually results from a related and possibly more substantive deficiency: the inadequate conception of what constitutes work that underlies much of our empirical data collection and our policies and programmes. This in turn has resulted in many adverse implications in terms of gender differences in recognised and unrecognised work. It is now being felt that this deficiency is generating misconceived policies which, instead of improving the wellbeing of workers, are actually worsening them.

So what do we mean by 'time poverty'? At its most banal level, it is understood as the shortage of time available to devote to purely personal requirements, including leisure and relational activities. There is a perception that time poverty, or the sense of not having enough hours in the day or week to perform all the activities one is required to perform or desires to undertake, is something common among middle-class professionals or those involved in high-stress

* This is the revised and combined version of the keynote address delivered at the UN Women conference at CISLS, Jawaharlal Nehru University, on 31 July 2014, and the T. G. Narayanan Memorial Lecture, delivered at the Asian College of Journalism, Chennai, on 11 December 2014. The bulk of this essay has been published in *METU Studies in Development* 43, April 2016.

managerial activities. Indeed the expressions 'money rich, time poor' or even 'affluenza' have increasingly been used in developed countries over the past decade to describe those with relatively high disposable incomes from well-paid jobs, who nonetheless lack time for leisure because of the time pressure of such jobs. Such problems are usually particularly acute for professional women, who face difficulties in achieving what is euphemistically called the 'work–life balance' since they continue to hold responsibilities in their households in addition to their paid employment. Such time poverty is often seen almost as a lifestyle disease, reflecting the way that those who are the beneficiaries of the current economic system choose to or are forced to organise their time in a rat race from which individual choice can make them separate.

But this essay argues that such time poverty among the better off accounts for very little of the total, and that genuine time poverty is more than a qualitative loss resulting from individual choices. Rather, most people who are time-poor are also income-poor and suffer from other (often multiple) deprivations. Further, the presence of time poverty adds to overall deprivation in a significant way that is rarely captured even in newer multidimensional measures of poverty.

The basic argument made here is that the poorer the people, the less are the chances to afford buying various goods and services from the market, and if these are not provided by public policy, then they can only consume them if they produce these goods and services themselves. This means that typically, in addition to having to work often long hours for relatively low wages, or paltry remuneration for self-employment, they must also engage in unpaid labour to meet the essential consumption needs of themselves and their family members. So the incidence of unpaid labour increases sharply as the income of a household falls.[1] This obviously means greater time deprivation in terms of less leisure time available.

But there is a further concern. Suppose that the conditions of work available to the members of a poor family are such that they are forced to spend long hours working for very low pay. They are still required to perform many unpaid activities—say, purchasing and processing food, cleaning the home to maintain a minimally sanitary environment, fetching water and/or fuel as well as other such essentials for daily use, caring for the young, the old and the sick members of the family, and so on. But imagine that the working hours (and possibly the hours of transport required from home to workplace) are such that they are simply not able to perform all of these activities, or at least do not have the time to perform them to a minimum satisfactory standard. Then time poverty translates into more than just loss of leisure—it adds to the material deprivation of that family because of the loss of the consumption that would have been enabled by the unpaid labour that there simply is no time for.

As it happens, standard poverty measures, which typically refer to money income as the relevant variable, effectively assume that all households have enough time to perform the (usually unpaid) activities required and do not take into account the variations in requirements of unpaid work that may well be driven by the money income available. This is why it has been argued (for example, by Vickery 1977) that if the threshold for determining the minimum non-poor consumption implicitly requires both money income and unpaid work products, then the official poverty standards do not correctly measure household needs. Since poorer households are less likely to be able to purchase goods and services to substitute for unpaid labour at home, they are therefore much more likely to have household members who have time deficits—in other words, who experience time poverty.

For many developing countries, including India, the problems are even starker: there are many unpaid work activities that simply cannot be outsourced because market substitutes or State provision simply do not exist in adequate measure (Antonopoulos and Memis 2010). Consider, for example, the fact that nearly 80 per cent of households in rural India still rely on collected firewood as the primary source of their energy needs for cooking, etc. Some households may simply be too poor to access processed fuel even when it is available—but in many parts of the country, this is not even available in adequate measure and therefore cannot be purchased. It is hard to envision how much of the time-consuming activity of walking long distances to collect firewood to meet household needs can be outsourced within the village. So this is unpaid labour that has to be performed, and cannot be substituted by purchased goods and services. Similarly, in both rural and urban India, the process of collecting and carrying water for drinking and other household uses is both arduous and extremely time consuming, especially for poor families. In some cases, this activity is necessary not only for family consumption but even for the small-scale production involved in, say, kitchen gardens or similar work. When such unpaid activities are necessary for household survival, they restrict the capacity of those involved in them to engage in paid work or remunerated activities, thereby adding to the income poverty of the household even as they are also associated with time poverty.

It is important to note that the existence of such unpaid work does more than add to the time poverty of those who must perform it. It also plays several important macroeconomic roles: it effectively subsidises the marketised part of the economy, which we tend to valorise through our obsession with measures of gross domestic product (GDP); and it subsidises State provisioning of goods and (especially) services, which are supposed to meet the social and economic rights of every citizen but end up getting delivered through such unpaid activities because of inadequate public delivery.

So far, we have discussed the household as a unit, but, of course, the time allocation among members of a household is also crucial. Here social constructs come prominently into play, particularly gender, which determines the allocation of both power and work responsibility within a household between men and women, boys and girls. It is well known [and now also sufficiently established by time-use surveys (TUS) across the world] that women and girls spend much more time on unpaid labour than men and boys, and that this contributes to their overall lack of status and empowerment because it also reduces their access to education and their ability to engage in paid work. TUSs conducted in different parts of the world tend to provide almost surprisingly similar results, with women and girls providing approximately 70 per cent of the total time involved in doing unpaid work for the household, in both 'economic' and 'care' activities.

The implications of time poverty for women in particular are immense, because they are associated with the 'double burden' of paid and unpaid work (Elson 1995) and extend into changing the nature of poverty and its implications. Thus, the unemployment–poverty link which has been noted for men in developing countries is not so direct and evident for women: many women are fully employed and still remain poor in absolute terms, and adding to their workload will not necessarily improve their material conditions. Many women in comparatively better-off households may well be time-poor because of the multiple demands imposed on them to meet the requirements of unpaid domestic activities.

This is corroborated by TUSs that link the time spent in various activities with the income level of the household. Let us consider the evidence from India. A TUS conducted by the Central Statistical Organisation (CSO) in 1998–99 (unfortunately still the most recent such survey, although a new one is now being planned) covered 18,628 households and 77,593 people in six major states in India: Gujarat, Tamil Nadu, Madhya Pradesh, Haryana, Odisha and Meghalaya. Some of the results (as analysed by Hirway 2010) are not surprising. For example, poorer households show greater time spent on unpaid work [in non-SNA (System of National Accounts) or not economically recognised activities] in a week, and women in general show much greater time spent on this than men. Women in ultra-poor households rank at the bottom in terms of the burden of total work, making them very clearly time-deficit and therefore doubly poor. But there are also some more surprising results. The survey found that women in rich households work much harder than ultra-poor men in terms of the time put into work. (This partly reflects the lack of paid work for poor men as well as the greater burden of unpaid work on women in their households.) The gender differences in time deficits indicated by the survey are quite stark: ultra-poor women have 10 fewer hours of personal time per week than ultra-poor men; and even in non-poor households, women have five-and a-half hours less of personal time per week than men.

So what does all this tell us about economic policies and the resultant material processes? First, it is evident that even for women's economic empowerment, the pressing policy concern is not that of simply increasing the volume of explicit female employment, since simply adding on recognised 'jobs' may, in fact, lead to a double burden upon women whose household obligations still have to be fulfilled.

Instead, concern has to be focused upon the *quality*, the *recognition* and the *remuneration* of women's work, as well as the *conditions* facilitating it, such as alternative arrangements for household work and childcare. All of these are critically affected by broader economic policies as well as by government interventions at micro and meso levels. And these together determine whether or not increased labour market activity by women is associated with genuine improvements in their economic circumstances.

Some governments have actually become more aware of this and have explicitly incorporated this concern into their economic policies. The National Plan for Good Living 2009–13 for Ecuador, which makes the improvement of quality of life of the citizenry a major priority, noted that liberating both work and free time are necessary elements. This clearly recognises the right to work, but it also recognises the right to 'relational time' in addition to private leisure, the time that is used for being an active participant of a society, community, group or family. This in turn requires the pursuit of 'a fairer social care regime in which care activities are valued, better distributed, meant to eradicate a sexual division of work so as to provide and receive care equitably' (Government of Ecuador 2009: 20).

Once we recognise the significance of unpaid work and its implications for poverty in its different dimensions and the way in which its logic is applied to economic policies, we can very well sum up that the contemporary mainstream economic thinking is clearly inadequate and even misleading in understanding the real economic reality in many ways. The first relates to the definition and measurement of work and employment, and second to a rather different but nonetheless very important indicator of income comparisons across countries.

Defining and Measuring Work

Work is typically thought of as an economic activity, and economic activities are typically defined as actions that involve the production, distribution and consumption of goods and services at all levels within a society. This, of course, begs the further question of what constitutes 'goods and services'. Pared down to its essence, it can be noted that any activity that can potentially be delegated is economic activity, which leaves only personal consumption and leisure as non-economic activities and requires a broadening of the common perception of what such activity is. For example, the activities associated with motherhood are typically seen as 'non-economic'. Yet breastfeeding can be outsourced through the hiring of a wet nurse, which then makes it an economic activity, with the wet nurse engaged in paid work. An even more extreme but recently proliferating example is that of surrogate motherhood, in which a woman is paid to be impregnated, carry a child in her womb and go through childbirth, making all these explicitly paid economic activities which in turn also contribute to national income to the extent of the remuneration received. Yet a woman who does this for her 'own' child rather than someone else's, and without any monetary reward, is classified as 'not in the labour force' in most if not all national statistical systems—and indeed, the very notion of 'maternity leave' from paid work suggests that the mother is, in effect, on some sort of holiday, rather than actively engaged in the work of producing a child.

Clearly, therefore, definitions of work and economic activity are not that simple. The standard definition of work is that used by the United Nations System of National Accounts (UN SNA 1993). Workers are seen as coterminous with economically active persons, and are those who are engaged in activities included within the boundary of production. This in turn includes (a) the production of all individual or collective goods or services that are supplied to units other than their producers, or intended to be so supplied, including the production of goods or services used up in the process of producing such goods or services; (b) the own-account production of all goods that are retained by their producers for their own final consumption or gross capital formation; and (c) the own-account production of housing services by owner-occupiers and of domestic and personal services produced by employing paid domestic staff. If this is taken to its logical conclusion, it should indeed include a very large range of human activity, especially once the second element of the production boundary is taken into consideration. Even so, some activities of social reproduction remain within an undefined and often shifting grey area, particularly the 'production' of children and the tasks associated with this.

The revised SNA of 2008 restricted the scope of the production boundary.

> Economic production may be defined as an activity carried out under the control and responsibility of an institutional unit that uses inputs of labour, capital, and goods and services to produce outputs of goods or services. There must be an institutional unit that assumes responsibility for the process of production and owns any resulting goods or knowledge-capturing products or is entitled to be paid, or otherwise compensated, for the change-effecting or margin services provided. (United Nations System of National Accounts 2008: 97–98)

Activities undertaken by households that produce services for their own use are excluded from the concept of production, except for services provided by owner-occupied dwellings and services produced by employing paid domestic staff (ibid.: 98). This effectively implies the exclusion of most services produced by households for their own use. Recognising that this makes quite a big difference, the UN Statistical Commission was at pains to explain why they were so excluded. It was noted that this exclusion was related *not* to any conceptual belief that these are not economic activities (indeed it was accepted that they are) but rather the result of the perceived difficulties of estimating and imputing values to such services, which were seen to be 'self-contained' within the family. So such activities, while recognised to be economic in nature, were excluded from the national accounts computations because of 'the relative isolation and independence of these activities from markets, the extreme difficulty of making economically meaningful estimates of their values, and the adverse effects it would have on the usefulness of the accounts for policy purposes and the analysis of markets and market disequilibria' (ibid.: 99).

However, a big breakthrough has come recently from the 19th International Conference of Labour Statisticians (ICLS) (International Labour Organisation 2013), which has distinguished between work and employment and expanded the concept of work: 'Work comprises any activity performed by persons of any sex and age to produce goods or to provide services for use by others or for own use'. The inclusion of the last phrase 'for use by others or for own use' provides the crucial difference, as it includes the production of goods and services performed in the home for other household members and for personal use. Several aspects of this definition are worth noting. First of all, work is defined irrespective of its formal or informal character or the legality of the activity. It only excludes activities that do not involve producing goods or services (for example, begging and stealing), self-care (for example, personal grooming and hygiene), and activities that cannot be performed by another person on one's own behalf (for example, sleeping, learning and activities for own recreation).

The significance of this definition is that it maintains that work can be performed in any kind of economic unit: government, corporations and enterprises, and households. Employment—defined as 'work for pay or profit'—therefore becomes a subset of work. This new and enlarged concept of work should dramatically change the way in which work is both recognised and measured.

But what is the Indian approach? Given the historical context of vagueness and imprecision, it is not surprising that Indian definitions of work have also been characterised by lack of clarity about what can be classified as 'work' in the sense of economic activity. At one level, the National Sample Survey Office (NSSO), from its inception has displayed a substantial degree of sophistication by introducing the concepts of 'principal' and 'subsidiary' activities, and seeking information on these in terms of 'usual status', 'current weekly status' and 'current daily status'. This was certainly an innovative way of trying to understand the nuances of work in largely informal economies, and it has since been emulated in several other developing countries. However, the NSSO has also had shifting definitions of work and economic activity, and these in turn still remain subject to substantial grey zones in which the classification into 'work' and 'non-work' remains arbitrary and often inconsistent.

In the early rounds of the NSS, until the 22nd Round (1967–68), the term 'work' was used as the basic category, defined in general terms as any work done for production of goods and services. However, domestic work by family members was not considered as 'work'.

Thereafter, from the 32nd (1977–78) to the 49th (January–June 1993) Rounds, the NSS shifted to the concept of 'gainful activity', which was defined as any activity pursued for pay, profit or family gain, or, in other words, any activity which adds to the national income. While normally these would be activities that result in production of goods and services for exchange, the NSS also included within this category of gainful work, all the agricultural activities in which a part or whole of the agricultural production was not sold but used for own consumption.

However, some activities that did result in earnings, such as prostitution, begging and gambling, were not considered to be 'gainful'. It was argued that this was 'by convention', although that is hardly a precise conceptual basis on which to define work, especially as these activities do generate incomes that are then included in national income. (It is worth noting that the NSS explicitly notes that the activity status of a person is to be judged irrespective of the situation, whether such activity is carried out illegally or not, say in the form of smuggling.) So clearly, legality is not the basis for exclusion of activities from the realm of 'economic' activities; rather it appears to be some inchoate and non-explicit notion of morality. The entire range of activities involved in social reproduction (described simply as 'the execution of household chores'), along with voluntary work for the community or for meeting social commitments, etc., was also not considered to be part of gainful activities.

From the 50th Round (1993–94) onwards, the NSS has moved to a notion of 'economic activity' rather than 'gainful' activity. As in the previous rounds, this included market activities and non-market activities in agriculture directed towards own consumption, including not only cultivation and post-harvest activities, but also gathering of uncultivated crops, forestry, collection of firewood, hunting, fishing, etc. In addition, it included another set of activities that were previously not included: those related to the production of fixed assets on own account, such as the construction of own houses, roads, wells, etc., and of machinery, tools, etc., for household enterprises and also construction of any private or community facilities free of charge. Involvement in such own-account construction either as labourer or supervisor has been construed as economic activity. However, the processing of primary products for own consumption has not been considered as economic activity. Once again, all domestic work has been excluded, as have been the miscellaneous activities such as prostitution, begging, gambling, etc., even though these generated earnings.

As a result, even to date and in the latest surveys, the NSS includes a broad category that it calls 'neither working nor available for work (or not in labour force)', which includes the following codes:

- 91: attended educational institutions;
- 92: attended to domestic duties only;
- 93: attended to domestic duties and was also engaged in free collection of goods (vegetables, roots, firewood, cattle feed, etc.), sewing, tailoring, weaving, etc., for household use;
- 94: rentiers, pensioners, remittance recipients, etc.;
- 95: not able to work owing to disability;
- 97: others (including beggars, prostitutes, etc.);
- 98: did not work owing to sickness (for casual workers only); and
- 99: children of age 0–4 years.

Lumping these disparate groups together and classifying them all as 'not working and not in the labour force' is deeply problematic for several reasons. It is very evident that codes 92 and 93 are fundamentally different from the other codes listed here because they do involve the production of goods and services that are potentially marketable and are therefore economic in nature. Indeed, when they are outsourced for payment by any household, they are included in both national income and in estimates of employment and therefore 'work'. Code 97 presents a different kind of anomaly: marketed activities that are not considered as work presumably for some moral reasons, though this is not stated explicitly (and also it is not clarified why, for example, smuggling should be acceptable if begging is not). The matter is further complicated by the fact that the NSSO also includes some unpaid work in its definition of work, by including 'unpaid helpers in household enterprises' among those defined as working.

The NSS has itself recognised this issue to some extent, in that it recognises paid domestic workers as workers:

> the procedure to be followed in ascertaining the activity status of a domestic servant who is a member of the employer's household is different from that adopted for other members of the household. It may be noted that engagement in domestic duties by such household members is not considered economic activity as defined for the survey. On the other hand, although a domestic servant staying in the employer's household and taking food from the common kitchen is, by definition, a member of the employer's household, he/she is also *engaged in domestic duties in return for wages* in cash and/or kind. Thus, *as a special case, domestic duties pursued by a domestic servant will be considered as an economic activity* and the activity status code as is applicable will be assigned to him/her. (National Sample Survey Office 2014)

It is extraordinary that this is treated as a 'special case' because there is no possible conceptual basis for denying that this is indeed work. And if it is work, then it should be work whether it is paid or unpaid.

Once we open our minds to this possibility, it is clear that we will have to rethink not only the way that our data is collected in the surveys, but also the interpretation of data that we already have from the previous and current surveys. In other words, and especially bearing in mind the definition proposed by the 19th ICLS (whose chairperson also happened to be the Chief Statistician of India), codes 92, 93 and 97 should be included within the definition of work, and contribute to the analysis of work participation rates.

But doing so dramatically changes the picture with respect to trends in work participation in the recent past. There has been much discussion on the evidence from recent NSS large sample surveys on employment, of the significant decline in women's workforce participation rates. Various explanations have been offered for this, including rising real wages that have allowed women in poor households to avoid or reduce involvement in very physically arduous and demanding work with relatively low wages and instead turn to focus more on 'domestic duties'. Implicit in this discussion is a notion of a household-level backward-bending supply curve, which allows women especially in poorer families to choose not to 'work' when their economic conditions allow it.

But once we include codes 92, 93 and 97 in the definition of work, then such a decline is no longer evident: rather it is simply that there is apparently a shift from paid to unpaid work. Figures 2.1 to 2.4 provide some evidence of this by looking at the different elements of work separately for males and females (all for the age group 15+ years) by rural and urban location. The data relates to usual principal activity status over the survey periods since 1999–2000. Once such work is factored in, and other paid but unrecognised work (the category 'others') is also included, then there is less evidence of significant decline in female work participation in recent times. Indeed, the decline in male work participation then appears to be stronger than that for women—and both declines can then be explained dominantly by increasing involvement in education.

Figures 2.1 and 2.2 provide evidence of this for rural and urban females (age 15 years and above) respectively. Once all the different forms of work—both paid/recognised and unpaid/unrecognised—are taken into account, then aggregate work participation declined by only 6.1 percentage points in rural areas and 3.8 percentage points in urban areas—and this decline can be mostly explained by increased involvement in education.

Figure 2.1: Rural Male Work Participation Rates, 1999–2000 to 2011–12

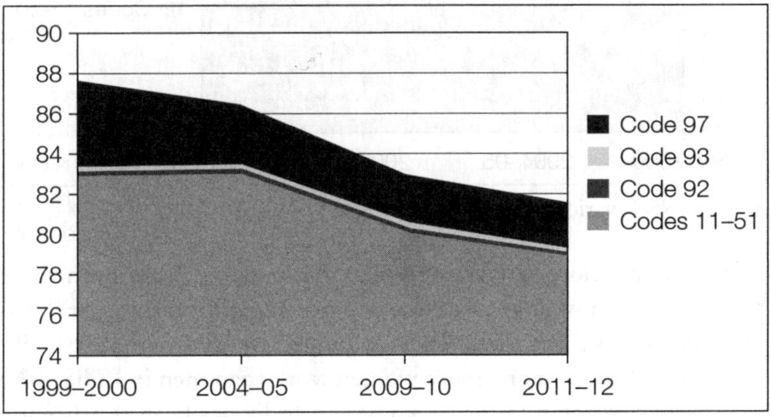

Source: NSS, various years.

Figure 2.2: Rural Female Work Participation Rates, 1999–2000 to 2011–12

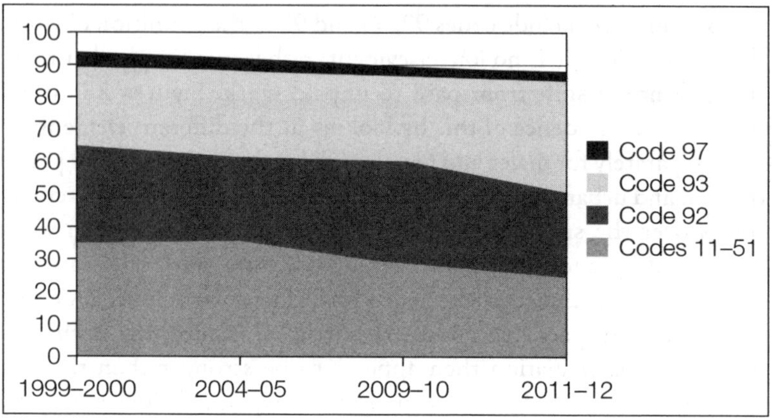

Source: NSS, various years.

Figure 2.3: Urban Male Work Participation Rates, 1999–2000 to 2011–12

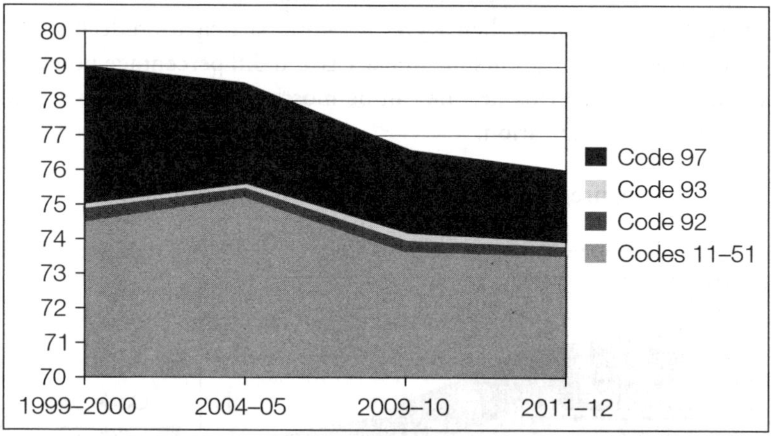

Source: NSS, various years.

Arguably the more interesting point that emerges from both these charts is just how many women are involved in working, in both paid and unpaid activities. Indeed, judged by this more expansive definition of work, many more women work than men in India—the work participation rate for all women in India has been consistently

Figure 2.4: Urban Female Work Participation Rates, 1999–2000 to 2011–12

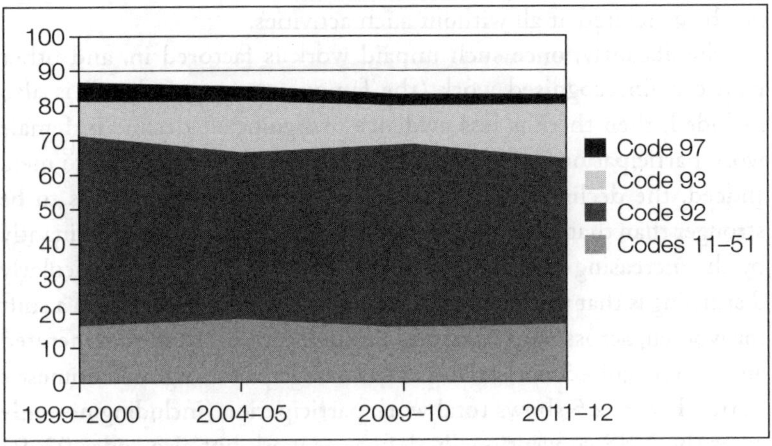

Source: NSS, various years.

higher than that for men. In 2011–12, across both rural and urban areas, the total female work participation rate (even after declining over the decade) was as high as 86.2 per cent, compared to 79.8 per cent for men. This is a very different picture from the conventional one that sees most women in India as 'not working'.

Some results are startling. So, while it is only to be expected that the proportion of men who are involved in domestic work (codes 92 and 93) would be lower than women, the difference is enormous. Thus, less than 1 per cent of men in both urban and rural areas have generally been involved in domestic work as their usual principal activity, but for women the proportion has generally been in excess of 60 per cent. This point needs to be emphasised much more, because the treatment of codes 92 and 93 within the category 'not in the labour force' implicitly suggests that such people are not engaged in activities that are socially necessary. Yet both these codes encompass activities that are absolutely essential for society, which simply must be undertaken. It is impossible to imagine either households or society functioning if these activities are not performed, which means that they must therefore be characterised as not only work, but essential work. To the extent that domestic and care services generally are provided privately within households, they obviously do not enter the national product, but on the other hand, the national product could not be generated at all without such activities.

Significantly, once such unpaid work is factored in, and other paid but unrecognised work (the famous category 'others') is also included, then there is less evidence of significant decline in female work participation in recent times, certainly when compared to men. Indeed, the decline in male work participation then appears to be stronger than that for women—and both can be explained dominantly by the increasing involvement in education. But what is particularly disturbing is that the data seems to indicate that there has been a shift for women, across both rural and urban locations, from remunerated and/or recognised work to unpaid and largely unrecognised domestic duties. Figure 2.5 shows total work participation (including not only what the NSS conventionally defines as work but also codes 92, 93 and 97) at the all-India level across both rural and urban areas for males and females above the age of 15 years. Not only is the female rate substantially higher than the male rate, but the gap between them has increased over this period from 5.6 percentage points to 6.4 percentage points.

Figure 2.5: Total Work Participation Rates, Including Codes 92, 93 and 97, 1999–2000 to 2011–12

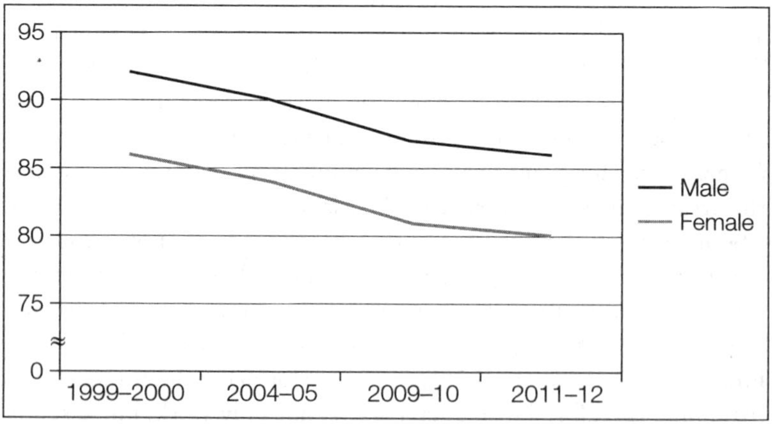

Source: NSS, various years.

There is an argument that enlarging the notion of work does not support measures of labour productivity that are based on current notions of employment. However, this argument misses the important point that much of the unpaid work covered in codes 92 and 93 directly and indirectly contributes to output, and therefore effectively subsidises the production of 'marketed' output. So this is what therefore enables the labour productivity that is captured using the restrictive notion of work. A more holistic framework that incorporates such work in the estimate of total labour use would provide a better sense of the true labour productivity in society.

This lack of recognition of a significant part of the work dominantly provided by women has several important economic and social implications. The unpaid–paid continuum of women's work serves to devalue both women and the work they do. Thus, when women do enter labour markets, their wages tend to be lower than those of men—not only because they are willing to work for lower wages but because so much of their work is available for free. India has one of the largest gender gaps in wages to be found anywhere in the world, with women's wages on average only around two-thirds that of men's wages.

Related to this, the occupations in which women dominate tend to be lower paid, and the wage penalty extends even to men doing similar work, such as in the low-paid care sector. This is certainly true of private employers. But in India, even the government has used these gender-segmented labour markets to provide public services on the cheap, by employing *anganwadi*—nursery or day-care—workers and helpers and Accredited Social Health Activists (ASHAs) as 'volunteers' who are paid only a fraction of the official minimum wages. Similarly, women are disproportionately employed by state governments as para-teachers, and auxiliary nurses and midwives (ANMs), and paid far less than regular employees.

It is evident that this unpaid work provides a huge subsidy to the recognised economy and to the 'formal sector', which rely both directly and indirectly on the goods and services produced by these unsung and unrewarded workers. Because this contribution is not recognised, it enables self-satisfied perceptions of rising aggregate labour productivity in the economy, which may be quite misplaced. This also means that public policy can continue to ignore the need to reduce and redistribute such unpaid labour, and can persist in the mistaken belief that GDP growth will simply generate enough 'good jobs' for everyone. For this to change, and for economic policy-making to become truly sensitive to the various gendered dimensions that enable it to occur as it does, it is crucial to understand the essential role played by the unpaid work performed by women.

Note

1. The better off a household is, the more likely that it can afford to buy many goods (such as, say, processed foods, prepared fuel, labour-saving devices) and services (related to care and housework). The more impoverished a family is, the more likely that members of that family will have to go out and work to deliver such goods and services to richer families, and then come home and provide for themselves these essential items through their own unpaid labour.

References

Antonopoulos, Rania and Indira Hirway, eds. 2010. *Unpaid Work and the Economy: Gender, Time Use and Poverty in Developing Countries.* London: Palgrave.

Antonopoulos, Rania and Emel Memis. 2010. 'Time and Poverty from a Developing Country Perspective'. *Working Paper No. 600*. New York: Levy Economics Institute of Bard College.

Central Statistical Organisation. 1998–99. *India: Time Use Survey 1998*. DDI-IND-MOSPI-CSO-TUS-1998–99, Central Statistical Organisation, New Delhi. Available at http://www.icssrdataservice.in/datarepository/index.php/catalog/142/overview (accessed 1 April 2020).

Elson, Diane. 1995. *Male Bias in the Development Process*. Manchester: Manchester University Press.

Government of Ecuador. 2009. *National Plan for Good Living 2009–13: Building a Plurinational and Intercultural State*. Quito: Ministry of National Planning and Development (Senplades).

Hirway, Indira. 2010. 'Understanding Poverty: Insights from the Time Use of the Poor'. In *Unpaid Work and the Economy: Gender, Time Use and*

Poverty in Developing Countries, ed. Rania Antonopoulos and Indira Hirway 22–57. London: Palgrave.

International Labour Organisation. 2013. *Resolution of the 19th International Conference of Labour Statisticians*, November. Geneva: ILO.

National Sample Survey Office. 2014. *Key Indicators of Employment and Unemployment in India 2011–12*, 68th Round. New Delhi: NSSO.

United Nations System of National Accounts. 1993. Available at https://unstats.un.org/unsd/nationalaccount/sna1993.asp (accessed 1 April 2020).

———. 2008. https://unstats.un.org/unsd/nationalaccount/sna2008.asp

Vickery, C. 1977. 'The Time-poor: A New Look At Poverty'. *The Journal of Human Resources* 12 (1): 27–48.

3

Women's Participation in Domestic Activities

Leisure, Care Services and Status Production

Vinoj Abraham

The labour force participation of women in India has attracted considerable scholarly attention since the early 2010s when a fall in female labour force participation rate (FLFPR) was noted (Abraham 2013; Himanshu 2011; Kannan and Raveendran 2012; Klasen and Pieters 2013; Mazumdar and Neetha 2011; Neff et al. 2012; Rangarajan et al. 2011; Thomas 2012, among others). All these studies have identified the declining FLFPR in both paid and unpaid 'work' as one of the distinguishing features of the Indian labour market. The FLFPR had declined from 23.7 per cent in 1993–94 to 16.1 per cent in 2017–18 for the rural areas and it had been stagnant at around 13–14 per cent in the urban areas during the same period. With the secular decline in FLFPR, the most dominant activity that females are now engaged in is 'unpaid domestic activities'.[1] More than 45 per cent of women in rural areas and 47 per cent of women in urban areas were engaged in such unpaid domestic activities in 2017–18 (Table 3.2).[2] In fact, if the available data is any evidence, with the very low share of paid labour participation, this category should be considered as the residual. Though such a staggeringly large share of women are engaged in unpaid domestic activities, there have been very few studies explaining this; rather, most studies have focused on the declining FLFPR.

Studies that do address this issue of domestic activities among women have, by and large, remained apologetic to women's work, claiming a large part of this unpaid domestic activity as disguised, unaccounted, invisible work for the output market. Hirway (2012) argued that the NSSO surveys, in their current modes of data collection and estimation, were incapable of capturing women's work. She posited that a substantial share of women who were engaged in what is accounted as non-work or unpaid domestic activity by the NSSO were in fact engaged in economic activities covered under the production boundary of the UN SNA. Category '93' of NSS economic activity status classification consists of 'attended domestic duties and were also engaged in (a) free collection of goods such as vegetables, roots, firewood, cattle feed, etc. and (b) sewing, tailoring, weaving, etc.', which needed to be accounted as work, even if unpaid. Using the Indian TUS conducted in 1998, she showed that though the NSS data accounts for only a negligible share of the females engaged in activity '93', when the weekly time spent on such activities is taken into account, the participation is not negligible. In another study, Hirway (2002) showed that often the work done by women at home would not be reported as work since paid manual work is stigmatised. Also, men from the households who report the activity status of women often do not report these activities as work. The intermediate stages of production, especially in agriculture and informal manufacturing, where women are actively involved, are perceived as non-work. The expansion of such home-based activities in the economy with liberalisation has probably caused a large share of women to be accounted as non-workers, giving the impression that women are missing from the labour force. Sudarshan and Bhattacharya (2009) also found through a sample survey that the NSS is an underestimation of actual women's work participation in urban Delhi.

Notwithstanding the arguments by scholars that this large presence of women in domestic activity probably is due to poor conceptualisation and accounting of women's work, it cannot be denied that the proportion of this population has been large and rising unabated since at least 1993–94. There have been no major definitional changes in these categories during the last three decades which would have accounted for the *rise* in the share of domestic activity among women. Moreover, the rise in this share of the female population has not been restricted to the liberalisation era. The share of females in domestic activities in rural areas was 30 per cent by 1983 which rose to 34.4 per cent by 1993–94, the pre-liberalisation era. In comparison, during the decade after liberalisation, 1993–94 to 2004–05, the share increased only to 35.5 per cent, a 1 percentage point increase compared to a nearly 5 percentage point increase in the pre-liberalisation decade. In urban areas there was a rise of about 5.5 percentage points during the period 1993–94 to 2004–05, but already by 1983 itself domestic activity among women was the most dominant activity. No doubt, some part of the rising share of domestic activity among women may be due to poor conceptualisation and accounting issues, but much understanding of this phenomena would be lost if we are blinded to the obvious—that the data at hand indeed is a reflection of the larger reality that women are increasingly engaging in domestic activities.

What makes these statistics not palatable is not so much the sheer size of these numbers, but the lack of an argument, a theory that would make these numbers within imagination. The absence of a theoretical perspective on this side of the Indian women's working world is again probably due to our own valuation of what work is and what is not. Much of the attention of women's work is focused on women's work for the output market whether for pay or not, whether visible or not. Yet we do know from our daily realities that women's work is much more than that. For instance, provisioning of care services to the household or family is central to women's domestic engagement and informs the main argument for double burden.

What we know less is *why*? Why do Indian women increasingly engage in unpaid domestic activity? Why is this trend being strengthened over the years? What encourages the enhanced 'domesticity' of Indian women? This essay contributes towards reopening some of the analytical constructs that could probably be helpful in explaining this phenomenon and further provide some rudimentary empirics in this direction.

THE ANALYTICAL CONTEXT: HOUSEHOLD AND WOMEN'S DOMESTICITY

Studies have signalled that it is probably the 'income effect' as in individual labour supply models that is the driving force behind the withdrawal of women from work and the shift towards domestic activities. With increasing income levels of the household, women withdraw from paid work and focus on domestic activities, as women are argued to have comparative advantage over men in such activities. But these are 'residual' arguments that provide reasons for why women need not participate in 'work' and hence could alternately engage in the residual activity of the domestic. In other words, these theories do not, in a very real sense, differentiate between leisure and unpaid domestic activity. Besides, they justify women's withdrawal from 'work' as escape from the double burden. They do not, in short, provide a reason as to why women are increasingly entering domestic activity, but give some justification for why women are not entering the labour market. Though from an apparent empirical point of view, the absence of one type of activity denotes the presence of another, that does not provide a theoretical justification to argue that one's absence leads to the presence of the other.

What we need is a theory that would reason out the expansion of domestic activity among Indian women, not as a residual activity, but whose reasoning would explain the causal linkages of the rise of domestic activity among Indian women. We have access to two streams of theoretical literature that accommodate domestic activity, not as a residual activity, but as a conscious choice, and enter the sphere of decision-making in its own right. Central to these approaches to domestic activity, and what makes them different from other approaches, is putting the focus back on the household/family.

Household Production

Household production models assume that the household time and purchased goods, made possible by paid work and non-labour income, are combined to purchase commodities that are then consumed (Becker 1965). The labour supply of married women would then be affected by two kinds of substitution effect, that is, substitution effect between market and household work, and between market work and leisure. As market wage rate increases, women tend to meet more of their household work/care services through purchased goods and services substituting household work with paid work. With high non-labour income, the negative income effect on women's paid work and preference for leisure dominates. The model implies that at higher levels of household income and/or spousal earnings, women's participation in the labour market would be low, and with higher levels of own labour wage rate, the probability of women's participation in the labour market would increase. While the household production model assumes that household production is essentially women's work, the *joint decision-making model* relaxes this assumption further and brings in the possibility of household work and market work as joint decision-making strategies of both spouses (Gronau 1977). Under this framework, both spouses being substitutes for household production, the relative productivity differences in household work between males and females, and their relative wage differentials in paid work, would determine who would supply labour for paid work, and how much time would be supplied for paid work.

However, household production models also assume perfect substitutability of labour between males and females, in both household activities and paid work, thus completely disregarding the gender relations that determine the household division of labour and relative position of women in the household. Missing in the above argument is then the gender relations within household/family and how the various choices of work, leisure and domestic activity are allocated.

The proponents of cultural studies and capitalist development bring gender relations to the core of household division of labour, and explain the distribution of work, leisure and domestic activity within the household. Cultural norms of patriarchy distribute power, which is the ability to influence the actions of others, unevenly and differently. With the development of capitalist organisation of production in patriarchal social systems, the shift from attached labour to wage labour and female labour marginalisation realigns the household division of labour among worker households. With rising income levels, the economic status of the male worker, the main breadwinner, in the labour market attains significance as the indicator for social status of the household, while women's paid work represents low social status and is stigmatised. With a decline in contribution to output market, lost autonomy and self-esteem, women remain disempowered and vulnerable, and importantly, are withdrawn to within the household providing care services and goods to the household. Her individual economic space now being lost, her ability to negotiate her survival and subsistence becomes largely dependent on the power-wielding members of the household, mostly the head of the household and/or her spouse. Dependent on these power centres for their own survival, she engages in production of status goods and services for the household, and negotiates, bargains, strategises every day in intra-household trading of status goods and services in return for her own economic wellbeing.

Status Production

Before we go into women and status production, let us take a look at what is 'status'. Status can simply be defined as the relative position of an individual/household with respect to its reference group. Status, like any other good or service gives utility to its consumers, and higher status is preferred to lower status. Social status thus could refer to the position of an individual or a household with reference to its social group. Now, if there are norms that are considered desirable by a social group, then individuals/households conforming to such social norms may acquire greater social status than units that do not conform, or only partially conform to such norms of the group. In patriarchal societies, thus conforming to the prevalent patriarchal social norms may produce greater status to the households. In order to acquire status in patriarchal societies, conforming to patriarchal norms is essential. However, to acquire such status, control over women, and women conforming to such norms, is necessary. Women thus become status producers for the households in patriarchal societies and it is these status goods and services that she trades within the household for her own wellbeing. What patriarchal norms do for the woman's choice between paid labour participation and unpaid domestic activity is that they allow the society to considerably reduce the opportunity cost of women's paid work and increase the opportunity cost of domestic activity by attaching status and status production to it.

Women engage primarily in two activities that enhances status to the household. One, she herself becomes the carrier of status, and the other, she produces goods and services that enhances status for the household. She becomes a carrier of status by accepting the norm that women's paid work deteriorates social status, while male paid work is status-enhancing. She becomes a carrier of status by ever trying to enact the stereotyped roles such as that of the dutiful wife, caring mother, respectful daughter, disciplined daughter-in-law, honourable sister and sister-in-law, and so on. By conforming to these stereotypes she adds status to the household. Second, her care services are valorised in society as indispensable for the family, and by producing these 'status goods and services' for the household, they enhance the status of the household. Status production theories suggest that women substitute paid labour with 'status production' activities such as education of children, healthcare of the members of the family, engaging in rites and rituals, etc., as survival strategies (Papenak 1979).

Women's domestic activity thus can be conceived as work, not for direct pay as in paid work, but as status labour, involved in producing status goods and services for the household. Her labour to follow the patriarchal norms, for instance, being a dutiful wife, is in this sense work, because she produces status for the household. Status goods thus produced by the woman can be bartered intra-household and it is the returns to her 'status labour' that ensures her economic security within households in a patriarchal society.

An essential feature of this argument is that women are part of a power relation within the household, and their position in the power relation is determined by their relationship with the other male members in the household. The degree of control that male members can have over her determines her position within the household, and in turn, determines her engagement in status production. To put it crudely, the more they are subjected to controls, greater would be their participation in status production and hence domestic activities.

Thus, though it may be true that most women engage in status production of some manner, when society has assigned roles of greater controls and subjugation of women in some relationships, it is these women who would be more domesticised and expend more labour on status production. In this context, relationships established through marriages, that is, affinal relations, may be more amenable to controls, rather than relationships of blood, that is, consanguineal relations. Within these relationship types themselves, the proximity to their loci of controls may further differentiate women in terms of domesticity.

To the above arguments made, we have some limited empirical evidences, which are discussed here. The data is extracted from the unit-level records of the NSS for the reports on the employment and unemployment situation in India. The data covers the period 1983 to 2011–12 primarily. I have also included, to the extent possible, the unit-level records of the Periodic Labour Force Survey (PLFS), the new incarnation of the NSS employment-unemployment surveys, implemented for the year 2017–18. That the sampling strategy followed by the two surveys are not entirely similar has raised issues regarding comparability of the two data sources, the NSS surveys and PLFS surveys. However, both are large samples covering the entire country. Hence, the broad national trends could be compared, though this may not be the case as we disaggregate the data. As a result, the comparison is limited to broad classification, and disaggregation is attempted only using the NSS data. Nevertheless, looking at the broad trends, it seems that the story would remain consistent with trends as seen upto the last employment–unemployment surveys of the NSS in 2011–12.

First, we analyse the trends in female labour participation, followed by an analysis of domestic activity participation of women. Further, we explore the domestic activity participation of women in various contexts such as marital status, relationship type with male members of the household, type of household in terms of nuclear families or extended families, and their place of stay in terms of natal homes or marital homes. It is expected that this type of classification of women in terms of marital status, relationship type with male members, household types and place of stay would bring out varying degrees of controls, and thus may provide some evidence for the argument of status production and domesticity. The last section provides the concluding remarks.

Female Labour Participation and Domestic Activity

The FLFPR has been declining in India since the 1970s. For rural areas, the FLFPR declined throughout the period from the 1970s till 2017–18, while for urban areas it had been stagnant at very low levels (Table 3.1). The FLFPRs using the Usual Principal Status (UPS) measure for rural females declined from 32 per cent in 1972–73 to 16.1 per cent in 2017–18, while for urban females the participation rates had been stagnant at around 13–15 per cent during the period 1972–73 to 2017–18. During the same period, however, there has been no decline in the male labour force participation rates (MLFPRs) both in the rural and urban areas. The MLFPRs had remained at around 54–55 per cent during the entire period both in the rural and urban areas.

With the declining FLFPRs, the single most important economic activity that is gaining prominence for women is the unpaid domestic activity (Table 3.2). The share of rural women engaged in domestic activity in 1983 was only 29.8 per cent, which increased to 45.1 per cent by 2017–18. In urban areas the share of women engaged in domestic activities increased from 38.5 per cent to 47.3 per cent during the same period. Domestic activity had become the dominant activity in the rural areas since 1999–2000, while in the urban areas this had been the most dominant activity by 1983 itself. Participation in education also increased from 7.6 to 24.6 per cent among rural women, and from 18.2 to 24.8 per cent for the urban women during the period 1972–73 to 2017–18, but the rise in participation in education was specific to the age group, up to 15 years, and the entire rise in education participation was accounted for within this age group.[3]

This large and rising share of women engaged in domestic activity, along with the declining share of women engaged in labour force,

Table 3.1: LFPR for All Ages (%), 1972–73 to 2017–18

	Rural Male		**Rural Female**		**Urban Male**		**Urban Female**	
	UPS	**UPSS**	**UPS**	**UPSS**	**UPS**	**UPSS**	**UPS**	**UPSS**
1972–73	55.2		32.0		52.6		14.3	
1977–78	54.9	55.9	26.2	33.8	53.2	53.7	15.0	17.8
1983	54.0	55.5	25.2	34.2	53.1	54.0	12.9	15.9
1987–88	53.2	54.9	25.4	33.1	52.8	53.4	12.9	16.2
1993–94	54.9	56.1	23.7	33.1	54.2	54.3	13.2	16.5
1999–2000	53.3	54.0	23.5	30.2	53.9	54.2	12.6	14.7
2004–05	54.6	55.5	25.0	33.3	56.6	57.1	14.9	17.8
2009–10	54.8	55.6	20.8	26.5	55.6	55.9	12.8	14.6
2011–12	54.7	55.3	18.1	25.3	56.0	56.3	13.4	15.5
2017–18	54.6	54.9	16.1	18.2	56.8	57.0	15.1	15.9

Note: UPS (Usual Principal Status) refers to activity done during the major part of the reference year; UPSS (Usual Principal and Subsidiary Status) refers to both the major and minor part of the reference year. For details, see concepts and definitions in NSSs on employment and unemployment.

Source: NSS Reports on Employment and Unemployment Situation in India and Periodic Labour Force Survey of India.

Table 3.2: Total Female Activity Status Distribution (UPS), 1983 to 2017–18

Activity Status	1983	1987–88	1993–94	1999–2000	2004–05	2009–10	2011–12	2017–18
Rural								
Labour force	41.2	42.5	37.3	23.3	24.6	20.8	18.0	16.1
All domestic	29.8	27.3	34.4	36.3	35.5	39.9	42.2	45.1
Education	7.6	7.2	11.7	18.4	21.3	23.8	25.1	24.6
Others	21.4	23.1	16.2	22.4	18.4	15.6	14.7	14.2
Total	**100.0**	**100.0**	**100.0**	**100.0**	**100.0**	**100.0**	**100.0**	**100.0**
Urban								
Labour force	25.2	25.4	23.5	13.0	14.5	12.8	13.4	15.1
All domestic	38.5	38.1	40.2	45.4	45.7	48.2	48.0	47.3
Education	18.2	18.4	21.8	25.1	25.1	25.6	26.0	24.8
Others	18.1	17.9	14.1	16.9	14.5	13.4	12.6	12.8
Total	**100.0**	**100.0**	**100.0**	**100.0**	**100.0**	**100.0**	**100.0**	**100.0**

Source: NSS Reports on Employment and Unemployment Situation in India and Periodic Labour Force Survey of India.

apparently, signals an income effect. Figures 3.1 and 3.2 plot the domestic activity participation rates of women across deciles of household monthly per capita consumption expenditure (HHMPCE) levels for rural and urban areas, respectively. It can be noted from Figure 3.1 for the rural areas, as the level of HHMPCE increases, the share of women engaged in domestic activities also increases and this trend is consistent in all years. The domestic participation rate of women was considerably lower in the lower deciles and vice versa. Also, it can be noted that the distribution of participation rates of more recent years dominates the older years, implying that in the more recent years, across all deciles there had been a rise in the share of domestic activities of women. In case of urban areas there was a non-linear relation, with domestic participation rates being low at the lower deciles, which peaks in the middle deciles and thereafter declines. This meant that women in the lowest and highest deciles had a lower share in the domestic activities, while it was the middle-income group which had the highest participation rates. But this inverted U-shaped relation flattens out in the more recent years, and looks similar to the trend in the rural areas. The relation between

Figure 3.1: Rural Female Participation Rate in All Domestic Activities (%), 1983 to 2009–10

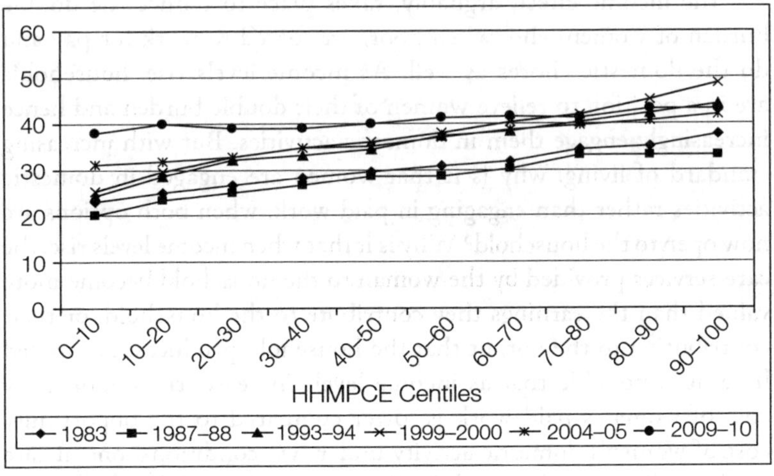

Source: Abraham (2013).

Figure 3.2: Urban Female Participation Rate in All Domestic Activities (%), 1983 to 2009–10

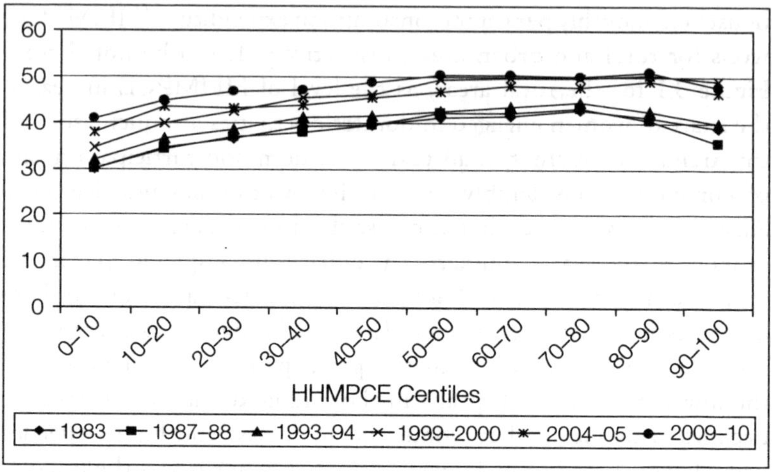

Source: Abraham (2013).

HHMPCE and female participation in domestic activities thus seems to support the argument that as the level of income increases, women tend to withdraw from the labour force and engage in domestic activities, argued as the income effect.

The income effect, arguably, takes place to reduce the double burden of women who, when poor, are forced to work for pay and do the domestic chores as well. As income levels rise, households are in a position to relieve women of their double burden and hence increasingly engage them in domestic activities. But with increasing standard of living, why is it that women are engaged in domestic activities rather than engaging in paid work, when both options are now open to the household? Why is it that when income levels rise, the care services provided by the woman to the household become more valued than the earnings they contribute to the household, or their contribution to the output that the household produces? As argued here, it is possible that as income levels increase, the opportunity cost of woman's paid work is lower compared to the opportunity cost of women's domestic activity under two conditions: one, if care work has limited substitutability between males and females; two, if there is stigma attached to women's paid work and/or status attached to women's domestic activity. Though for the sake of abstraction we can separate out care work and status production as analytically two categories, in empirical terms it may be extremely difficult to distinguish these two aspects because one of the important dimensions of status production is care work itself.

To argue the case that status and status production may indeed be one of the important factors that are associated with increasing domestic activity, we now look at domestic activity patterns of women across different relationship types.

Domestic Activity across Relationship Types

This analysis is based on the premise that one of the important ways through which a woman's position in a household is determined is based on the type of relationship she has with the household. Relations of marriage in patriarchal societies produce greater control over women, hence, as argued earlier, their need for greater status production. Thus, her position as a spouse in the household may be relatively more vulnerable as compared to her position as an unmarried daughter, while she may have relatively greater autonomy when she is the head of the household herself. With greater autonomy she may expend much less labour on status production and may spend more labour on paid work.

Table 3.3 shows the domestic activity participation rate of women according to their relationship status with the head of the household. The category 'Self' accounts for women who are heads of the household. All other categories are self-evident. It can be noted from the table that the domestic participation of women in their roles as spouses is much higher than any other relationship status. On an average, women in their roles as spouses of heads of the household or spouses of married children accounted for the largest share in domestic activity. For instance, in the year 2017–18, 74.62 per cent of the spouses of heads of the household were engaged in domestic activity, and 81.4 per cent of the spouses of children were engaged in similar activities. No other category of women crossed a share of more than 51 per cent. The share of women in women-headed households

Table 3.3: Domestic Participation Rate by Relationship Status (UPS, %), 1999–2000 to 2017–18

	Relation to Head of Household									
	1	**2**	**3**	**4**	**5**	**6**	**7**	**8**	**9**	**Total**
					Total					
1999–2000	30.6	64.3	47.5	72.8	11.6	3.8	37.9	40.1	32.1	38.2
2004–05	30.7	62.5	39.2	72.3	11.6	3.6	37.7	37.7	14.4	37.9
2009–10	29.9	70.6	39.7	76.9	10.5	3.4	41.8	40.3	23.1	42.3
2011–12	32.7	73.6	55.3	80.0	10.0	3.1	39.7	43.1	22.7	43.8
2017–18	28.7	74.2	51.3	81.4	12.2	3.1	41.7	47.8	20.8	45.8
					Rural					
1999–2000	30.1	58.4	44.6	69.8	11.6	4.0	37.3	38.4	27.7	35.8
2004–05	28.9	56.5	36.9	69.5	11.7	3.7	36.2	35.4	23.8	35.3
2009–10	28.4	66.1	34	74.5	10.8	3.6	41.3	38.0	24.2	40.1
2011–12	31.4	70.1	54.9	79.0	10.2	3.1	38.6	42.9	10.9	42.2
2017–18	28.3	72.3	52.6	81.4	12.9	3.4	39.7	48.4	22.1	45.1

(Contd)

Table 3.3: (*Contd*)

	Relation to Head of Household									
	1	**2**	**3**	**4**	**5**	**6**	**7**	**8**	**9**	**Total**
					Urban					
1999–2000	32.0	81.2	56.9	85.3	11.5	2.9	39.8	44.7	35.6	45.3
2004–05	35.3	79.4	46.3	82.5	11.2	3.3	42.1	43.2	9.8	45.6
2009–10	33.6	82.0	54.2	84.5	9.8	2.7	43.1	45.2	21.8	48.2
2011–12	35.4	82.2	55.9	83.2	9.5	2.8	42.4	43.7	32.8	48.0
2017–18	29.4	78.7	49.4	81.5	10.4	2.2	46.1	46.8	19.5	47.3

Note: 1—self; 2—spouse of head of household; 3—married child; 4—spouse of married child; 5—unmarried child; 6—grandchild; 7—father/mother/father-in-law/mother-in-law; 8—servants/employees/other non-relatives; 9—others.

Source: Estimated from unit-level data of the NSS on Employment and Unemployment Situation in India, various rounds, and Periodic Labour Force Survey of India.

accounted as domestic activities was only 28 per cent, and unmarried children accounted in the same status was only 12.2 per cent.

It needs to be recognised from this analysis that though the overall participation rate of women in domestic activities is high as remarked here, this is not uniform across relationship types. The position of women in their respective households seems to play a deterministic role in their activity. While women who were married were largely engaged in domestic activities, women who were unmarried in general seem to have a lower participation in domestic activities. Thus, it seems to point out that marital status is an important marker for participation in domestic activities for women, and also their relationship with the head of the household, as blood relation or relationship through marriage seems to mediate their activity status, being engaged in domestic activities or not.

In terms of trends, the participation in domestic activities conditioned on this relationship status with the head of the household seems to be further strengthened during the period 1999–2000 to 2017–18. The share of women married to the head of the household engaged in domestic activity was 64.3 per cent in 1999–2000, which increased to 74.2 per cent by 2017–18. In case of the spouse of married children, this share increased from 72.8 to 81.4 per cent during the same period. These two categories of women were the only types, among all women, to show a consistent rise in their shares engaged in domestic activity. For all other categories, be it married child, self or unmarried child, there was no substantial change in trend during this period. Thus, evidently, the increase in domestic activity rate during the period 1999–2000 to 2017–18 is largely driven by the increasing share of domestic activity among married women. This indeed shows that not only is marital status an important marker of domestic activity, but also, over time, the socially assigned role of women as caregivers is gaining strength such that an overwhelmingly large share of married women play out this role.

Comparing rural and urban areas, the share of women in domestic activities is much higher in the urban areas, as noted earlier. However, the interesting aspect to note here is that though the urban areas have higher domestic participation shares, this is evident only in case of spouses of heads of households and spouses of children, while in all other categories the urban and rural areas are largely comparable. For instance, for women who were heads of households, the share of women in domestic activities ranged between 28 and 31 per cent in the rural areas and between 32 and 35 per cent in urban areas. While for the spouse categories, for the spouse of the head of the household, the rural range was between 58 and 72 per cent and for urban areas it was between 79 and 82 per cent. In case of the spouse of a married child, the rural ranged between 69 and 81 per cent, and for urban areas it was between 82 and 85 per cent.

In terms of trends, too, this rural–urban difference is visible only in case of these spouse categories. For rural areas, the share of women as spouses of the heads of households in domestic activity increased from 58.4 per cent in 1999–2000 to 72.3 per cent in 2017–18, a rise of nearly 14 percentage points during the period. But for urban areas, the share was more or less constant at 79 to 82 per cent. Similarly, as the spouse of a married child, the shares in rural areas increased from 70 to 81.4 per cent during the period, while for urban areas there was only a marginal decline from 85.3 to 81.5 per cent. These trends, too, seem to suggest that the domestic activity status of women is getting strengthened in the rural areas, and their shares are converging with those of the urban areas. From this, it may be possible to argue that over time, the rural women, too, are increasingly engaged in domestic activities, just as their urban counterparts, and it is the shift in activity status of married women in the rural areas that is causing the overall domestic activity participation rates to rise over time. While in the case of unmarried women or women-headed households, there was no visible rise in domestic activity participation.

A comparison across HHMPCE decile categories shows that levels of household income and domestic activity rates of 'spouses of heads' and 'spouses of other married male members' moved in the same direction in 1999–2000 (Table 3.4). For instance, the gap between the first decile and tenth decile for these two groups was 33.1 percentage points and 20.6 percentage points, respectively. In none of the other categories was the gap between the rich and the poor so large as in case of the spouses. It may be interpreted that as

Table 3.4: Domestic Activity Rate by Relationship Status across Income Categories, 1999–2000 to 2017–18

					Relation to Head					
					1999–2000					
Decile	**1**	**2**	**3**	**4**	**5**	**6**	**7**	**8**	**9**	**Total**
1st	25.9	47.6	44.0	58.5	8.6	2.9	33.3	30.6	35.7	25.8
2nd	22.7	52.1	43.6	66.8	10.1	3.0	34.5	32.3	47.9	30.0
3rd	24.7	54.2	45.2	71.9	12.1	3.7	34.4	39.5	21.6	33.2
4th	28.6	58.0	43.2	71.4	12.7	4.1	36.6	39.7	52.7	35.3
5th	27.8	61.4	40.4	71.6	12.1	4.2	38.3	42.0	24.0	37.3
6th	30.7	62.5	46.6	75.7	13.6	4.1	39.1	41.2	17.6	39.2
7th	31.7	67.5	55.2	74.9	13.9	4.7	42.0	42.2	27.9	41.8
8th	31.5	71.8	47.6	78.4	13.5	3.1	40.0	41.6	34.8	43.9
9th	38.0	77.4	57.5	81.5	12.3	5.4	40.8	46.8	27.8	48.1
10th	35.1	80.7	55.1	79.1	7.9	2.7	40.4	44.0	35.0	49.4
Total	30.6	64.3	47.5	72.8	11.6	3.8	37.9	40.1	32.1	38.2
10th minus 1st	9.2	33.1	11.1	20.6	–0.7	–0.2	7.1	13.4	–0.7	23.6
					2011–12					
Decile	**1**	**2**	**3**	**4**	**5**	**6**	**7**	**8**	**9**	**Total**
1st	26.5	68.2	62.3	83.3	11.2	4.5	38.8	44.0	20.9	36.9
2nd	33.4	75.5	52.5	80.4	11.2	2.1	42.0	42.3	11.0	40.9
3rd	32.1	72.7	63.5	78.6	11.3	2.7	37.6	49.0	33.5	42.0
4th	31.5	74.9	42.3	78.2	10.5	4.5	40.7	46.3	25.2	43.1
5th	32.7	71.9	60.1	80.3	10.6	1.4	40.9	36.7	38.7	43.1
6th	30.9	70.3	62.6	79.8	11.1	4.0	34.8	43.0	17.1	43.5
7th	29.4	70.8	45.1	82.3	9.4	2.0	38.8	43.6	3.4	44.2
8th	35.8	73.5	51.4	80.8	9.4	3.5	37.4	45.7	43.3	46.5
9th	36.8	76.8	55.5	82.0	7.9	3.4	41.8	41.0	42.4	49.1
10th	33.7	79.6	48.7	73.2	4.6	1.6	45.3	39.0	25.9	49.8
Total	32.7	73.6	55.3	80.0	10.0	3.1	39.7	43.1	22.7	43.8
10th minus 1st	7.2	11.4	–13.6	–10.1	–6.6	–2.9	6.5	–5.0	5.0	12.9

(*Contd*)

Table 3.4: (*Contd*)

	2017–18									
Decile	**1**	**2**	**3**	**4**	**5**	**6**	**7**	**8**	**9**	**Total**
1st	23.9	71.3	56.5	80.9	14.5	3.9	38.1	47.2	19.8	40.8
2nd	24.4	69.1	31.8	84.6	14.1	1.6	43.4	45.4	19.6	40.9
3rd	28.1	75.1	58.0	83.7	12.1	2.8	41.7	47.7	18.7	44.5
4th	38.5	73.5	50.6	81.2	14.7	2.7	40.5	53.6	36.0	45.6
5th	31.6	72.7	54.4	83.6	12.4	3.6	38.7	46.2	7.4	46.8
6th	31.2	73.2	49.6	82.9	13.4	3.9	42.2	51.0	37.7	47.9
7th	27.9	74.5	51.2	82.9	11.6	4.3	38.1	46.6	40.8	48.0
8th	31.0	75.9	48.6	80.4	9.3	2.3	45.4	48.0	16.2	49.0
9th	29.1	76.9	41.3	78.2	8.6	1.9	43.2	47.7	26.7	48.8
10th	24.9	76.7	44.7	68.4	5.8	1.1	50.7	42.7	15.3	49.2
Total	28.7	74.2	51.3	81.4	12.2	3.1	41.7	47.8	20.8	45.8
10th minus 1st	1.0	5.4	–11.8	–12.5	–8.7	–2.8	12.6	–4.4	–4.5	8.4

Note: 1—self; 2—spouse of head of household; 3—married child; 4—spouse of married child; 5—unmarried child; 6—grandchild; 7—father/mother/father-in-law/mother-in-law; 8—servants/employees/other non-relatives; 9—others.

Source: Estimated from unit-level data of the NSS on Employment and Unemployment Situation in India, various rounds, and Periodic Labour Force Survey of India.

the levels of income in the households rise, it is the spouses within the households that increasingly engage in domestic activity, while women belonging to other categories are only marginally affected by rise in income. Even though participation of women belonging to other categories also has a positive relation with income, their response to income is at a much lower level compared to spouses. This gives some evidence to the argument that higher income levels provide heads of households and other male members the option of engaging their spouses in domestic activities, while women whose decision-making are not linked with male relations through marriage engage less in domestic activities even at higher levels of income.

But this positive relation between income levels and domestic activity of spouses is considerably muted in 2017–18. This is because of the fact that a large share of women belonging to the relatively poorer households got engaged in domestic activity by 2017–18. In fact, between 1999–2000 and 2017–18, the largest rise in domestic participation was among the poorest, such that the difference in domestic participation between poor and rich has narrowed down. For instance, the gap for spouses of head of households between the poorest (first decile) and the richest (tenth decile) was only about 5.4 percentage points in 2017–18. The gap between these two groups in 1999–2000 was more than 33 per cent. A very similar trend is visible in cases of the spouses of children as well.

At the same time we do not see any consistent and large change with regard to women belonging to other categories. Thus, the changes during the period 1999–2000 to 2017–18 did not have any major impact on women's decision to join domestic activity in case of women belonging to other categories. But for spouses, the changes in this period made engaging in domestic activity more attractive. If it can be assumed that between 1999–2000 and 2017–18 there has been considerable rise in income, then it can be argued that with income rise among the poor, the household decision was to engage such women in domestic activities. Such a decision is probably linked with status attached to domestic activity for spouses. The fact that other women are not affected by income changes adds support to the argument that probably status/stigma considerations are an important component in decision-making when it comes to a choice between women's paid and unpaid work.

Domestic Activity and Type of Family

From the previous section, it is evident that women's participation in domestic activities is primarily associated with their nature of marital relation. It follows then that there are two possibilities as to why marriage encourages domestic activities. One possibility is the increased care services that the household requires owing to childbearing and child rearing. The other possibility is that marriage attaches stigma/status to women's activity status. To examine the role of care services in the activity status of married women, we look into their participation patterns when they are living in nuclear families as against extended families. We identify nuclear families as those households where only the father, mother and unmarried children are cohabiting. All other households are considered as extended families. Such a classification may be helpful in identifying the role of care services based on the argument that care services provided by women are not limited to childcare, but also to care services rendered to other male members of the household and care provided to the elderly and the incapacitated as well. It could be argued that since nuclear families are typically smaller in size than extended families, the demand for care services would be higher in extended families compared to nuclear families, hence a larger share of women in extended families engage in domestic activities. Alternatively, it is also possible that since there is only one adult married woman in most nuclear families, the burden of caregiving falls entirely on her, making her services indispensable to the rest of the household, while in extended families the presence of other women reduces the individual burden of caregiving for female members of the household.

Analysing the data after such a classification we find that there is no significant difference between the domestic activity share of women in nuclear families and extended families, and this observation is consistent over time (Table 3.5). In both types of households we find that the domestic activity share of 'spouses of head of household' is higher compared to women-headed households. For instance, in 2011–12, the share of women belonging to women-headed households engaged in domestic activity in nuclear households was 28.4 per cent, while it was 74.6 per cent for spouses of heads of households in the same type of households. In case of extended households, the women's share in domestic activities for nuclear families was 40.3 per cent and for spouses it was 71.5 per cent. Further, between 1999–2000 and 2011–12 the share of women as spouses of heads engaged in domestic activities increased by around 10 percentage points, whether they were in nuclear households or extended households. However, one noticeable trend is the rising domestic activity share of women in women-headed households in extended families, both in rural and urban areas. In rural areas, their share increased from 33.5 per

Table 3.5: Domestic Participation Rate by Relationship Status and Type of Household, 1999–2000 to 2011–12

		1	2	3	4	5	6	7	8	9	Total
					Total						
1999–2000	Nuclear	28.4	64.9	NA	NA	10.7	NA	NA	NA	NA	35.2
	Extended	34.8	63.3	47.5	72.8	14.1	3.8	37.9	40.1	32.1	41.3
2011–12	Nuclear	28.4	74.6	NA	NA	9.3	NA	NA	NA	NA	41.4
	Extended	40.3	71.5	55.3	80.0	12.5	3.1	39.7	43.1	22.7	46.8
					Rural						
1999–2000	Nuclear	28.4	58.6	NA	NA	10.7	NA	NA	NA	NA	32.4
	Extended	33.5	58.1	44.6	69.8	14.0	4.0	37.3	38.4	27.7	39.3
2011–12	Nuclear	28.2	71.2	NA	NA	9.4	NA	NA	NA	NA	39.6
	Extended	37.3	67.7	54.9	79.0	12.9	3.1	38.6	42.9	10.9	45.3

(Contd)

Table 3.5: (*Contd*)

					Urban						
1999–2000	Nuclear	28.1	81.7	NA	NA	10.5	NA	NA	NA	NA	43.0
	Extended	38.0	80.1	56.9	85.3	14.4	2.9	39.8	44.7	35.6	48.2
2011–12	Nuclear	28.9	82.5	NA	NA	9.0	NA	NA	NA	NA	45.9
	Extended	46.2	81.5	55.9	83.2	11.3	2.8	42.4	43.7	32.8	50.7

Note: 1—self; 2—spouse of head of household; 3—married child; 4—spouse of married child; 5—unmarried child; 6—grandchild; 7—father/mother/father-in-law/mother-in-law; 8—servants/employees/other non-relatives; 9—others.

Source: Estimated from unit-level data of the NSS on Employment and Unemployment Situation in India, various rounds.

cent to 37.5 per cent and in urban areas their share increased from 38 to 46.2 per cent. Given these trends, it can be seen that the type of household is not an important determinant for the activity status for women. Whether they belonged to nuclear families or extended families, their share in domestic activities remained by and large similar, and the categorisation that mattered was their status as spouse to the head of the household. From this, it may be safe to argue that while care services provided by women indeed did matter in their participation in domestic activity, this did not explain their increasing share in domestic activity in the recent years.[4] Rather it is their marital status and their position within the household, be it in nuclear or extended households, which seem to matter in their participation in domestic activity.

Domestic Activity and Place of Stay

From the NSS data it is possible to classify the place of stay of women into their natal homes and marital homes. Natal homes are their place of birth while marital homes are the homes that women marry and move to. It can be posited that the position of women, whether married or not, in their natal home is different from that of being in their marital home. While patriarchal norms govern the life of women in both types of homes, these norms are imposed with greater rigour in their marital homes. Status/stigma attached to their economic activities becomes more relevant in the context of their marital homes than their natal homes.

The data available in NSS does not provide any clear classification on their place of stay. But it is possible to approximate this classification by reclassifying the households according to relationship with the head of the household. By assuming that living with one's parents, if we can consider that an individual is living in her/his natal home, and living away from one's parents and living with their spouses and other affinal kin after marriage, if we can consider that this individual is living in her marital home, then such a classification can be redrawn from the NSS data on the relationship status of the individual. Table 3.6 shows a comparison of the share of women engaged in domestic activities living in their natal homes and marital homes,

Table 3.6: Share of Women's Participation in Domestic Activity by Marital Status and Place of Stay (Age $\geq$ 25), 1999–2000 to 2011–12

		Rural			Urban			Total		
		Natal Home	Marital Home	Total	Natal Home	Marital Home	Total	Natal Home	Marital Home	Total
1999–2000	Never married	29.5	NA	32.6	29.4	NA	33.3	29.4	NA	32.9
	Currently married	44.4	59.2	58.3	54.1	81.0	79.6	46.3	64.8	63.7
	Widowed	26.3	47.8	33.2	32.8	54.1	36.2	28.1	49.1	34.0
	Divorced/separated	20.6	31.0	25.2	26.7	77.0	33.8	22.0	44.2	27.2
	Total	**32.0**	**59.1**	**53.5**	**36.5**	**80.9**	**70.9**	**33.2**	**64.8**	**58.0**
2011–12	Never married	35.1	NA	36.3	26.6	NA	28.3	30.1	NA	31.9
	Currently married	51.3	70.5	69.4	60.3	81.8	80.5	53.6	73.8	72.6
	Widowed	25.9	59.1	32.2	38.7	57.0	39.5	30.0	58.6	34.4
	Divorced/separated	18.6	64.8	27.6	29.7	75.1	33.0	23.3	70.9	29.8
	Total	**33.7**	**70.5**	**63.3**	**39.6**	**81.7**	**71.9**	**35.8**	**73.7**	**65.8**

Source: Estimated from unit-level data of the NSS on Employment and Unemployment Situation in India, various rounds.

according to their marital status. Since this table looks specifically at marital status, we have analysed this only for women belonging to the age group of 25 or above.

First, looking at the marital status, currently married women are the ones that are most prone to engage in domestic activity compared to unmarried, widowed or separated women. For instance, in 2011–12, nearly 73 per cent of the currently married women were engaged in domestic activity, while the corresponding share of unmarried women was only 32 per cent, separated/divorced women only 30 per cent, and widows only 34.4 per cent. In urban areas, the share of currently married women in domestic activity was as high as 80 per cent in 2011–12, while in rural areas it was 69.4 per cent. In both rural and urban areas, the share of women not currently married, be it unmarried women, divorced/separated women or widows, their participation in domestic activities was much lower compared to the currently married women. Thus, it can be argued that their marital status, as being currently married, was the most important characteristic of women engaged in domestic activity. This follows that it is essentially the presence of a male spouse that acts as a conduit for women's engagement in domestic activity, not necessarily being a woman per se. The fact that the absence of a male spouse in case of unmarried, divorced/separated women or widows creates space for women to engage in activities other than domestic activities supports this argument.

Another important aspect to note is the change in the shares over time. Between 1999–2000 and 2011–12, it is only in case of currently married women we find a substantial rise in the share of women engaged in domestic activities. Between the two periods, their share increased from 63.7 to 72.6 per cent, while in case of the unmarried, widowed and separated, the respective shares either declined or saw only a marginal rise. This, in effect, means that it is the increasing domesticity of the currently married women that is driving the entire rise in domestic activity during this period, while for women who did not have spousal presence, their domestic activity was very low and stagnant during the entire period. Thus, it follows that since care work was not an important reason for the rise in domestic activity among women while marriage was an important reason, and moreover, within marriages also it was essentially the presence of the male spouse that drove the domestic activity of women, it may be reasonable to conclude that the presence of women in domestic activity, apart from providing care work, provided some form of utility to the male spouses of the household. This utility may be related to status gained by the household by not letting one's female spouse go out for paid work. By following the norm of the society that women's work is stigmatised, the household derives some utility, while her presence in domestic activity may add to the status of the household.

Now looking at the share of women in domestic activity according to their place of stay, natal home or marital home, it can be seen that their place of stay has substantial effect on their propensity to engage in domestic activity. In the year 2011–12, while nearly 74 per cent of the women living in their marital homes were engaged in domestic activity, only 36 per cent of the women living in their natal homes were engaged in domestic activity. This gap between the women living in marital homes and natal homes is equally large in both urban areas (81.7 per cent and 39.6 per cent, respectively) and rural areas (70.5 per cent and 33.7 per cent, respectively). Also, between 1999–2000 and 2011–12, while the share of women in domestic activity living in marital homes increased from 65 to 74 per cent, by 9 percentage points, the corresponding change for women in natal homes was only by about 2.5 percentage points, from 33.2 to 35.8 per cent. This rise in the share in marital homes largely occurs in the rural areas, while in the urban areas, though the shares are very high, they do not increase. Thus, the rise in domestic activity during the period 1999–2000 to 2011–12 to a large extent was explained by the rise in domesticity among women living in their marital homes, especially in the rural areas.

The difference in share of participation between natal homes and marital homes is visible across all marital classification. Whether it is currently married, widowed or separated women, their domestic participation is higher if their place of stay is their marital home, compared to corresponding women in their natal home. It is interesting to note that for currently married women, when they live in their natal homes, their domestic participation is considerably lower at 53.6 per cent, compared to living in their marital homes, where their participation share is 73.8 per cent. It is true that domestic participation has increased for currently married women whether they lived in natal homes or marital homes, but the levels of participation are different between the two types of houses. For natal homes, the participation of currently married women increased from 46 to 53.6 per cent during 1999–2000 to 2011–12, while the corresponding rise in marital homes was from 65 to 74 per cent. The rise in participation for women in marital homes was higher in the rural areas compared to urban areas, where though the levels were high, the rise was only marginal. From this, it can be argued that apart from being currently married, their place of stay also mattered in their decision on engaging in domestic activity. Further, this gives some evidence to the argument of status creation for the marital homes by married women.

Conclusion

This study aimed to analyse the rising share of women in unpaid domestic activities, as against the declining female labour participation rates. This issue has received only scant attention in literature despite its phenomenal size and growth in the last three decades, as analytically this category is considered a residual activity, and most studies have tried to explain the changes in domestic activities as a fallout of the declining female labour participation rates. This study tried to instate that domestic activity among women is not a residual activity; rather, it is central to women's work life in a patriarchal society. Analytically, though individual labour supply models and household production models do provide insights into decision-making with regard to paid work and unpaid work of women, these models do not take gender relations into consideration. Alternative theoretical constructs of capitalist development and culture is helpful in explaining the domestication of females with the rise of capitalism in patriarchal societies. The disempowered woman through the process of marginalisation within the society engages in status production for the household, who values status as a desirable good.

Rudimentary empirical evidences are provided to support this argument, though they are not conclusive. Empirical evidences show that FLFPR had been declining and there exists a negative relation between income levels and female labour participation rates. In contrast, engaging in domestic activity seems to have increased over the years, and they have a positive relation with income levels. However, not all women are equally affected by a rise in income. In fact, the income effect seems to be affecting only the married women. Relationships within households seem to have a strong effect on the activity status women assume. Being a female spouse tended to enhance their possibility of being engaged in domestic activities while unmarried women did not seem to be affected. Marital status was an important marker that defined one's role. Yet, there was little evidence to show that it was the demand for care services that increased domestic activities among married women, as shown by the similarity in participation of married women in nuclear families and extended families. However, their place of stay, in their marital home, seem to accentuate domestic participation, while women in general, even married women, living in their natal homes had a lower domestic participation rate. These indicators do suggest that women who are probably subjected to greater control by males through marriages, living in their marital home with rising income levels, have a greater possibility of engaging in domestic activities. These domestic activities are not necessarily restricted to childcare, and may, to a large extend, represent women's status labour for status production. However, it may be cautioned that the evidences provided are only preliminary in nature. To authenticate the arguments made here on status production, a deeper analysis on the processes of status production is required.

Notes

1. The NSSO of India defines 'unpaid domestic activities' as the following: attended domestic duties only, or attended domestic duties and was also engaged in free collection of goods (vegetables, roots, firewood, cattle feed, etc.), sewing, tailoring, weaving, etc., for household use. This category is different from a similarly titled category, 'unpaid family

worker', wherein one worked as a helper in a household enterprise. An unpaid family worker is assumed to directly contribute to the household's production-related activities, while domestic activities are assumed not to make a direct contribution to the household's production-related activities though it certainly contributes indirectly to production.

2. Estimated from the unit records of the NSS unemployment surveys and the PLFS, respectively.
3. For a detailed analysis of education and age group-wise participation of women in education, see Abraham (2013).
4. To understand whether the rising domestic activity participation rates were driven by the demand for care services, we compared the participation rates across childless households, and households with different numbers of children; however, no significant differences were noted. Further, it may also be safe to assume that with declining fertility rates and increasing nuclear families, the burden of caregiving may be declining. These evidences thus stand against the argument that it is increasing care provisioning that is leading to increase in domestic activities among women.

References

Abraham, Vinoj. 2013. 'Missing Labour or Consistent "Defeminisation"?'. *Economic and Political Weekly* 48 (31): 99–108.

Becker, Gary S. 1965. 'A Theory of the Allocation of Time'. *Economics Journal* 75: 493–517.

Gronau, Reuben. 1977. 'Leisure, Home Production, and Work: The Theory of the Allocation of Time Revisited'. *Journal of Political Economy* 85 (6): 1099–1123.

Himanshu. 2011. 'Employment Trends in India: A Re-examination'. *Economic and Political Weekly* 46 (37): 43–59.

Hirway, Indira. 2002. 'Employment and Unemployment Situation in 1990s: How Good Are NSS Data?'. *Economic and Political Weekly* 37 (21): 2027–36.

———. 2012. 'Missing Labour Force: An Explanation'. *Economic and Political Weekly* 47 (37): 67–72.

Kannan, K. P., and G. Raveendran. 2012. 'Counting and Profiling the Missing Labour Force'. *Economic and Political Weekly* 47 (6): 77–80.

Klasen, Stephan and Janneke Pieters. 2013. 'What Explains the Stagnation of Female Labor Force Participation in Urban India?'. *IZA DP No. 7597*. Germany: Institute for the Study of Labor.

Mazumdar, Indrani and Neetha N. 2011. 'Gender Dimensions: Employment Trends in India, 1993–94 to 2009–10'. *Economic and Political Weekly* 46 (43): 118–26.

Neff, Daniel, Kunal Sen and Veronika Kling. 2012. 'The Puzzling Decline in Rural Women's Labor Force Participation in India: A Re-examination'. *Working Paper No. 196*. German Institute of Global and Area Studies.

Papenak, H. 1979. 'Family Status Production: The "Work" and "Non-work" of Women'. *Signs* 4 (4): 775–78.

Rangarajan, C., Padma Iyer Kaul and Seema. 2011. 'Where Is the Missing Labour Force?'. *Economic and Political Weekly* 46 (39): 68–72.

Sudarshan, R. M., and S. Bhattacharya. 2009. 'Through the Magnifying Glass: Women's Work and Labour Force Participation in Urban Delhi'. *Economic and Political Weekly* 64 (48): 59–66.

Thomas, Jayan Jose. 2012. 'India's Labour Market during the 2000s: Surveying the Changes'. *Economic and Political Weekly* 47 (51): 39–51.

4

Capitalism and Unpaid Work in India

A Conceptual and Methodological Proposition

Chirashree Das Gupta, *Isha Ralli* and *Mohit Gupta**

In India, in the decades since the early 2000s associated with high economic growth, a literature largely based on empirical work has evolved around women's work and women's labour in attempts to examine recent trends in work participation, migration, discrimination, casualisation and informal employment. The explanations of the trends are, however, far from satisfactory. Declining work participation has seen weak causal attribution to education (Gandhi et al. 2014). Higher education remains socially exclusive and accessible to a tiny minority and thus cannot explain work participation patterns for women who have no access to higher education. Moreover, work participation decline is evident in groups or cohorts well past the age in which education can account for non-participation in the workforce (Lahoti and Swaminathan 2013).

In the attribution of causal explanation, the implicit belief is that women's 'exclusion' is despite the economic growth process

* This essay acknowledges gratefully and draws on the work done in the AUD-NUPI (Norway) Collaborative Research Project on 'The State, Globalisation and Industrial Development in India: The Political Economy of Regulation and Deregulation' by the three authors as well as their research in the UN Women project on 'The Macroeconomics of Gender, Labour and Property Rights in India'. The authors are grateful for the comments received on the draft version of this essay from Janine Rodgers, Ritu Dewan, Surajit Mazumdar and Satyaki Roy.

and so policy should concentrate on ways of 'inclusion'. But is it established beyond doubt both empirically and theoretically that 'exclusion' is despite the macroeconomic process and not because of it? Not only is the employment neutrality of India's recent economic growth trajectory since the early 2000s significant, but also the associated process of decline of share of wages in gross value added and imbalances of demand and output constitute the material basis of this growth trajectory (Chandrasekhar and Ghosh 2002; Mazumdar 2010; Mohanty and Reddy 2011; Pieters 2010; Roy 2014)? If that is so, it can be argued that the growth trajectory is not based on 'exclusion'; rather, this growth is based on a very specific kind of 'inclusion' by way of oppressive labour hierarchies without which this particular trajectory of growth would be impossible. This is our first point of departure.

Another strand of literature has attempted exploration of links between particular aspects of macroeconomic policies, for example, compression of social expenditures under fiscal conservatism and the structure of tax regimes in its impact on women (Hui 2013). This literature is robust in forging links which explain intensification of trends in the last two decades, since 2000–01. However, this literature has two gaps. It has picked on particular aspects of the link between tax regimes and property rights and not the complex gamut of macroeconomic policy change. All components of macroeconomic policy are related and so causality is far more complex than one-to-one mappings of few variables in terms of linear causal connections. Second, it has not been able to establish causality in situations where the trends precede the changes in the macroeconomic framework since 1991 (for example, patterns of women's work participation rates). A third group of literature has looked at the labour market and established systemic patterns of discrimination in employment opportunities and institutions of religion, caste and gender (Papola 2012; Sengupta and Das 2014). While this literature has established the trends, it has, like the first set of literature, been less forthcoming on establishing correlation and causality with larger macroeconomic processes. Conclusions based on establishing causality between policies of macroeconomic reforms, while rich in findings, do not delve into the question of continuity and change before and after the economic reforms. This is our second point of departure.

A Methodological Proposition

Shifting from the focus on employment and wage shares, the recent attention to the question of unpaid work both at the global level and more specifically in the Indian context has largely been due to much-needed intervention(s) by feminist economists (Braunstein et al. 2011; Hirway and Jose 2011). These interventions have centred around two propositions mostly established by empirics. First, the macroeconomy is constituted by both paid and unpaid work. While paid work can be undervalued, unpaid productive and reproductive work (with an emphasis on care work) done by women are not valued at all in their contribution to the macroeconomy (Boserup 1970; Hussmans 2004; Lewenhak 1992). Second, this problem of different standards of valuation is due to the prevalence of gender discrimination and exclusion in labour markets which have three dimensions—demonstrated discrimination in the structure of labour markets, exclusion from public resources (health, education, nutrition, tax devolution, etc.), and exclusion from (or discrimination in) access to credit and financial markets.

Rich in its empirical rigour, this understanding of unpaid work can be traced to two conceptual propositions. The first is the 'plug-in' narrative which inserts gender as a variable in standard neo-classical market models based on the dichotomy between equity and efficiency in goods and factor markets (Fontana and Wood 2000; Sinha 2009). Another variant plugs in gender in computable general equilibrium (CGE) models using social accounting matrices (Fofana et al. 2009; Weichselbaumer and Winter-Ebmer 2005). The second is based on the 'inclusion-exclusion' narrative with estimates of exclusion in both goods and factor markets, public expenditure and public resources, and the processes of 'work' valuation in the macroeconomy. Both these strands of literature essentially amend and extend the neo-classical water-tight classification of human activity into 'work' and 'leisure' to paid work, unpaid work and leisure. Thus, it modifies the neo-classical assumption of all 'work' being paid to underscore that there is a gamut of human activity which is neither paid work nor leisure and can only be classified as 'unpaid work'.

The plug-in narrative demonstrates both in the Indian and the global context the extent of gender discrimination and exclusion in the labour market and public resources, but does not provide any explanation beyond the proximate for it. It assumes that women's work is no different from any other form of waged work and hence the debate gets confined to whether and to what extent unpaid work should be valued and monetised. The specificity of labour in its spatio-temporal and systemic dimensions is beyond the conceptualisation of the economy. It also distils away from the myriad forms of unpaid work in terms of intensified work regimes represented in 'marginal work', the phenomenon of shadow work and the lengthening of the working day under flexible labour regimes where the work–leisure dichotomy fails to address the continuum of human activity that qualifies as 'work'. The underlying assumption of the ahistorical society of *homo economicus* prevails. Such a conceptualisation of the role of economic agents not only privileges men over women as economic agents (Ferber and Nelson 1993; Kalpagam 1986), but also has no room to examine the role of social institutions in structuring institutions of investment and economic growth. In the Indian context, such literature is almost non-existent except for the work of Dewan (2011) who underscores the macroeconomic basis of the 'construct' of patriarchy in India.

The 'inclusion-exclusion' narrative, on the other hand, attributes the demonstrated discrimination to patriarchy. But patriarchy in this framework is exogenous to the macroeconomy and to the economic system. It is 'social' as opposed to the 'economic'. Hence, while the first set of literature has an underlying theory (neo-classical conceptualisation of the economy) and the second apparently has none or has claims to be heterodox, both converge in the policy paradigm based on the market-system as the best self-correction mechanism for the macroeconomy based on the false dichotomy between the 'economic' and the 'social'. The first argues for monetisation of unpaid work within the market system while the second argues for 'social' and 'political' solutions (by the State) avoiding interventions in the 'economic' (namely the market).

Thus, the apparently contending conceptualisations of paid and unpaid work based on different techniques in the economics literature have a common underpinning perspective—conceptualisation of capitalism as a market system, populated by homo economicus operating on the basis of methodological individualism, in which patriarchy falls in the ambit of the social and political and hence is institutionally linked to State and society, while the domain of the economy is around the market. The ahistorical abstraction of homo economicus-based market systems is inadequate in its explanatory capacity of change because of this false dichotomy between economy and society.

There has been seminal work in the field of political economy of institutions which has established the causal links of gender, race and class in the structure of labour regimes under capitalism, and between property rights, patriarchy and caste specifically in the Indian context to unravel the relationship between paid and unpaid labour in capitalism (Brown 2013; Davis 2011; Elson 1979; Fine 1992; Ghosh 2009; Mazumdar 2007; Mazumdar et al. 2013; Ranadive 2004; Sen 2001; Sharma 1984). The macroeconomic links between patriarchy, labour and property rights have been central to the understanding of both continuities and changes in the nature of gender inequality and patriarchy in the context of both developed and developing countries (Bannerji et al. 2001). This involves a delineation of patriarchy in the processes of social production and reproduction (Beneria and Sen 1981; Moghadam 1996). These links are neither universal nor independent of time and space. So it is important to examine the specific patriarchal basis of the macroeconomy in establishing how policy frameworks and institutions interact with social relations in specific contexts and over time in structuring investment, capital formation and labour processes, which in turn shape the nature of economic growth in particular societies.

But the role of patriarchy in the design of the macroeconomy-spanning property rights, labour regimes and the process of economic growth has so far been an understudied area, especially in developing country contexts. Our point of departure is rooted in two interconnected paradigms provided by a Marxist Feminist understanding of capitalism. The first is that patriarchy is endogenous to the construct of the macroeconomy. The second is the centrality of both paid and unpaid social labour as opposed to the concept of 'work' in the construction and reproduction of the accumulation regime under capitalism. Thus, the actual patriarchal construct of the macroeconomy within which the social hierarchy of paid and unpaid labour operates institutionally is very much a historical process in its social and economic specificity both in terms of time and space.

This departure is based on a number of propositions which can be summarised as follows: first, capitalism in its systemic dimension has been dependent on both paid and unpaid labour from its very inception in which the wage-surplus relationship can only be explained through the relationship between paid and unpaid labour in the creation and appropriation of value. Second, while it is a global system, it functions on the basis of several institutions which have both spatial and temporal specificity. Third, of these, the combination of international market systems and nation States constitute the institutional terrain of the construction of regimes of accumulation. Fourth, the continuities and changes in the role of paid and unpaid labour in the accumulation process can only be established through the interstices of institutional hierarchies. Fifth, in the Indian context this hierarchy for historical reasons is constituted not only by patriarchy but also caste and religion in defining the relationship between paid labour, unpaid labour and the nature of the economic surplus which is appropriated as profit.

All of these are most vividly encapsulated in the conceptual category of the 'marginal worker' whose survival and sustenance depends on a continuum of different kinds of paid and unpaid labour—entailed in intensified work regimes, the phenomenon of shadow work and the lengthening of the working day under flexible labour regimes, all of which contribute to the skewed distribution of the value created in favour of surplus and against wages. This mode of labour deployment itself can be the propellant of a growth trajectory largely reliant on labour cheapening. This is our central proposition.

This methodological approach to the question of the causal relationship between modes of labour deployment to growth is in some ways antithetical to the ways in which the relationship between paid and unpaid work has been understood in the dominant literature. The quantum and nature of paid labour in our proposition is heavily dependent on the structure and quantum of unpaid productive and reproductive labour in a given social context. Both in turn determine the proportion of economic surplus that can be appropriated as profit. Using this methodological proposition based on a material historical premise, in the second part of this essay, we examine the continuities and changes in the relationship between paid and unpaid labour in India after Independence in the construct of the macroeconomy.

Political Economy of Institutions

The cyclical nature of growth accompanied by high volatility is persistent in its systemic dimension regardless of shifts in policy regime in India since Independence (Das Gupta 2016). This indicates the prevalence of structural constraints and dimensions in the economy in the post-Independence period. In this essay, our focus is on one significant structural dimension—the construction of the labour hierarchy in India after Independence. In continuation of the colonial legacy almost in its entirety within the macroeconomic context over time, capitalism in independent India has been based solely on the logic of labour cheapening. This, however, was not inevitable. At Independence there were opportunities to explore many paths, given the domestic and international context as well as the aspirations in India that had built up through the anti-colonial struggle. However, the political power of capital with respect to the Indian State grew in the first two decades after Independence (Chenoy 2015; Chibber 2003; Das Gupta 2016). It is this factor which determined the macroeconomic context within which the labour hierarchy built on caste, patriarchy and religion got institutionalised.

At Independence, the most important manifestation was a huge labour surplus based on a labour hierarchy constituted by patriarchy, caste and religion. This meant that labour cheapening was the basis on which the capitalist class had also developed in India, given the twin benefits of an extraordinarily large reserve army and the possibility of appropriation of a large amount of unpaid labour both within the family structure and in the social relations defined by institutions of caste, patriarchy and religion. This process of labour cheapening spans both the sphere of production and reproduction. Thus, the structure of the macroeconomy cannot be understood without its institutional premises.

To depart from this colonial legacy and ensure competitiveness within a capitalist organisation of society, four interventions were considered after Independence: (a) substantive land redistribution; (b) laws upholding the rights of labour universally in all employer–employee relationships; (c) property rights rearrangement, breaking the ties of religion, caste and patriarchy; and (d) a progressive taxation structure to ameliorate unpaid reproductive labour through adequate investment in universal health, education and social security.

All of these were not utopian ideas but real possibilities at the time of India's becoming an independent sovereign republic, given the balance of class forces and political configurations in Parliament and outside. However, all four propositions lost out in the final making of legal institutions in India. The way in which this strategic dilution was effected is discussed in the following sections.

Property Rights and the Question of Land Redistribution

On the question of substantive land redistribution, the main barrier was the power of landlords who had enough social and political power both inside Parliament and outside, but more importantly in the state legislatures. In the Constitution adopted in 1950, Article 31 guaranteed the right to property, Article 19 (g) protected the right to practise any profession, or to carry on any occupation, trade or business, and Article 15 (3) provided for special provisions for women and children within the larger right to no discrimination.

On one hand, using these constitutional provisions, landlords went to court against the different versions of the land tenure regulation acts and the abolition of the Zamindari Act, pleading protection for 'their women and children' and their right to property and freedom to carry on occupation, trade and business. On the other, there were larger agitations and legal battles on the implication of the right to no discrimination both on the question of protection and affirmative action for Dalits, Adivasis and minorities.

The first amendment of the Indian Constitution in 1951 was a response to this political situation. The dominant understanding of the amendment from the point of view of both jurisprudence and social theory has been to interpret it as progressive. This has largely been based on the reading of the amendment of Article 15 which established the right of the state for taking affirmative action for Scheduled Castes (SCs) and Scheduled Tribes (STs), and upheld the right to do the same for women, children and religious and ethnic minorities. Also, Article 19 is often considered only in the singular dimension of upholding freedom of speech. What has been significantly missed in such readings is the premise of class compromise that underwrites the amendment in the continuities and changes that constituted the three articles and their interrelationship.

Given that land reforms were under the domain of the states rather than the Centre, the amendment qualified the right to property in the following ways:

Article 31 was qualified by the insertion of 31A which said:

> Saving of laws providing for acquisition of estates, etc.-(1) Notwithstanding anything in the foregoing provisions of this Part, no law providing for the acquisition by the State of any estate or of any rights therein or for the extinguishment or modification of any such rights shall be deemed to be void on the ground that it is inconsistent with, or takes away or abridges any of the rights conferred by, any provisions of this Part: Provided that where such law is a law made by the Legislature of a State, the provisions of this article shall not apply thereto unless such law, having been reserved for the consideration of the President, has received his assent.

'Estate' was defined in relation to any local area, to have the same meaning as that expression or its local equivalent has in the existing law relating to land tenures in force in that area, and included any *jagir, inam* or *muafi*[1] or other similar grant. 'Rights' was defined in relation to an estate, and included rights vesting in a proprietor, sub-proprietor, under-proprietor, tenure-holder or other intermediary, and any rights or privileges in respect of land revenue. Hence, all social relations were encompassed in the status quoist conceptualisation of the hierarchy of 'rights' in an 'estate'.

Right to property became a statutory right rather than a fundamental right through a process that was finally completed in 1955 with the fifth amendment. But this very process also opened up the route to discretionary legislative power to uphold property rights of landlords in state legislatures. It also enabled discretionary executive power in the office of the President to veto progressive land reform legislation in case the powers of landlords were circumvented in the process of law-making in state legislatures.

The first amendment listed 13 existing acts in central and state legislatures in the ninth schedule which meant these could not be challenged in the judiciary. Later, the 14th and 34th amendments added further acts on land reforms to the ninth schedule. However, in the same amendment, Article 19 (g) was amended as follows:

> [. . .] nothing in the said sub-clause shall affect the operation of any existing law in so far as it relates to, or prevent the State from making any law relating to-
>
> (i) the professional or technical qualifications necessary for practising any profession or carrying on any occupation, trade or business, or
>
> (ii) the carrying on by the State, or by a corporation owned or controlled by the State, of any trade, business, industry or service, whether to the exclusion, complete or partial, of citizens or otherwise.

It further stated that:

> No law in force in the territory of India immediately before the commencement of the Constitution which is consistent with the provisions of article 19 of the Constitution as amended by sub-section (1) of this section shall be deemed to be void, or over to have become void, on the ground only that, being a law which takes away or abridges the right conferred by sub-clause (a) of clause (1) of the said article, its operation was not saved by clause (2) of that article as originally enacted.

Thus, the amendment effectively validated all laws on occupation, trade and business that pre-dated the Constitution and left it open to both 'business as usual' and legal interpretations for the judiciary. This facilitated landlords in case law using Article 15 (3) and Article 19 (g) to challenge any appropriation of estates or curbing of revenue rights under Article 31, thus providing a way to circumvent the ninth schedule listings. It also facilitated circumvention of tax imposition or curtailing of business operations in the interest of protecting citizens. This facilitation has continued across policy regimes up to the present period (for some examples, see AIR 1952 Mad 203; AIR 1952 Bom 16; AIR 1952 Mad 565; AIR 1951 All 674; 1967 SCR [2] 762; AIR 1964 Guj 82; 2002 [6] ALD 548).

Thus, land reforms remained an unfinished agenda except for the minimum abolition of zamindari.[2] This was evident in the way the contradictions in the Indian Constitution were used by landlords and the class compromise arrived at by the central legislature to perpetuate and institutionalise the status quo of social relations. Not only did this institutional legitimisation of the status quo lead to concentration of property, it institutionalised social inequality in all its dimensions. For example, Article 23 prohibited *begari*.[3] But given the amended status of Article 31 (discussed earlier) along with the legalisation of all existing social relations under the garb of freedom through the introduction of 19 (g), begari could not be institutionally stopped. The same provisions rendered Article 38 toothless in its aim to minimise inequality of income, status and opportunities by legitimising all concrete social relations based on class, caste, patriarchy and religion. The definition of estate also made Article 39 redundant (the objective of which was equitable distribution of the community for common good) because the control of the propertied over ponds, lakes, forests, grazing lands, etc., all came under the wide definition of estate protected by Article 31A.

Moreover, this legal framework by being silent on the status of parallel structures of social adjudication perpetuated those. Thus, not only were *joru* and *jameen*[4] legitimised as signifiers of status, but institutions of social oppression and adjudication (for example, *khap* panchayats,[5] caste panchayats, religious boards and trust, etc.) were also legitimised through the combination of Article 31 and Article 19. Thus, beyond the narrow scope of limited affirmative action for identified oppressed groups, by 1951 the Constitution had institutionalised the existing property rights and labour hierarchies in all its dimensions.

This had four implications: first, it underwrote the demand constraint in the economy and perpetuated the huge labour reserves inherited from the colonial period. Second, it ruled out a classical capitalist transformation in ruling out a process of development through creation and channelling of a substantive agrarian surplus into industry. Third, it perpetuated one of the strongest links in preserving the links between caste, gender and property relations in the hierarchy of definitions of property rights. Fourth, it ensured the perpetuation of labour regimes based on extra-economic coercion with legitimisation of the unpaid labour regime based on caste, religion and patriarchy. Thus, class relations in constituting the labour process consisted of creation of economic subsistence and surplus reliant heavily on unpaid labour. The variety and forms of unpaid labour in both social production and reproduction and hence the macroeconomy was a complex interstice of caste, religion and patriarchy. This has both spatial and temporal variations but unpaid labour is the universal on which this labour hierarchy was institutionally constructed.

Definition of the 'Worker' and 'Work' in Fixing Labour Rights

In the context of legally defining employer–employee relationship, interventions were required on the question of labour laws which saw the greatest contest around what is work and who is a worker. The 1947 version of the Industrial Disputes Act had defined work to cover all forms of labour, including domestic labour. But the Federation of Indian Chambers of Commerce and Industry (FICCI), Associated Chambers of Commerce and Industry of India (ASSOCHAM) and the All-India Organisation of Industrial Employers were vehemently opposed to this formalisation of all employer–employee relationships. FICCI launched a full-scale battle to limit the domain of adjudication and trade union formation. Finally, in 1956, the employers succeeded. 'Work' was narrowed down to formal factory labour in India based on the definition of 'factory' from the Factories Act, and this definition of the workspace by extension defined who the worker was. All labour rights in terms of right to formation of unions, wage negotiations and standardisation and other rights (for example, social security and welfare entitlement) were formulated based on this narrow definition of 'work' and 'worker'. Thus, 'informalisation' was built into the existing structure of the labour market by defining 'work' in relation to the workspace, that is, a specific kind of factory and by extension the 'worker'. Subsequent political struggles of different sections of workers led to specific, piecemeal legislation legitimising further segmentation (for example, the Contract Labour Act of 1970, Sales Promotion Employee (Condition of Service) Act of 1976, etc.).

Moreover, wage repression formed the last pillar of this labour-cheapening process right after Independence (Das Gupta 2016). The institutional basis of capital accumulation in India was laid down in the first decade after Independence based on two institutions. The first was through the labour regime that was established through the narrow definition and recognition of 'work' and hence the definition of paid work. This legitimised the hierarchy of social relations based on caste, religion and gender that formed the class basis of the predominantly mercantile capital accumulation regime in India. This structure has shown resolute structural continuity across all subsequent policy regimes and is one of the key reasons for the continuity of the main propellant of the Indian transition—the widening scope of unpaid and unrecognised work of various kinds forming the very bottom of the pyramid of labour cheapening. Intensification of unpaid reproductive labour based on the sexual division of labour, caste as a hierarchical system of extraction of coercive labour, various forms of pushing the production boundary of unpaid labour, acute wage repression, intensification of work and re-emergence of semi-feudal conditions of bondage are all reflected in the increasing share of surplus at the cost of wage in India. This constitutes a two-fold causal chain in capitalism. Unpaid labour in social reproduction and production keeps wages down and hence maintains cheap labour. Paid labour entails acute wage repression, intensification of work and re-emergence of semi-feudal conditions of bondage due to the existence of the reserve army, pauperisation and debt, and thus extends the continuum of unpaid labour within paid labour in both production and social production.

The second was through the property rights and taxation structure that was developed, which spanned corporate governance, taxation and personal laws. The property rights and taxation structure privileged Hindus over Muslims, Christians, Jews and Parsis through the institution of the Hindu Undivided Family (HUF) as a separate legal property-holding taxation entity with special privileges. The process through which the HUF was institutionalised, and its ramifications, are elaborated in the next section.

Property Rights, Corporate Governance Structures, Tax Laws and Personal Laws

By 1967, with the publication of the Hazari Report, it was clear that monopoly capital in India consisted of the predominance of a few representative units of organisation of capital in most areas of industry and trade. The key houses of business, both old and new, found ways to maintain control over decision-making through the institutional structure of the 'family-run business house'. While the entity of the 'business group' has been emphasised in the literature (Mazumdar 2006), the familial basis of ownership and control remains an understudied area (Das Gupta 2013).

This section elaborates the unique interstices of gender, property and religion in the facilitation of the family-run business house as the locus of organisation of monopoly capital in India. The peculiar form of the HUF as a distinct entity of property-holding for the purpose of direct taxation has only recently been recognised in the literature (for example, Dewan 2009; Hui 2013). The first aspect is significant in the organising of the institutional basis of concentration of capital combining the modalities of ownership and control. The second has implications for both accumulation and concentration (Das Gupta 2013).

There were two ways in which the family control over the organisational structure of business groups and the ownership of wealth generated through these structures were maintained. The first had to do with the legal provisions of 'corporate governance' structures which facilitated the optimum mix of various forms of registered companies like partnerships, private limited companies, unregistered and registered public limited companies under the umbrella group through interlocking shareholdings. These were done within the enabling legal provisions of the Indian Partnerships Act of 1932 and the Companies Act of 1956. Apart from risk-spreading, this also ensured avenue to escape the minimal restrictions on expansion under Monopolies and Restrictive Trade Practices (MRTP) after 1973. It was also important for labour deployment and control with employers often making sure that each company only had less than seven employees and pre-empting any possibility of trade union formation under the stipulations of the Trade Union Act of 1926 (Das Gupta 2010).

The second way of maintaining familial basis of ownership and control was by accrediting the HUF as a distinct legal entity. To corroborate, the singular political action in the first decade after Independence was the codification of Hindu personal laws—a political process that continued for more than nine years, from 1947 to 1956. This had very significant implications for the subsequent institutionalisation of the HUF as the locus of organisation of the business group. First, under the codification process, a Hindu was defined as anyone who was not a Muslim, Christian, Parsi or Jew, and thus by default included followers of other institutionalised religions like Buddhism, Jainism and Sikhism as Hindu, along with theistic practices outside the domain of organised religion.

Second, it institutionalised monogamy and made polygamy illegal for Hindus; but it also instituted recognition of both Dayabhaga and Mitakshara property holdings (a compromise over the original draft which had proposed to do away with custom laws in defining hereditary rights on property) and marriage only between two Hindus into the ambit of the code. Adoption and succession was to be defined in jurisprudence by 'custom laws' institutionalising male lineage of descent based on caste rules of endogamy and exogamy as the 'natural' inheritors of property and the expropriation of any right to property of children born outside marriage. Third, it created the legal space for any Hindu male to break away from the 'joint family' and start a new HUF, as long as he was married. Even as families went nuclear, the HUF could be perpetuated as a legal entity as each nuclear family marked the beginning of a new HUF. Thus, the patriarchal basis of the property rights structure was institutionalised in the organisation of wealth and property in India. Women were denied any property right on land on the feeble plea to prevent 'fragmentation of land' and thus were granted only maintenance and not ownership/coparcenary rights in a HUF. Even the tenancy rights in agricultural land were specifically exempted from the Hindu Succession Act of 1956[6] (Agnes 2011). Women were denied equal share in all property till the 2005 amendment which gave daughters equal right to property under Mitakshara laws, but not to wives and daughters-in-law.

This led to disjunction between states' land enactment, affecting devolution of agricultural land and the personal laws affecting the devolution of personal property. This has given different states enough room to bring gender bias in land laws and also define their rules of devolution different from the order of devolution of land under personal laws. The north Indian states of Haryana, Himachal, Jammu and Kashmir, Uttar Pradesh and Delhi, for instance, have strong preferences for male succession in devolution in their tenure laws, while others like Gujarat, Maharashtra, Andhra Pradesh, West Bengal, and others do not specify the order of devolution and thus it is assumed that it would be defined by personal laws (Saxena 2012).

The state-level disparities are also evident in state-specific laws pertaining to HUF and proportion of HUF across different states. A few states account for the major proportion of HUFs in the country. Over time, this concentration has intensified. These are the so-called high-income states. Particularly, the four states of Maharashtra, Gujarat, Punjab and Haryana and Delhi constituted around 31 per cent of the total number of HUF during 1961, and by 1989 this proportion had increased to around 47 per cent. On the other hand, it is the proportion of HUF in the middle-income states like Tamil Nadu, Karnataka, Kerala, Andhra Pradesh and West Bengal, as well as in low-income states (Bihar, Rajasthan, Odisha, Uttar Pradesh and Madhya Pradesh) which had declined during this period. The share of HUF in the middle-income states has declined slightly from 31 to 28 per cent, while the proportion of the HUF in the category of low-income states has shrunk considerably from 37 to 23 per cent (Table 4.1). Thus, over time, beginning from a more balanced distribution of HUF, there has been a shift towards a greater degree of concentration of HUF in the high-income states. The Indian government stopped releasing state-specific data on HUFs after 1989.

Table 4.1: Percentage Share of HUFs, 1961–89

Type of States	1961	1971	1980	1989
High-income states (Maharashtra, Gujarat, Delhi, Haryana, Punjab)	32	43	43	48
Middle-income states (Kerala, Tamil Nadu, Karnataka, Assam, West Bengal, Andhra Pradesh)	31	31	36	29
Low-income states (Bihar, Madhya Pradesh, Rajasthan, Odisha, Uttar Pradesh)	37	27	20	23

Note: Totals are very near to but may not add up to exactly 100 per cent, as contributions of some states and Union territories having insignificant number of HUFs have been left out. Decimals are approximated to the nearest whole number.

Source: Authors' calculations based on Statistical Abstracts of India, various years.

While some of the southern states abolished the recognition of HUF beginning with Kerala in 1976, Haryana in 1987 on the contrary abolished Hindu women's right in self-acquired property. The state-level variation in HUF can be attributed mainly to the preferential tax provisions offered to HUF and the institutionalisation of patrilineal principles in property rights codes which are discussed further in the next section. What is important, however, is that with the aid of two definitions, that of a Hindu and that of the HUF, religion, caste and patriarchy were installed as the institutional basis of determining property rights. Hence, contrary to principles and processes of secularisation, Hindu personal law became state law in India through codification.

This process preserved the patriarchal rules of limiting inheritance rights of women to property and assigned the karta[7] as the patriarch of the family with legal powers to represent and structure the holding of property (Sachdeva 1987). According to the Hindu Succession Act before the 2005 amendment, a daughter could not reside in the family home unless she was single or divorced, and could not claim her share of property as long as the men of the family continued to live in it. The status of the karta and the HUF as a form of property-holding in a body incorporate were not affected by the 2005 amendment. The status of the karta was preserved in its implication for inheritance rights as well as in the HUF as a tax entity. Thus, a Hindu male can be a karta in more than one HUF.[8]

Under the Income Tax Act of 1961, a HUF is assessed for income tax as a distinct unit of assessment. Thus, the main avenue of family control of property was through the use of HUF as a legal tax entity, separate and distinct from individuals and corporates (which were firms defined under the Companies Act and the Partnership Act). While all other body corporates recognised in corporate and individual income tax laws are defined on the basis of company law, the HUF as a legal entity in Indian tax law is defined on the basis of Hindu personal law.

The state perpetuated the HUF as a taxable entity under the Wealth Tax Act of 1957 and the Income Tax Act of 1961. This was a continuation in its status from the colonial income tax laws of 1876 and 1922. The preferential position was ensured by ruling that a member of a HUF is not taxable for income and wealth tax for any sum which s/he receives as a HUF member[9] out of the income of the family (even though the family may not have paid the tax on its income). So the privilege cannot be ascertained by how much tax a HUF pays, but how much of its wealth or income is not taxed at all by virtue of being declared as 'family income'. Moreover, the provisions ensured that an individual can organise her/his wealth across multiple HUFs or could perpetuate HUF by partial partition of a bigger HUF and thus reduce her/his tax liability[10] (Das Gupta and Gupta 2017). The Wealth Tax Act of 1957 and Income Tax Act of 1961 were drawn up with higher exemptions and lower rates for HUF (as compared to other assesses), institutionalising the low effective direct taxation that was to follow across policy regimes. All this was done on the recommendations of direct tax committees formed after Independence. The Wanchoo

Committee (1971) and Raj Committee (1972) pointed out the clear discrimination in favour of Hindus.

Apart from income tax and wealth tax, other forms of direct tax like gift tax and capital gains tax also privileges HUF in certain ways because of loopholes in the tax structure. For instance, gift tax was put in place in 1958 and was abolished in 1998. Later, after several amendments, it was established that for gifts with consideration of more than Rs 50,000 in a year, an individual or HUF would be taxable. But the HUF could easily evade this tax [for example, in *Vineetkumar Raghavjibhai Bhalodia versus ITO* (2011)], because of two counter-provisions in the Income Tax Act. Section 56 (2)(vii) gives exemption to relatives to give and receive gifts, while Section 10 (2) exempts an individual from any income received from family income. This together established that gifts received by HUF from an individual are not subjected to gift tax. Thus, it was ruled in this case that HUF is a group of relatives and so members can gift from family income without any tax consideration. Similarly gifts at the time of marriage are exempt from tax, whether from a friend, relative or colleague. Hence, if a member of the HUF is getting married, the gift can be shown to be made to the HUF, and it will be exempt from tax in the hands of the HUF. Movable or immovable property received through a will by way of inheritance which can form the corpus of HUF is also exempt from gift tax.

The capital gains tax was put in place in 1956 after the recommendation of the Kaldor report according to the provisions of which capital gains made on sale of assets are subjected to taxation. In case of long-term capital assets, however, if any residential property or urban agricultural property that is held by the HUF is sold and there is capital gain, the HUF can save tax on these gains by reinvesting the proceeds into another property by following the provisions of exemptions at par with individuals, offered to this entity by various provisions in Section 54 of the Income Tax Act.

Thus, the direct taxation structure offers copious ways of exemptions to HUF as a taxable entity, sometimes explicit or because of inherent contradictions in the direct tax structure. These exemptions as a result have translated into the trends in falling effective tax rate, not only for HUFs but for all forms of corporate organisation because of interlocking. These trends are discussed in the next section. At the same time, India's elite resisted any attempt to raise effective rates of direct taxation. Simultaneously, the logic of the fiscal constraint was also raised by FICCI from 1956 to 1965 to resist all moves on questions of universalising health, education and social security (Das Gupta 2016). Thus universal welfare provisioning was ruled out two decades before the shift to neo-liberalism, not only because of the woeful inadequacy of direct taxation, but also because of special privileges given to the majority religious community in India.

Trends in Effective Direct Taxation Rate since Independence

While the focus on expenditure cuts by the state are important in the causal connection with intensification of unpaid work and the extension of the share of unpaid labour within paid labour, there are two other dimensions which need to be taken into account. The first is the trend in effective direct taxation rates. In a situation where the direct market-based distribution of the economic surplus is highly skewed against labour and is largely reliant on the extraction of unpaid labour of various kinds, resource mobilisation of the state through a progressive direct taxation regime has been the classical option to provide for not only a minimum socially acceptable level of nutrition, health, education, housing, sanitation and social security, but also reduce the amount of unpaid labour that forms the basis of production and reproduction which powers the macroeconomy.

The problem of direct tax mobilisation in India in the post-liberalisation phase was attributed to high rates of taxation and sources of 'inefficiency' traced to the administrative structure of taxation and proliferation of multiple taxes (Rao and Singh 2005). Thus, the emphasis has been on 'rationalisation' of tax rates in the architecture of tax reforms.[11] The post-liberalisation period has seen tax exemptions and tax subsidies being awarded to corporates (Das Gupta and Mazumdar 2018; Mazumdar 2014) as a major incentivising policy tool. In the very period in which the debate on taxation and tax mobilisation in India has gained ground, and in a period when the ratio of direct tax to indirect tax collection has moved in favour of

Figure 4.1: Three-yearly Average Effective Income Taxation Rates, 1955–2000

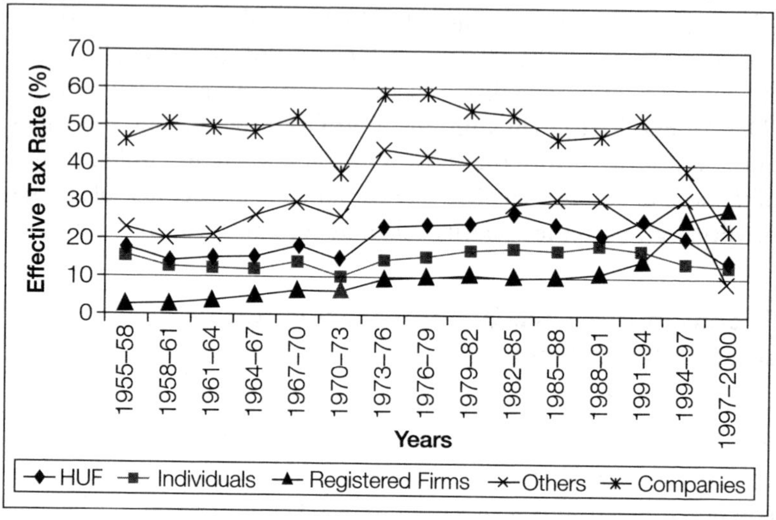

Source: Authors' calculations from Statistical Abstracts of India, various years.

direct tax, the full import of these trends is not available for analysis as the central government stopped releasing detailed data on direct taxation between 2000 and 2012. Within these constraints, we have compiled income tax data from various volumes of the Statistical Abstract of India and computed effective rates of income tax for the different assesses in India.

There are three broad trends evident in Figure 4.1. From 1954 to 1965, the decades of planning in India, effective rates of taxation were largely constant at different levels for all categories except the registered firms (sole-proprietorships and partnerships) which showed a steady increase.

From 1972 to 1973, the effective taxation rate (ETR) for all units of taxation increased till 1975, coinciding with the period of monopoly regulation with the implementation of the MRTP Act. From 1974 to 1975, there was significant divergence in trends. Between 1972 and 1985, the ETR of HUFs showed a steady increase. This could be explained by two significant policy changes—the equalisation of rates of taxation for HUF as compared to individuals, and the doing away of special privileges of HUF in many states in southern India.[12]

However, from the mid-1970s, limited liability companies and others (trusts, cooperatives, registered societies, etc.) saw a steep decline in effective taxation rates right up to 1999–2000, with limited liability companies recording an ETR of less than 10 per cent in 2000. Also, registered firms (with unlimited liability) had the lowest ETR at Independence while companies had the highest ETR. The registered firms have seen a gradual but continuous rise in effective rates of taxation across policy regimes. This rise has been accelerated after 1991. Thus, by 2000, registered firms showed much higher ETR compared to limited liability companies. Moreover, the ETR for HUFs had converged with that of individuals even though the structure of the HUF is that of a business entity (Das Gupta and Gupta 2017).

Two methodological propositions follow. First, the institutional structure of asset, wealth and property-holding in India being a maze of interlocked family and business entities spanning all five categories needs to be recognised as the comprehensive unit of taxation. However, the only legislation in India that recognised this comprehensive unit (the MRTP Act) was one of the first regulations to be repealed in 1991 after strategic dilution of monopoly regulation since the late 1970s (Das Gupta 2016; Mazumdar 2006). Moreover, there is no systemic compilation of data by the Indian State on interlocking tax entities and extent of direct and indirect ownership of economic assets and property by family-owned business groups.

Second, larger corporate entities constitute the category of companies (with limited liability) while smaller firms (proprietorships and partnerships with unlimited liability) would mainly constitute the category of 'registered firms'. This broad generalisation, of course, does not take into account 'limited liability' partnerships which come under the Limited Liability Act of 2008 (Das Gupta 2010). Keeping this qualification in mind, the macroeconomic direct tax trends in our analysis seem to suggest that larger corporate entities face lower ETR compared to smaller entities corroborating Rao's (2015) findings.

This trend of declining effective direct taxation of property, assets and income which set in after 1975–76 and intensified after 1991 with lower ETRs for large corporate entities is the causal explanation of the so-called resource crunch in the economy, specifically in the period of high growth after 1991. Thus, the state's role in the labour-cheapening process by increasing the burden of unpaid labour for social reproduction, as well as declining support for paid employment enhancing production is evident in the conscious policy paradigm founded on different ways of lowering effective taxation rates to drive growth after 1991.

Causal Explanation of Labour Deployment (Before and After 1991)

The last aspect relates to the nature of labour deployment which has driven this growth. Thus, the causal connection in our methodological paradigm is from labour deployment to growth rather than the usual way of growth as the causal explanation for labour deployment in the 'exclusion' paradigm (see the first section of this chapter). Here, we demonstrate some implications of our conceptual and methodological proposition in an analysis of the intensified labour regime that forms the basis of India's growth trajectory, entailing the growing component of unpaid labour to paid labour ratio in the nature of labour deployment itself, centred around the intensification of marginal work of the labour force in India after 1991.[13]

Table 4.2A: Number of Main Workers Per Marginal Worker in the Rural Child Workforce in India (4–15 Years), 1981–2001

	Rural Male			Rural Female		
Sector	**1981**	**1991**	**2001**	**1981**	**1991**	**2001**
Cultivators	12	8	1	1	1	0
Agricultural labourers	18	14	1	3	3	0
Allied activities (primary)	37	16	1	4	3	1
Mining	33	38	4	7	12	3
Household industry	25	13	1	3	4	1
Non-household industry	37	33	2	5	7	1
Construction	45	35	2	4	10	1
Trade	22	20	2	2	3	1

(*Contd*)

Table 4.2A: (*Contd*)

Sector	Rural Male			Rural Female		
	1981	1991	2001	1981	1991	2001
Transport and communication	35	36	3	5	6	2
Other services	23	20	1	5	4	1
Overall	11	11	1	2	2	1
Overall (2011)		2			1	

Table 4.2B: Number of Main Workers Per Marginal Worker in the Urban Child Workforce in India (4–15 Years), 1981–2001

Sector	Urban Male			Urban Female		
	1981	1991	2001	1981	1991	2001
Cultivators	15	7	2	2	1	1
Agricultural labourers	17	15	1	5	4	1
Allied activities (primary)	15	21	2	4	4	1
Mining	43	64	5	22	20	4
Household industry	19	21	2	3	6	1
Non-household industry	37	62	5	11	13	3
Construction	28	54	3	14	25	2
Trade	23	43	4	2	9	2
Transport and communication	30	71	5	11	16	4
Other services	28	31	3	15	14	2
Overall	24	27	3	5	6	2
Overall (2011)		14			10	

Source: Census of India, General Economic Tables of Census years 1981, 1991, 2001 and 2011.

Table 4.3A: Number of Main Workers Per Marginal Worker in the Rural Working-age Workforce in India (15–59 Years), 1981–2001

Sector	Rural Male			Rural Female		
	1981	1991	2001	1981	1991	2001
Cultivators	71	112	14	2	2	2
Agricultural labourers	34	68	3	3	3	1
Allied activities (primary)	36	42	6	2	2	1
Mining	96	161	10	10	12	4

(*Contd*)

Table 4.3A: (*Contd*)

Sector	Rural Male			Rural Female		
	1981	1991	2001	1981	1991	2001
Household industry	60	66	6	2	3	1
Non-household industry	60	105	8	3	4	2
Construction	44	82	4	4	11	2
Trade	52	110	10	3	5	2
Transport and communication	61	122	11	5	8	3
Other services	99	186	12	8	9	3
Overall	54	94	6	2	2	1
Overall (2011)		4			1	

Table 4.3B: Number of Main Workers Per Marginal Worker in the Urban Working-age Workforce in India (15–59 Years), 1981–2001

Sector	Urban Male			Urban Female		
	1981	1991	2001	1981	1991	2001
Cultivators	60	53	18	2	2	2
Agricultural labourers	32	45	3	4	4	1
Allied activities (primary)	61	84	10	5	6	3
Mining	163	359	24	49	40	7
Household industry	76	74	9	4	4	2
Non-household industry	137	214	19	8	11	4
Construction	49	92	6	14	23	3
Trade	122	238	18	7	18	5
Transport and communication	122	226	18	30	50	12
Other services	124	228	24	25	25	8
Overall	98	150	14	7	8	4
Overall (2011)		10			4	

Source: Census of India, General Economic Tables of Census years 1981, 1991, 2001 and 2011.

Table 4.4A: Number of Main Workers Per Marginal Worker in the Rural Senior Citizen Workforce in India (60 Years and Above), 1981–2001

Sector	Rural Male			Rural Female		
	1981	1991	2001	1981	1991	2001
Cultivators	67	71	12	2	2	2
Agricultural labourers	32	41	3	3	3	1

(*Contd*)

Table 4.4A: (*Contd*)

	Rural Male			Rural Female		
Sector	**1981**	**1991**	**2001**	**1981**	**1991**	**2001**
Allied activities (primary)	21	24	5	2	2	1
Mining	39	75	8	10	12	4
Household industry	51	48	6	2	3	1
Non-household industry	39	53	7	3	4	2
Construction	14	57	4	4	11	2
Trade	47	81	10	3	5	2
Transport and communication	55	86	10	5	8	3
Other services	44	65	7	8	9	3
Overall	52	59	6	2	2	1
Overall (2011)		4			1	

Table 4.4B: Number of Main Workers Per Marginal Worker in the Urban Senior Citizen Workforce in India (60 Years and Above), 1981–2001

	Urban Male			Urban Female		
Sector	**1981**	**1991**	**2001**	**1981**	**1991**	**2001**
Cultivators	49	61	17	4	2	3
Agricultural labourers	24	38	3	5	5	1
Allied activities (primary)	30	41	7	5	5	3
Mining	69	133	14	201	27	4
Household industry	71	56	10	4	6	2
Non-household industry	112	138	17	8	7	4
Construction	60	90	5	19	23	3
Trade	132	189	21	6	20	5
Transport and communication	133	168	15	13	31	7
Other services	63	92	14	16	17	5
Overall	68	91	12	7	7	3
Overall (2011)		8			3	

Source: Census of India, General Economic Tables of Census years 1981, 1991, 2001 and 2011.

Between 1991 and 2001, there was a remarkable shift in trend in the reliance of the growth trajectory on drastic increase of marginal work by men and boys in both rural and urban India, secularly spread across all sectors as compared to the period between 1981 and 1991. Though sectoral data is not available yet for 2011, this trend of increase of the share of marginal workers to that of main workers continues across age and sex in both rural and urban India at the aggregate level with a sharpening of this trend for male workers in rural India. In urban India, the same trend is visible except for an increase of male child workers as main workers. The trends also illustrate the in-built patriarchal macroeconomic structure in the reliance of the economy of marginal work of women and girls secularly spread across all sectors before 1991 and an intensification of the process after 1991 (Tables 4.2A to 4.4B).

These secular trends pay put to the argument about specificity of the sectoral nature of growth or the specific basis of 'exclusion' after 1991. Apart from the much commented upon employment-neutrality of the growth trajectory after 1991, the reliance of the trajectory on marginal work is evident in every sector of the economy. In fact, this process before 1991 showed a clear evidence of reliance on patriarchal division of labour with the increasing component of marginal work the macroeconomic basis of which has been laid out in the first section of this essay. However, after 1991, there is a very steep rise in the share of unpaid labour of men and boys, as well as intensification of unpaid labour of women and girls.

Examining workforce participation rates (WPR) by educational status, we find that in the period 1981–91, fewer rural and urban men and women with the qualification of being 'graduate and above' were part of the workforce. But between 1991 and 2001, the Census data shows that more educated rural and urban men and rural women have been part of the workforce, as can be seen with the rise in WPR in the categories of 'literate', 'matric but below graduate' and 'graduate and above'. Moreover, between 2001 and 2011, there is a reversal of trend for educated rural and urban men, whereas more rural and urban women in the same categories of education, 'matriculation and above', have been part of the workforce. So, education suggests an inverse correlation with work participation only between 2001 and 2011 for rural and urban men with access to undergraduate and postgraduate education, and not for women. This result is contrary to the dominant argument about education as an explanation for 'missing women' in the rural (or even urban) workforce. Additionally, the number of main workers per marginal worker by educational status shows the same result as we saw in the sector classifications earlier, that is, post-1991, a steep rise in marginalisation of work for men and intensification of the same process for women.

Between 1981 and 1991, more rural women of all age groups entered the workforce, while rural men's participation in the workforce started declining in the very same period. The same trends are evident for urban men and women except for the rise in the 'below 15' age group for urban boys and girls (and rural girls), indicating intensification of child labour.

Post-1991, the results change. For rural and urban men, the only age groups showing any rise in WPR are those in the category of above 40 years. Between 2001 and 2011, for urban men, the age groups of 'below 15' (once again indicating rise of child labour) and '25–29' along with the older age groups of '50–59' and '60+' show a rise. Urban women's workforce participation has risen for all age groups post-1991 with no exceptions whatsoever, going by the Census data with all its definitional limitations. But for rural women between 1991 and 2001, work participation fell for the 'below 19' age group. However, between 2001 and 2011, there was an overall fall for all age groups except for women above 50 years of age. Thus, in the period 2001–11, both rural and urban, both male and female workforce participation has risen specifically for the older age group of above 60 years.

Sporadic expansion of work participation is evident between 1991 and 2001 but becomes muted between 2001 and 2011. The dominant trend is that of a rearrangement of labour deployment after 1991. This has four main features. The first is the reversal of trends entailed in the drastic reduction of men from main to marginal workers after 1991. The second is the intensification of marginal work by women in the same period as a continued feature since the 1980s. The third is the rearrangement of the workforce with rising shares of rural women and girls and urban women, men, girls and boys in the workforce as compared to rural men and boys. The fourth is increasing reliance on the work of children, older working-age workers and senior citizens, which makes all discussion on the so-called demographic dividend redundant.

Thus, the *longue durée* of post-Independence capitalism in India can most cogently be explained in all its dimensions in the institutionalised substitution of paid labour by unpaid labour. This process is held in place through the patriarchal basis of holding structures, property rights, tax privileges and definitions of work and worker to facilitate labour cheapening as the sole basis of profitability and capital accumulation in India, privileging the male Hindu capitalist since the first decade of Independence. Combining these with ways of controlling labour deployment on the basis of gender, religion and caste identity appeals to feudal patriarchy in the name of tradition, and using bogeys to deny security of citizenship rights to Muslims and Dalits (with both direct coercion expropriation and violence, and using indirect modes of labour control), along with intensified deployment of children, older working-age and senior citizens, the macroeconomic system after 1991 works to perfection in its ability to deliver growth through labour cheapening, primarily on the basis of intensified marginal work. Thus, neither 'inclusion' nor 'exclusion' is an outcome of the growth trajectory. It is the nature and process of 'inclusion' rather than 'exclusion' in the organisation and reorganisation of paid and unpaid labour which is the causal explanation of the growth and expansion trajectory of Indian capitalism after Independence.

Notes

1. Jagir is a feudal land grant given with right to land revenue collection; inam is a land grant given to a religious person or sect with right of collection of land revenue; and muafi is remission of land revenue to the owner.
2. Land ownership system in India where the landowner owned vast tracts of land and had complete power over the peasantry to extract land rent, tax and tribute.
3. A form of forced labour without any remuneration.
4. Joru is wife, and jameen is land.
5. Caste groups that act as quasi-judicial bodies, mainly in north India.

6. It was only in 2005 that the amendment in the Indian Succession Act deleted Section 4 (2) and brought agricultural land at par with other property.
7. The male patriarch who is the head of a HUF.
8. The Delhi High Court's landmark judgement in December 2015 (*Sujata Sharma versus Manu Gupta Delhi High Court*) has stipulated that women can be karta of a HUF if she is a coparcenary in the HUF.
9. Section 10 (2) of the Income Tax Act of 1961 and Section 5 (2) of the Wealth Tax Act of 1957 exempts HUF property from income tax and wealth tax.
10. An amendment in 1979 did away with the partial partition of HUF.
11. Reports on India's Tax Reforms, Academic Foundation, 2003.
12. Kerala Joint Family Abolition Act (1976), Andhra Pradesh Amendment Act (1986), Tamil Nadu Amendment Act (1990) and Karnataka Amendment Act (1990).
13. All analysis in this section is based on Census data. The analysis excludes Jammu and Kashmir and Assam, as figures for these states are not available for all three Census years. The 1981 Census gives data on the child workforce from 0–14 years. This leaves scope for a small overestimation for 1981.

References

Agnes, F. 2011. *Family Law and Constitutional Claims: Volume 1*. New Delhi: Oxford University Press.

Bannerji, H., S. Mojab and J. Whitehead, eds. 2001. *Of Property and Propriety: The Role of Gender and Class in Imperialism and Nationalism*. Toronto: University of Toronto Press.

Beneria, L., and G. Sen. 1981. 'Accumulation, Reproduction, and "Women's Role in Economic Development": Boserup Revisited'. *Signs* 7 (2): 279–98.

Boserup, E. 1970. *Woman's Role in Economic Development*. London: George Allen and Unwin.

Braunstein, E., I. van Staveren and D. Tavani. 2011. 'Embedding Care and Unpaid Work in Macroeconomic Modelling: A Structuralist Approach'. *Feminist Economics* 17 (4): 5–31.

Brown, H. 2013. *Marx on Gender and the Family: A Critical Study*. Chicago: Haymarket.

Chandrasekhar, C. P., and J. Ghosh. 2002. *The Market that Failed*. New Delhi: Leftword.

Chenoy, K. M. 2015. *The Rise of Big Business in India.* Delhi: Aakar Books.

Chibber, V. 2003. *Locked in Place: State Building and Late Industrialisation in India.* Princeton: Princeton University Press.

Das Gupta, C. 2010. 'Globalisation, Corporate Legal Liability and Big Business Houses in India'. *Cambridge Journal of Economics* 34: 895–913.

———. 2013. 'The Tenacity of the Hindu Undivided Family: Gender, Religion and Tax Concessions'. *Economic and Political Weekly* 48 (40): 73–75.

———. 2016. *State and Capital in Independent India.* New Delhi: Cambridge University Press.

Das Gupta, C., and M. Gupta. 2017. 'The *Hindu Undivided Family* in Independent India's Corporate Governance and Tax Regime'. *South Asia Multidisciplinary Academic Journal (SAMAJ)* 15. Available at http://samaj.revues.org/4300 (accessed 21 April 2020).

Das Gupta, C., and S. Mazumdar. 2018. '"Fiscal Federalism" in India since 1991: Infirmities of Sound Finance Paradigm'. In *Quarter Century of Liberalisation in India: Essays from Economic & Political Weekly,* 148–167. Delhi: Oxford University Press.

Davis, A. Y. 2011. *Women, Race and Class.* New York: Random House.

Dewan, R. 2009. 'Indian Taxation Systems and Policies: A Gendered Critique'. In *Macro Economics and Gender,* ed. Ritu Dewan and K. Seeta Prabhu, 117–38. New Delhi: Zubaan.

———. 2011. 'Twelfth Plan: Patriarchy as Macroeconomic Construct'. *Economic and Political Weekly* 46 (42): 19–21.

Elson, D., ed. 1979. *Value: The Representation of Labour in Capitalism.* London: CSE Books.

Ferber, M. A., and J. A. Nelson. 1993. *Beyond Economic Man: Feminist Theory and Economics.* Chicago: University of Chicago Press.

Fine, B. 1992. *Women's Employment and the Capitalist Family: Towards a Political Economy of Gender and Labour Markets.* London: Routledge.

Fofana, I., J. C. Parra and Q. Wodon. 2009. 'Exports, Labor Income, Gender and Poverty: A Social Accounting Matrix Analysis for Senegal'. In *Gender Aspects of the Trade and Poverty Nexus: A Micro-Macro Approach,* ed. M. Bussolo and R. Hoyos. Washington, DC: World Bank and Palgrave Macmillan.

Fontana, M., and A. Wood. 2000. 'Modeling the Effects of Trade on Women at Work and at Home'. *World Development* 28 (7): 1173–90.

Gandhi, A., J. Parida, S. Mehrotra and S. Sinha. 2014. 'Explaining Employment Trends in the Indian Economy: 1993–94 to 2011–12'. *Economic and Political Weekly* 49 (32): 49–57.

Ghosh, J. 2009. *Never Done and Poorly Paid: Women's Work in Globalising India*. Delhi: Women Unlimited.

Hazari, R. K. 1967. *Industrial Planning and Licensing Policy: Final Report*. New Delhi: Planning Commission, Government of India.

Hirway, I., and S. Jose. 2011. 'Understanding Women's Work Using Time-use Statistics: The Case of India'. *Feminist Economics* 17 (4): 67–92.

Hussmans, R. 2004. 'Measuring the Informal Economy: From Employment in the Informal Sector to Informal Employment'. *ILO Working Paper No.* 53. Geneva: ILO, Bureau of Statistics.

Hui, N. 2013. 'Gender Implications of Tax Policies'. New Delhi: Centre for Budget and Governance Accountability.

Kalpagam, U. 1986. 'Gender in Economics: The Indian Experience'. *Economic and Political Weekly* 21 (43): WS59–66.

Lahoti, R., and H. Swaminathan. 2013. 'Economic Growth and Female Labour Force Participation in India'. *Working Paper No. 414*. Bangalore: Indian Institute of Management.

Lewenhak, S. 1992. *The Revaluation of Women's Work*. London: Earthscan.

Mazumdar, I. 2007. *Women Workers and Globalisation: Emergent Contradictions in India*. New Delhi: Stree.

Mazumdar I., Neetha N. and I. Agnihotri. 2013. 'Migration and Gender in India'. *Economic and Political Weekly* 48 (10): 54–64.

Mazumdar, S. 2006. 'Business Groups and Concentration in the Private Corporate Sector in India'. Unpublished PhD thesis, Jawaharlal Nehru University.

———. 2010. 'On the Sustainability of India's Non-inclusive High Growth'. *ISID Working Paper 2010/12*. New Delhi: Institute for Studies in Industrial Development.

———. 2014. 'Union Budget 2014–15 and the Myth of UPA's "Populism"'. Available at http://www.vikalp.ind.in/2014/03/union-budget-2014-15-and-myth-of-upas.html (accessed 2 February 2016).

Moghadam, V. M. 1996. *Patriarchy and Economic Development: Women's Positions at the End of the Twentieth Century*. Oxford: Clarendon Press.

Mohanty, M., and V. N. Reddy. 2011. 'Some Explorations into India's Post-Independence Growth Process, 1950/51–2002/03: The Demand Side'. *Economic and Political Weekly* 45 (41): 47–58.

Papola, T. S. 2012. 'Social Exclusion and Discrimination in the Labour Market'. *ISID Working Paper 2012/04*. New Delhi: Institute for Studies in Industrial Development.

Pieters, J. 2010. 'Growth and Inequality in India: Analysis of an Extended Social Accounting Matrix'. *World Development* 38 (3): 270–81.

Raj, K. N. 1972. *Report of the Committee on Taxation of Agricultural Wealth and Income*. New Delhi: Ministry of Finance, Government of India.

Ranadive, B. T. 2004. 'Caste, Class and Property Relations in India'. In *Caste and Democratic Politics in India*, ed. G. Shah, 100–22 New Delhi: Anthem South Asian Studies.

Rao, M. G., and N. Singh. 2005. *Political Economy of Federalism in India*. New Delhi: Oxford University Press.

Rao, K. 2015. 'Corporate Taxes and Exemptions: What Does the Proposed Agenda Mean?'. *Economic and Political Weekly* 50 (120): 27–29.

Roy, S. 2014. 'Towards Employment Augmenting Manufacturing Growth'. *ISID Working Paper 168*. New Delhi: Institute for Studies in Industrial Development.

Sen, S. 2001. 'Gender and Domesticity: Liberalisation in Historical Perspective'. *UNEAC Asia Papers No.* 4. Available at http://www.une.edu.au/__data/assets/pdf_file/0018/19026/Sen.pdf (accessed 24 August 2014).

Sachdeva, U. S. 1987. *Hindu Undivided Family: Law Judiciary and Bankers*. Delhi: UDH.

Saxena, N. C. 2012. *Women, Land and Agriculture in Rural India*. New Delhi: UN Women South Asia.

Sengupta, A., and P. Das. 2014. 'Gender Wage Discrimination across Social and Religious Groups in India: Estimates with Unit Level Data'. *Economic and Political Weekly* 49 (21): 71–76.

Sharma, M. 1984. 'Caste, Class and Gender: Women's Role in Agricultural Production in North India'. *Working Paper No. 57*. University of Hawaii.

Sinha, A. 2009. 'Engendering Macroeconomic Modeling for Policy Analysis'. In *Engendering Macroeconomics and Macroeconomic Policies*. UNDP and Zubaan.

Wanchoo, K. N. 1971. *Final Report of the Direct Taxes Enquiry Committee*. New Delhi: Ministry of Finance, Government of India.

Weichselbaumer, D., and R. Winter-Ebmer. 2005. 'A Meta-analysis of the International Gender Wage Gap'. *Journal of Economic Surveys* 19 (3): 479–511.

5

Exploring Paid and Unpaid Work Dichotomy

A Care–Employment Perspective

Neetha N.

The marginalisation of unpaid work, especially non-economic activity from macro statistics and discussions on macroeconomy and policies is well acknowledged. This is because it is often assumed that such work has no bearing on the production, price of the output and adds nothing to the national income. Accordingly, it is often viewed that nothing is gained by collecting statistics on these activities or studying it.

There is a large and robust evidence base about the extent to which women perform unpaid work, and its contributions to both the economy and human development outcomes. A clear division between paid and unpaid work and between women's reproductive and economic work may be possible in the case of economies where markets are fully developed and have penetrated to all sectors of the economy and society. Unpaid work in many developing countries constitutes two broad components which are interrelated. There are some activities which are part of the broader definition of economic activities, but not paid for. The other set of unpaid work accounts for all that is outside the realm of production, which are conceptualised as social reproduction which includes not only direct care work of various kinds but also the routine housework such as cleaning, cooking and other household maintenance activities. Though both are unpaid work, they are different in terms of the relations to the larger economy and society, and therefore strategies for intervention vary considerably.

In the context of India, the line between unpaid work related to social reproduction and other types of unpaid work (for example, work in subsistence agriculture or family businesses) is fuzzy. Further, a large proportion of women constantly move back and forth between reproductive work and 'economic' work through the day or these activities are undertaken simultaneously. This is especially so where women are engaged in 'economic' activities for household consumption carried out in the home.

However, unpaid economic work is included in calculations of GDP and systems of national accounting and increasingly recognised in development programming and food security initiatives. In contrast, housework and unpaid care work[1] have remained out of statistical data collection, economic calculations and policy discourses, which is a reflection of the social understanding of such work, furthering its undervaluation. After years of exclusion from development debates, unpaid reproductive work is now gaining recognition, which is evident from the consensus that is emerging in the negotiations around the post-2015 development agenda (the Sustainable Development Goals or SDGs).

It is well acknowledged that the labour force participation of women in India has always been low and has fallen since 1999–2000. One of the reasons cited by women, who are out of the labour force by principal status, for their non-participation in employment is the non-availability of any other member to carry out domestic duties. This reason accounted for 62.8 per cent of women aged 15 and above who reported as not part of the labour force in the principal status. Thus, unpaid housework and care work is evidently an important issue of women's non-participation in employment.

Since the nature of unpaid reproductive work, its intensity and dimensions vary depending on the lifecycle of women, it is important not only to acknowledge the linkage between the two but also to understand how the two are related at various stages of women's lives. When one looks at the linkages between employment and reproductive work, childcare and related housework is an important component of unpaid reproductive work for many women. However, the intensity and importance of child-related unpaid work vary across women of various age groups.

In this context, the essay attempts to understand the linkages between paid work and unpaid reproductive work through an analysis of women's employment and its trends over time. As a background to this analysis, the next section conceptualises reproductive work in terms of gendered capitalist division of labour, articulating the systematic devaluation of household labour by patriarchal capitalism. Following that, a detailed review of the NSS data systems (the widely used statistics on 'work') through the vantage point of unpaid work is attempted. The essay points out that though the data is largely silent on unpaid work which falls beyond the definition of economic activities used in the survey, some dimensions of unpaid work could be analysed using the data source. The fourth section of the essay captures the possible links between paid work and unpaid work and reproductive work using the available macro-data. Though employment data from the PLFS is available for 2017–18, given its limitations and comparability with previous NSS quinquennial rounds, the analysis is limited to the period 1990–2000 to 2011–12. Further, with 2017–18 data, there have been no reversals; rather there is a sharpening of the already existing trends for female employment, which make the issues raised in this essay more relevant and critical. Finally, the conclusion highlights the need to generate adequate and reliable statistics for furthering the understanding and debates around unpaid reproductive work and its gender implications.

Conceptualising the Undervaluation of Housework

It is now fairly acknowledged that undervaluation of housework is to be located in the ideological dichotomies between home and work, 'labour' and 'domestic labour', 'women's work' and 'work', which are also crucial in understanding the subordination of women. These dichotomies are rooted in a particular political economy and theoretical context, the understanding of which is essential to open up the debates around and issues on unpaid work.

Divisions of labour across processes and tasks in capitalist economies leads to hierarchies among workers. The position of every individual in the hierarchy is determined by the social attributes of individuals, of which gender is an important variable alongside other social divisions such as caste or race. Since capital only values what can be measured by wages, devaluation of domestic labour makes the productive value of women's work murky.[2] In the capitalist division of labour, patriarchy assumes a central role both in terms of creating hierarchies of labour and in deciding who would fill these spaces. The gendered division of labour is most expressed in the construction of a divide between market and non-market (household) oriented labour. Since patriarchy governs the gendered division of work in a capitalist society, women are bound to be degraded to a private sphere. To quote Folbre (1991), 'the concept of the unproductive housewife was a by-product of a new definition of productive labour that valorised participation in the market and devalorised the non-market work central to many women's lives'. This undermines their contribution to the society and economy, perpetuating subordination of women both economically and socially. The division of work across gender increases as market economies develop with women finding it difficult to enter all spheres of production. The spheres of production are not only rendered as public sphere with this system, but they are also segmented on the basis of social relations and power equations. Post (2008) argues:

> With patriarchy, both defined by and defining capitalism, women are relegated to the private sphere and generally denied access to the public. Thus the systemic devaluation of domestic labour has been instrumental to the capitalist mode of production as it is largely outside the realm of the market. Domestic labour, under this system, is thus categorized as "women's work," legitimizing its lack of valuation and by perpetuating an ideological construction placing social expectations and norms on women to perform such labour. Within the capitalist framework, this division is further bifurcated in terms of waged domestic labour and unwaged domestic labour, the latter being explicitly devalued, but both are devalued overall.

This understanding governs framing of economic concepts and thereby policies. Thus, concepts like national income and its compositions are not neutral representation of the economy but are social constructions. The various concepts that define the current understanding of national income are thus based and ordered within a theoretical perspective which is located within the social institution of patriarchy.

The concept of 'the economy' as it exists today is located very much within the neo-classical and Keynesian economics framework. The concept of production followed in national accounts is still neo-classical though there have been changes in the accounting system with Keynesian influence with clear distinctions drawn between market and non-market activities, with market centrism (Nelson 1993). The mainstream definition of 'work' is often associated with market-oriented activity which is guided largely by the definition of production followed. Here, work does not convey anything more than the fact that a monetary return is often associated with it and that the output which is the result of labour could be easily marketed and thus valued.

The mapping of the concept 'work' as it is used in data systems delineates a paid/unpaid regime in which unpaid labour is socially and economically devalued and paid work is valued over unpaid work and a conscious denial of the social reproduction work/unpaid care work. Thus, the classification of activities for the calculation of national income divides all activities into two: those which contribute to the national income and those which are outside. Unpaid work takes place both within the production boundary as well as outside the production boundary, broadly what is referred to as social reproduction. The feminist challenge to the national accounts and other measures of the economy originates from the fact that the production boundary excludes, and thus renders invisible, much of the work and production done in subsistence production and the household (Elson 2005; Hirway 2008). Given the division of work in many societies, a majority of work in these spheres is done by women. Thus, according to Waring (1988), 'devaluing of women's work is woven into the very fabric of contemporary economic theory and practice'. With the increased monetisation of the economy, the categories of work for which valuation is possible also increased alongside a large section of the population entering into paid work outside home. This monetisation of the economy has not only further marginalised the work that was not carried out for monetary returns or for the market, but also those who performed these activities. Thus, the present-day national accounts and employment statistics which are entrenched in Keynesian and neo-classical economic theories render unpaid work in the households invisible and worthless.

Nonetheless, some problems were recognised and incorporated later into production and national income accounting. Few countries in the 1970s and 1980s included subsistence production in the national accounts, but it was the push by the women's movement in the 1970s which highlighted non-market production and undervaluation of women's work (Razavi 2007). The move towards standardisation of national income accounts culminated in the UN SNA in 1953. Though this SNA has been revised over the years, the important ones being in 1968 and 1993, the fundamental principles of the system continued. The underlying principle that the economy is defined by market/economic production remained, with small changes in the definition of 'production boundary' to accommodate subsistence production. This not only continues to hold and strengthen the hierarchy between market and non-market work, but also between economic and non-economic work, or productive and reproductive work.

NSS Data on Unpaid Work

The poor conceptual understanding and the lack of interest in unpaid work and its dimensions is visible in national statistics. Non-availability and inadequacy of data on unpaid work is an issue both with reference to unpaid economic work as well as the work outside the production boundary. Census and NSS definition of work makes a distinction between economic and non-economic work based on the Indian System of National Accounts (ISNA). Both the data systems capture unpaid economic work. However, Census does not collect separate data on unpaid economic work and hence the statistics cannot be used for any estimation of unpaid economic work.

The most regular and hence largely used statistics on 'work' is the Employment and Unemployment Surveys of the NSSO, which captures unpaid economic work at various levels. Though the data is largely silent on unpaid work that falls beyond the definition of its economic activities, some dimensions of unpaid work which falls in the fringes of the unpaid economic and non-economic activity could be analysed using this data source. Though NSS data has improved over time in terms of its capacity to capture various dimensions of work, the estimates on women's employment based on NSS data is still an underestimate. For the unpaid work segment that is counted as workers, the category that is relevant in NSS data is that of contributing family workers/helpers.

There are three broad sets of issues regarding data on unpaid 'economic' work, with reference to NSS data. One is the issue of invisibility and undercounting of unpaid economic work which is captured under the statistics on employment. Even in the context of recent declines in FLFPR, it has been argued that a 'large part of the missing labour is missing only from the NSSO data but is very much there in the labour force ... It appears "missing" because of the inability of the NSSO surveys to capture it adequately' (Hirway 2012). Underestimation of women's work and its different dimensions are part of the macro-datasets on employment. The issue of invisibility is much less for wage work as monetary rewards make them recognisable as workers and hence the issue is largely with reference to the self-employed, of which a large segment is unpaid workers.

Second, the limited data on unpaid work is often hidden under the category of self-employment, leading to its invisibility in analysis and policy interventions. To quote Mazumdar and Neetha (2011), 'the present commonly used method of lumping paid and unpaid workers together without differentiation is hardly the best method for analysis of employment trends, particularly among women'. The NSS shares raw data with users, hence it is possible to conduct a disaggregate analysis of unpaid workers (contributing family workers/helpers). The publication of statistics on contributing family workers/helpers as part of the report itself is a sign of recognising these workers who constitute a large proportion of women workers even in urban areas, thereby communicating gender progressive signals.

The other and the most crucial issue is the limited definition of unpaid economic work that is followed in the data systems. To examine this, it is important to look at the definition followed in the NSS Employment and Unemployment Surveys. The discussions further are based on the information provided by Ministry of Statistics and Programme Implementation in its various reports. The term 'economic activity' as defined in NSS includes the following two broad categories:

1. All the market activities performed for pay or profit which result in production of goods and services for exchange.
2. Of the non-market activities, (a) all the activities relating to the primary sector which result in production (including free collection of uncultivated crops, forestry, firewood, hunting, fishing, mining, quarrying, etc.) of primary goods for own consumption and (b) activities relating to the own-account production of fixed assets, which include production of fixed assets including construction of own houses, roads, wells, etc., and of machinery, tools, etc., for household enterprise and also construction of any private or community facilities free of charge.[3]

Going by these, the processing activities of primary products produced by the households for household consumption are not considered as economic activity. However, these fall within the production boundary, according to the UN SNA 2008. Given the social and economic division of work, many women are surely to be involved in such activities spending considerable time. This demands a revision of the concept of work followed in the ISNA taking into account SNA 2008.

Apart from the data on contributing family workers/helpers, some limited information on few unaccounted, unpaid activities is available from NSS schedules. The survey collects some additional information from those who are categorised as 'out of labour force' according to the principal status approach and who report their status as attended domestic duties (codes 92 and 93). However, the information is limited to 'specified domestic activities which resulted in economic benefits to their households'.

Additional questions are canvassed during the survey to those who are out of the labour force by principal status[4] (men and women) to collect information on a range of activities which are undertaken for household consumption. Each person, categorised as usually engaged in domestic duties in the principal status (that is, codes 92 or 93) is asked whether he/she pursued certain specified activities more or less regularly for household consumption along with their normal domestic chores. These activities are (1) maintenance of kitchen garden, etc.; (2) work in household poultry, dairy, etc.; (3) free collection of fish, small game, wild fruits, vegetables, etc., for household consumption; (4) free collection of firewood, cow dung, cattle feed, etc.; (5) husking of paddy for household consumption; (6) grinding food grain for household consumption; (7) preparation of *gur*[5] for household consumption; (8) preservation of meat and fish for household consumption; (9) making baskets and mats for household use; (10) preparation of cow dung cakes for use as fuel in the household; (11) sewing, tailoring, weaving, etc., for household use; (12) tutoring of own/others' children free of charge; (13) bringing water from outside the household premises and for rural areas; and (14) bringing water from outside the village separately for distances up to 1 km, 2–5 km, and 6 km and above.

From the perspective of the activity classification, these activities are grouped by NSS into three—Category (i): activities relating to agricultural production such as the maintenance of kitchen garden, work in household poultry, dairy, etc., including free collection of agricultural products for household consumption; Category (ii): processing of primary products produced by the households for household consumption; and Category (iii): other activities for own consumption but resulting in economic benefits to households.

Activities under Category (i) fall within the production boundary according to UN SNA 2008 as well as the ISNA. However, as time criterion is followed in defining the work status, women who may not have engaged in such activities for less than 30 days during the reference year are not counted as subsidiary workers.

As discussed earlier, activities under Category (ii) are to be considered as economic activities according to the recommendations of UN SNA 2008, but the Indian definition of SNA does not, so far, consider them as economic activities if they are for own consumption.

It is possible to arrive at a wholesome statistics on unpaid work within the production boundary from Categories (i) and (ii). Thus, Categories (i) (separating those who are counted as subsidiary workers) and (ii) put together could be used to obtain an upper bound to the number of persons usually engaged in unpaid economic activity, irrespective of their intensity of participation during the reference year, which gives some better, though basic, insight into the unpaid economic work undertaken by women. Further, the inclusion of these would give a better picture of women's economic contribution as captured by women's work participation rate. This has been a consistent demand by many scholars.

Interestingly, neither SNA 2008 nor ISNA includes processing activities of primary products for household consumption if these products are acquired. Thus, if the woman is involved in husking the paddy or making gur from raw materials that are acquired, these activities are not counted as economic activity. Thus, for activities 5 to 9, NSSO publishes separate data for that which is part of SNA 2008 (processing of own produce) and that of those outside the production boundary (processing of acquired produce). Activities listed under categories 10 to 14 are also not counted as economic activity both by SNA 2008 and ISNA.

The data on those who have attended domestic duties (codes 92 and 93) in their principal status consists of three broad groups: (a) those who are subsidiary workers (spending adequate time in economic activity); (b) those who are workers but are not counted as subsidiary workers as the time that they spent on such activities are nominal; and (c) those who do not undertake any of the specified activities that makes them qualified to be a worker as per the existing definition of work.

Comparable data on those who attended domestic duties in the principal status is available since the 50th Round of NSS.[6] However, the data is available only for women with principal status as 'out of labour force' and is limited to mere participation rate, irrespective of the nature and intensity of involvement. Many women who are workers in usual status may also be engaged in several activities, but the survey is silent on these, as the questions are asked only to those who are out of the labour force by principal usual status. Thus, the statistics on unpaid work based on NSS data do not capture the issue of the double burden of women workers and their multitasking.

This warrants a wider definition of work that could capture activities and time allocations of women. TUSs are the principal source of such data, which records all activities irrespective of their status. In the discussions on unpaid work, an important issue that has been raised is that of time poverty, as the burden of multiple activities constraints women from making choices on how they allocate their time. This not only leads to increased work intensity but also trade-offs, and women at all income levels are vulnerable to time poverty. However, the issue of time poverty could be particularly severe for poor women, who have limited assets and poor returns to their labour.

Linkages between Women's Employment and Unpaid Reproductive Work

Do unpaid work and the social reproduction role of women affect and determine their entry and their presence in some segments? It is difficult to arrive at any firm conclusion from the macro-data as the existing statistics on women's work is highly limited. Women's labour force participation is low and has always been much below that of men, suggesting a clear gender gap. Further, there has not been any increase in participation rate even with high economic growth. To make the matter worse, participation rates have shown a decline since 1999–2000, making the long-term trend as one of decline. To understand the unpaid/care work dimensions of employment, it is important to examine the trends across different age groups, as reproductive care work demands vary considerably across women of different age cohorts as discussed elsewhere also.

The participation rate varies across various age groups and is the highest for the age group 35–44 years. Figure 5.1 shows that participation rates have declined for all age groups, but the extent of decline

Figure 5.1: LFPR across Age Groups (Usual Status), 1999–2000 to 2011–12

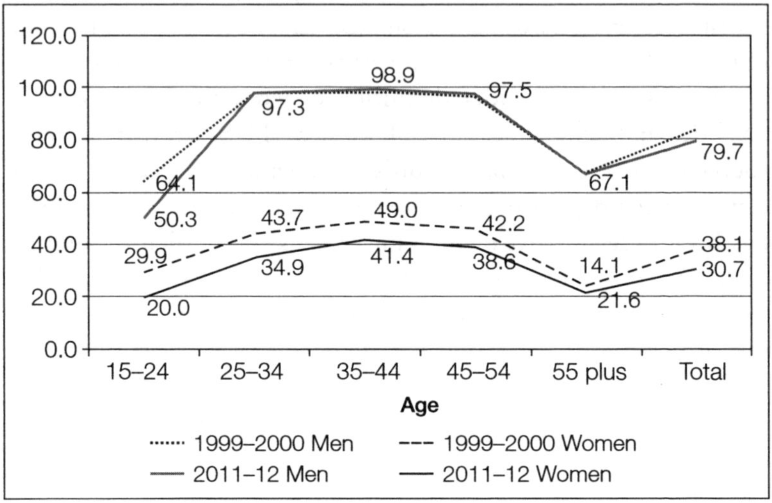

Source: Employment and Unemployment Reports, NSSO, various rounds.

has been highest for the age group of 15–24 years. The decline for this group is anticipated with their increased presence in education. The age group 25–34 years comes second in order with a decline of 8.8 percentage points. It is this age group for whom childcare responsibilities, demanding the presence of an adult caregiver, are most important. The age group 25–34 years comprises many sub-age groups and for each of the different categories there has been a decline in LFPRs.

A related variable, which is important in examining their productive work dimension of employment alongside age, is that of participation in economic activity across marital status of women. Unmarried women have the lowest participation rate across years, rooted in the restrictions on women's mobility. However, the trend over time is revealing. Though the decline in participation rate is visible across all categories, the decline has been the highest for currently married women (Figure 5.2).

The 'currently married' category comprises women from different age groups for whom the nature and requirement of care would be

Figure 5.2: LFPR across Marital Status (Usual Status), 1999–2000 to 2011–12

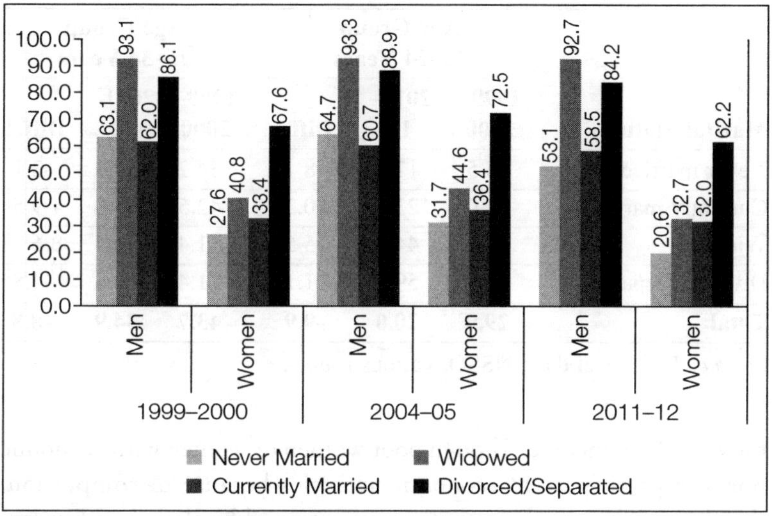

Source: Unit-level data, NSSO, various rounds.

different. It is understood that the demand for housework is high among younger age groups of women and the nature of housework is elaborate and continuous. Thus, it is critical to look at this age group among currently married women to get a better picture of the relation between housework and paid work. In Table 5.1, the participation rate is given for the two critical age groups. It shows that it is for the younger age group for whom the decline in participation rate is particularly sharp. The nuclearisation of households which leaves individual families to take care of housework and childcare seems to be at work, with many married women in this age group withdrawing from work. As evident in the table, it is striking that for the age group of 25–34 years, the participation rate shows an increase for unmarried girls over the period, while for currently married women there is a marked decline. This does reflect on the importance of women's house/care work and its limiting role in women's participation in economic activities.

The option to participate or not may not be available to all women, as many would be compelled to undertake paid employment

Table 5.1: LFPR for Women across Select Age Groups and Marital Status (Usual Status), 1999–2000 to 2011–12

	Age Group 15–24 Years			**Age Group 25–34 Years**		
Marital Status	**1999–2000**	**2011–12**	**Diff.**	**1999–2000**	**2011–12**	**Diff.**
Never married	25.5	17.5	–8	54.2	56.3	2.1
Currently married	34.0	23.7	–10.3	42.5	33.0	–9.5
Widowed	59.7	44.2	–15.5	71.4	77.4	6
Divorced/separated	60.6	59.5	–1.1	71.4	66.6	–4.8
Total	**29.9**	**20.0**	**–9.9**	**43.7**	**34.9**	**–8.8**

Source: Unit-level data, NSSO, various rounds.

for want of an income. Though poor women or women with economic burdens participate in economic activities because of compulsion, the choice of economic activities are restricted by their care burden. Thus, for those who are in employment, the nature of employment is an important variable that could throw some light on the relation between care work and employment.

Self-employment is the most important category of employment for all, but especially for women. The share of self-employed women in total employment does not show any signs of a decline over the years. Self-employment accounted for 55.1 per cent of women in 1999–2000, and over time the share showed a small increase with a share of 56.2 per cent (Table 5.2). As per the definition of self-employment followed in the NSS survey, the category comprises three different segments such as employers, own-account workers (OAW) and contributing family workers/helpers. Given the larger social restrictions on women's work, it is possible that women workers could be concentrated in those economic activities that could be carried out at homes along with men. Thus, it is natural to have a larger proportion of women in the category of contributing family workers. However, their shares across age cohorts could reveal some insights into the linkages between unpaid reproductive work and employment. Thus, within the subcategories of self-employed, a larger

Table 5.2: Distribution of Workers by Status of Employment (%), 1999–2000 to 2011–12

	1999–2000		2004–05		2011–12	
Activity Status	**Men**	**Women**	**Men**	**Women**	**Men**	**Women**
Self-employed	50.8	55.1	54.3	61.0	50.7	56.2
Regular wage/salaried worker	18.3	8.0	18.4	9.1	20.4	13.4
Casual worker	30.8	36.9	27.2	30.0	28.9	30.3
Total wage workers (regular wage/salaried worker + casual worker)	49.2	44.9	45.7	39.0	49.3	43.8
Grand total (self-employed + total wage workers)	100.0	100.0	100.0	100.0	100.0	100.0

Source: Employment and Unemployment Reports, NSSO, various rounds.

concentration of women from particular age groups may be seen in segments where there could be an easy flow between reproductive work and economic work.

Of the self-employed, for the age groups 15–24 and 25–34 years, where the significance of childcare is high, the proportion of unpaid family helpers is also the largest (Table 5.3). Unpaid economic work is mostly undertaken in family farms and enterprises and thus it allows women to move easily back and forth between reproductive work and economic activities through the day or to undertake both simultaneously. Another important category is OAW, which includes subcontracted wage work carried out in homes. This activity mostly undertaken at home also permits some flexibility in economic work, allowing women to meet their care responsibilities.

Apart from the nature of work, the sectoral distribution is also worth exploring as concentration in particular sectors could be influenced not only by an understanding of women's role in households but also on account of women's choices of sectors based on their judgement of the nature and extent of household responsibilities. The broad sector-wise distribution shows the predominance of agriculture in total female employment, which accounts for almost the entire share

Table 5.3: Percentage Distribution of Self-employed Women across Different Age Groups by Employment Status, 1999–2000 to 2011–12

	1999–2000			2004–05			2011–12		
Age Group	**OAW**	**Employer**	**Unpaid Helpers**	**OAW**	**Employer**	**Unpaid Helpers**	**OAW**	**Employer**	**Unpaid Helpers**
15–24 years	19.7	0.2	80.1	19.0	0.1	80.9	24.0	0.0	76.0
25–34 years	28.3	0.7	71.1	27.0	0.6	72.4	34.3	0.2	65.5
35–44 years	35.5	1.0	63.5	32.2	1.1	66.7	38.9	0.9	60.2
45–54 years	33.5	1.2	65.3	30.2	1.1	68.6	39.1	0.9	60.0
55+ years	37.8	2.1	60.1	31.3	2.6	66.1	38.1	1.9	60.0
Total (for all age groups)	**30.2**	**0.9**	**68.9**	**27.8**	**1.0**	**71.3**	**35.3**	**0.7**	**64.0**

Source: Unit-level data, NSSO, various rounds.

of the primary sector (Figure 5.3). In agriculture, as is well documented, women are largely non-wage workers who are part of the family labour. As discussed earlier, it is difficult to separate housework from economic work in these forms of labour where the flow is continuous. The female share of employment in the secondary sector has stagnated over time, while that of service sector increased, though at a much lower level compared to that of primary sector.

Figure 5.3: Distribution of Workers across Broad Industrial Divisions, 2011–12

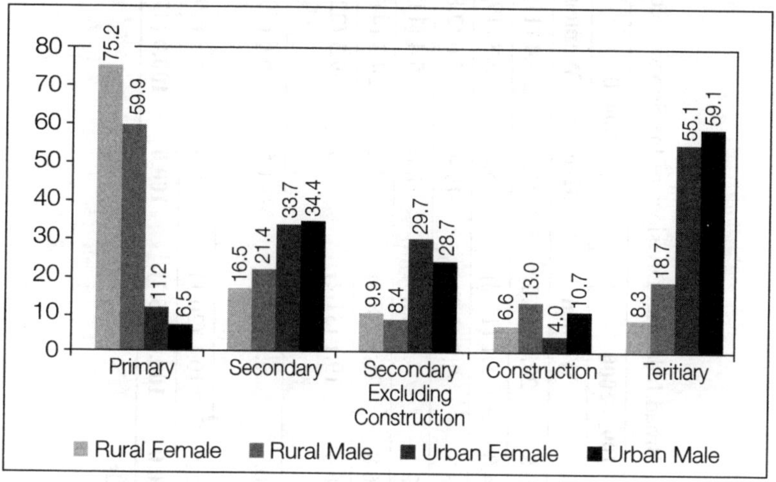

Source: Unit-level data, NSSO, various rounds.

The service sector consists of a range of sub-sectors, which are divergent in terms of skill categorisations and employment conditions. Table 5.4 gives the distribution of women across various broad sub-sectors of the service sector.

From the table, it is clear that within the limited share of women in total services, there is segregation across sectors/occupations that are considered female-friendly from the perspective of care work. Community, social and personal services, which include education, health, domestic work and a range of other services, accounts for the second largest sector next to manufacturing, especially in urban areas.

Education is seen as an acceptable occupation for female employment for its ability to combine paid work with childcare because

Table 5.4: Distribution of Workers across Broad Industrial Divisions of the Service Sector, 1999–2000 to 2011–12

Service	1999–2000		2004–05		2011–12	
	Men	**Women**	**Men**	**Women**	**Men**	**Women**
Trade	40.8	27.8 (12.0)	41.3	24.4 (11.2)	39.7	22.7 (11.0)
Hotels and restaurants	4.8	5.1 (17.7)	5.2	5.8 (19.5)	6.2	5.2 (15.4)
Transport, storage and communication	18.3	2.7 (2.9)	19.4	2.6 (2.8)	19.2	1.8 (2.0)
Public administration and defence	12.1	7.5 (11.0)	8.6	5.4 (11.8)	6.8	4.4 (12.2)
Education	6.8	21.1 (38.4)	7.2	24.3 (41.9)	7.6	27.0 (43.5)
Other community, social and personal services	8.4	19.1 (31.2)	7.0	9.3 (22.3)	6.2	11.5 (28.6)
Private households with employed persons	0.7	6.7 (64.0)	1.5	16.6 (70.9)	1.2	11.7 (67.2)
Other services	8.0	10.1 (20.1)	9.9	11.5 (19.9)	13.0	15.7 (20.7)
Total	**100.0**	**100.0 (16.7)**	**100.0**	**100.0 (17.6)**	**100.0**	**100.0 (17.8)**

Source: Unit-level data, NSSO, various rounds.

of work timings. Work schedules of teachers coincide with those of children's schooling, so women teachers can return with their children and are present to do their routine household responsibilities. Education accounts for the largest share of female employment within the sector, accounting for 27 per cent of women workers in this category of services. In education, female teachers at the primary level have increased steadily over the period, though women's presence is increasing in other segments as well. Though education accounts for the largest segment in terms of growth in this category, private households with employed persons assumes special significance. The number of women engaged in private households with employed persons shows a phenomenal increase within a short period and the share of the sector has increased from 6.7 to 11.7 per cent. This phenomenal increase means that paid domestic work is next in importance to education in women's employment in the service sector. The flexibility and timings of paid domestic work, which allows women to combine paid work with their own housework, is one of the reasons for women's preference to take up such employment. The natural link of this occupation to women's housework is, of course, a critical factor which explains the increasing share of women in the total employment of the sector. Education and paid part-time domestic work are preferred employment for the potential to combine paid and unpaid care work.

The most important feature which may be noted in the trends and patterns is that female employment continues to concentrate in areas akin to women's care responsibilities or where they can easily combine both care work and 'employment'. Thus, the growing areas of paid employment are those which appear to have a 'natural' link to women's care work and the timings of which are seen to enable them to fulfil their domestic 'responsibilities'. It is assumed that women can combine paid work and housework or other unpaid care work.

Labour Force Participation of Women in Households with Small Children

Given the demographic profile of the population and the social understanding of women's household functions and responsibilities, childcare is one of the most important components of unpaid care work in our contexts. Childcare responsibilities are at their peak before the age of schooling. The entry of children to *anganwadi* centres or play schools is usually after age of three years. Hence, it would be insightful to analyse the pattern of women's participation in the labour market with the presence of children below three years of age. The household data collected by NSS gives details of household members including their age. However, it is not possible to locate any relationship between individual men and women with children in the households. What is possible is to analyse the participation of women in the labour market with the presence of small children in the household, irrespective of their relationship with them. One intermediate way is to exclude 'never married' from the analysis, though, even in this case, the possibility of the presence of children other than sons and daughters in households cannot be completely ruled out.

The data provides some insights into the delimiting role of childcare in women's participation in economic activity. The labour force participation of women declines with increased presence of small children up to the age of three in the household, while for men there seems to be an inverse relation. The pressure on men to earn for the family with the increased number of children could be an explanation of their increasing LFPR with the presence of more young children in the household. The opposite seems to happen for women (Figure 5.4). Thus, it seems that women from households where there are no small children are more likely to be in the labour force which is evident across years with higher LFPR for this category.

The presence of small children can have differential influence on women in different age groups, as the presence of older siblings can relieve women from some amount of childcare responsibilities. Further, though childcare demands could be higher and intensive for children in the younger age groups, the older children also require care, though of a different nature. To examine these dimensions, Figure 5.5 captures the relationship between age of women and childcare demands across different age categories of children and its relation to LFPR.

Figure 5.4: LFPR of Men and Women in the Age Group of 15–55 Years across Number of Children below Three Years in the Household, 1999–2000 to 2011–12

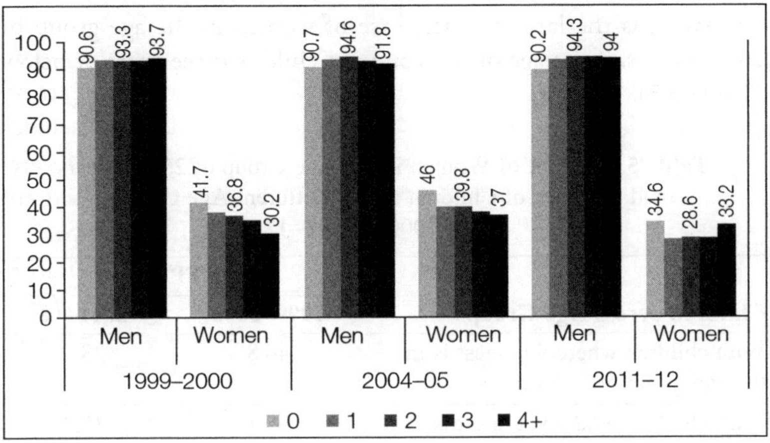

Source: Govindan (2016).

Figure 5.5: LFPR of Women across Various Age Groups across Age of Children in the Household (15–55 Years), 2011–12

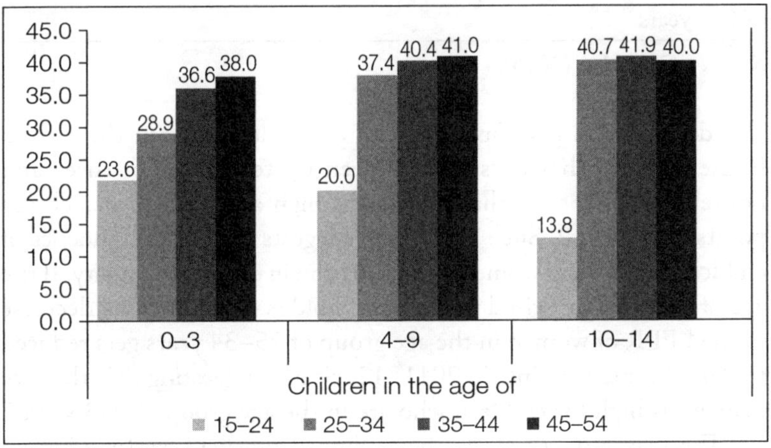

Source: Govindan (2016).

The participation rate of women is lowest when the age group of the children is below three years for all groups of women. Within all age groups of women with children below three years, the lowest participation is for the age cohort of 15–24 years, 23.6 per cent (Figure 5.5). The data over various years shows that the decline in the LFPRs of women due to the existence of small children in the household is the largest in the case of women in the age group of 25–34 years, if the age of the youngest child is three years or below (Table 5.5).

Table 5.5: LFPR of Women in the Age Group of 25–34 Years and Presence of Children across Different Age Groups, 1999–2000 to 2011–12

	LFPR	
Children across Age Groups	**1999–2000**	**2011–12**
With children where youngest is in the age group of 0–3 years	40.8	28.9
With children where youngest is in the age group of 4–9 years	45.8	37.4
With children where youngest is in age group of 10–14 years	48.6	40.7
No children in the age group of 0–3 years	46.7	39.0

Source: Govindan (2016).

The difference in participation rates of women between those from households not having small children up to the age of three and households with such children was as high as about 10 percentage points in 2011–12. Such a wide gap suggests the critical influence of childcare in limiting women's participation in economic activity. If the age of the youngest child in the household is 4–9 years, the decrease in the LFPR of women in the age group of 25–34 years gets reduced to 8.4 percentage points in 2011–12, clearly suggesting that the care demand is high for children who are in the age group of 0–3 years.

The macro-data reflects the findings from field-level studies on women workers across sectors (Ghosh 2002; Mazumdar 2007). Married women were few or absent in certain categories of jobs, which was partly due to the employer's preferences, again determined by their care functions. This is true in the case of a range of sectors such as garments, modern services which are at different layers of the heirarchy. The pressure of paid work and the perception of housework do influence their decision to continue at work as well as the nature of their particpation. In a study of women workers in Delhi, it was found that many unmarried women did not consider themselves working after marriage or childbirth (Neetha and Mazumdar 2010). Even those who wanted to remain in the labour force after marriage did not anticipate themselves working in the same sector or firm, given the work-related demands.

The selection of certain categories of work by women is also determined by their role in housework. The fact that domestic wokers can work close to their dwellings, which allows for some flexibility in terms of managing paid work with unpaid care responsibilities, is found as a major reason for women's preference for paid domestic work over construction work or other informal-sector wage work (Palriwala and Neetha 2010). Domestic workers mostly add or deduct the number of tasks or employers according to their household care demands. These insights make it obvious that patriarcial demands and expectations on women prevail, which restrict their participation in economic activites. Further, such expectations continue, irrespective of entry into economic work, which influence their sector of employment, terms and conditions of work.

Employment Aspirations of Women Engaged in Domestic Duties

Many women who report themselves as principally engaged in domestic work report some economic activity that fetches the household some additional income. Such participation, if nominal, or is a borderline case of economic activity, would not be reflected in the usual indicators of employment. However, the NSS, through a set of probing questions, collects some information on their participation in economic activities, which are minimal.

Among women of age five years and above usually engaged in domestic duties in terms of their principal and subsidiary statuses taken together, about 55 per cent in rural areas and 19 per cent in urban areas pursued one or more economic activities in 2011–12, which were nominal. These activities were related to (a) agricultural production such as the maintenance of the kitchen garden, work in household poultry, dairy, etc., including free collection of agricultural products for household consumption; and (b) processing of primary products produced by the households, for households' consumption. These activities suggest the possibility of a labour–care dichotomy. The activities that these women are engaged mostly with are free collection of goods and fuel, household poultry and dairy, sewing, tailoring, weaving, grinding of food grains, etc. Their unpaid, familial responsibilities decrease their opportunities for paid work outside their premises which will affect their care responsibilities. Since the work is performed within the familial, 'private' sphere, the extent of work they do is also obscured. This suggests the difficulty in separating and measuring paid and unpaid work and the ease of flow between the two.

The related information collected also shows that the demand for home-based work is on the increase, which could be explained in terms of economic pressure on households alongside the social pressure on women to remain within the boundaries of households. This is evident from the proportion of those who are out of the labour force showing willingness to take up economic work, provided such work is done at home. About 33 per cent in rural areas and about 27 per cent in urban areas reported their willingness to accept work if the work was made available at their household premises. Among the women of age 15 years and above who reported willingness to accept work at the household premises, about 70 per cent in rural areas and about 69 per cent in urban areas preferred 'part-time' work on a regular basis, while about 23 per cent in rural areas and about 26 per cent in urban areas wanted regular 'full-time' work. These insights further confirm the criticality of housework in women's life and its restrictive impact on women's entry into economic work, its nature and status.

Conclusion

The discussion here reveals that in the given social order on which existing eonomic structures are built, women are bound to be unduly concentrated in unpaid work categories. Even within paid work, women's work is defined and limited by their household roles, both as a matter of choice as well as labour market options. On the other hand, labour market expectations on women are still based on the assumption that women are free to undertake and devote any amount of time at any time in the day in paid work. Thus, what is disturbing is the fact that there has been no acknowledgement of these pressures, as visible in the absence of any policy initiatives towards maternity leave, childcare leave, crèches, etc. This leads to conentration of women in sectors which are considered women-friendly in terms of women's larger household roles.

The most important concern emerging from the discussion is the lack of reliable data on the various dimensions. Given the critical role of unpaid work in underlining women's contribution (both within the spheres of production and reproduction) and gender inequality, regular and reliable statistics on unpaid work is a must. Though micro-level studies are useful and are required, these cannot be substitutes for macro-data collected by well-equipped and trained state agencies. TUSs, which are quantitative summaries of how individuals allocate their time over a specified period of time, can provide a good source of data for understanding unpaid work both within the production boundary as well as outside. Though occasional interest is shown in TUS by policy-makers, it is often not given its importance due to many reasons. To quote Hirway (2009), 'it is frequently argued that TUS is not a high priority survey for India, as there are many other areas which demand higher priority. It is also argued that TUS is a costly survey and the country cannot afford mainstreaming it at this stage.' This position resonates the division and hierarchy between paid and unpaid work and the indifference for the latter, entrenched in the patriarchal understanding of the economy, an issue discussed earlier.

Notes

1. In the subsequent discussions, the term 'reproductive work' is used for all activities which are captured under unpaid housework as well as unpaid care work.
2. Value in a capitalist economy is market determined (exchange value), while in other modes of production it is the use value which is important.

3. A person may be engaged in own-account construction in the capacity of either a labourer or a supervisor. Certain activities like prostitution, begging, etc., which though fetched earnings, were not considered as economic activities. Activity status of a person was judged irrespective of the situation, whether such activity was carried out illegally in the form of smuggling or not.
4. Only 0.5 per cent among males belonged to this category as against 42.2 per cent of females in 2009–10.
5. Gur is the Hindi word for jaggery made from sugarcane or date palm tree.
6. Though the quinquennial round of NSSO was initiated since the 27th Round, the 27th Round made no distinction between the principal and subsidiary worker which the subsequent rounds did. Since the data on domestic duties is collected only from those whose status as per principal status is out of labour force in all the surveys since the 32nd Round, the data is not comparable with that of the 27th Round.

References

Elson, D. 2005. 'Unpaid Work, the Millennium Development Goals, and Capital Accumulation'. Paper presented at UNDP-Levy Institute Conference on Unpaid Work and Economy: Gender, Poverty, and the Millennium Development Goals, 3–5 October, Levy Economics Institute of Bard College, New York.

Folbre, Nancy. 1991. 'The Unproductive Housewife: Her Evolution in Nineteenth-century Economic Thought'. *Signs: Journal of Women in Culture and Society* 16 (3): 463–84.

Ghosh, Jayati. 2002. 'Globalisation, Export-oriented Employment for Women and Social Policy: A Case Study of India'. *Social Scientist* 30 (11/12): 17–60.

Govindan, Raveendran. 2016. 'The Indian Labour Market: A Gender Perspective'. Discussion Paper No. 8 for Progress of the World's Women 2015–2016, UN Women, New York.

Hirway, Indira. 2008. 'Multiple Uses of Time Use Statistics in Developing Countries'. In *Towards Mainstreaming Time Use Surveys in National Statistical System in India*, Ministry of Women and Child Development. New Delhi: UNDP and World Bank.

———. 2009. 'Mainstreaming Time Use Surveys in National Statistical System in India'. *Economic and Political Weekly* 64 (49): 56–65.

———. 2012. 'Missing Labour Force: An Explanation'. *Economic and Political Weekly* 48 (37): 67–72.

Mazumdar, Indrani. 2007. *Women Workers and Globalisation: Emergent Contradictions in India*. Stree: Kolkata.

Mazumdar, Indrani and Neetha N. 2011. 'Gender Dimensions: Employment Trends in India, 1993–94 to 2009–10'. *Economic and Political Weekly* 46 (43): 118–26.

Ministry of Statistics and Programme Implementation. 2001. 'Concepts and Definitions Used in NSS'. Golden Jubilee Publication, Government of India, New Delhi.

———. 2008. *Background Paper for the Workshop on Conceptual Issues in Measurement of Employment-unemployment*. New Delhi: Ministry of Statistics and Programme Implementation.

Neetha N., and Indrani Mazumdar. 2010. 'Report on the Conditions and Needs of Women Workers in Delhi'. Unpublished mimeo, Centre for Women's Development Studies, New Delhi.

Nelson, Julie A. 1993. 'The Study of Choice or the Study of Provisioning?: Gender and the Definition of Economics'. In *Beyond Economic Man: Feminist Theory and Economics*, ed. Marianne A. Ferber and Julie A. Nelson. Chicago: University of Chicago Press.

Palriwala, Rajni and Neetha N. 2010. 'Care Arrangements and Bargains: Anganwadi and Paid Domestic Workers in India'. *International Labour Review* 149 (4): 511–27.

Post, Eric. 2008. 'The Gendered Division of Labor: The Wages for Housework Movement, and the Law'. Available at https://www.academia.edu/827795/the_gendered_division_of_labor_the_wages_for_housework_movement_and_the_law (accessed 12 September 2017).

Razavi, Shahra. 2007. *The Political and Social Economy of Care in a Development Context: Conceptual Issues, Research Questions and Policy Options*. Gender and Development Programme Paper No. 3. Geneva: United Nations Research Institute for Social Development.

Waring, Marilyn. 1988. *Counting for Nothing: What Men Value and What Women are Worth*. Toronto, Buffalo: University of Toronto Press.

6

Labour Relations within the Household

A Study of Women Domestic Workers in the National Capital Region

Archana Prasad and *S. Krithi*

The relationship between class, gender and social discrimination has formed one of the main areas of focus in recent studies on domestic work. In classical scholarship, domestic work has been seen as unpaid and unaccounted for women's work, which is grounded in the traditional division of labour. Hence, the fight for domestic workers' rights has largely been seen in terms of 'recognition' and the politics of recognition has become the hallmark of all struggles for decent working conditions. In this essay, 'domestic work' refers to 'household work' performed for a wage by those living inside or outside the household. It includes any household work like sweeping, cleaning utensils, washing clothes, cooking, child and elderly care, and any other manual work performed for the maintenance of the household. This category of labour is part of the growing informalisation of labour in the current stage of corporate capitalism, where there is an increase in the commodification of domestic work, thus converting the home into a workplace. The home is increasingly getting integrated into the larger labour market by employing wage labour for domestic work. The invisibility and non-recognition of work is also related to this integration of the home into wider commodity and labour markets. In this essay, we deal with the second trend identified here.

The question of domestic work has almost always been seen from the lens of 'decent work' and the need to recognise housework in the larger system of national accounts. The argument is that the traditional social division of labour ensures that domestic labour is undervalued and stigmatised in public perception. According to this theory, the concentration of women workers in low-wage domestic labour and the indecent conditions of work are determined by social perceptions and gender hierarchies. Within this theory, social structures are given primacy and domestic work is treated as a distinct form of work with special characteristics (Jain and Banerjee 1985). Hence, the real enemy is the social discrimination within the labour markets and not the capitalist system which systematically reproduces exploitative conditions of wage labour within the home (John 2013; Ray and Qayum 2009). This misunderstanding arises from the misconception that labour relations within domestic work have to be treated as a specific case and not as a part of the larger problem of informalisation of labour relations under the current stage of capitalist development.

While it may be argued that social reproduction of patriarchal structures is closely linked with the domestication of work, it is interesting to see how the formation of a class of domestic labourers is mediated by gender and caste factors (Neetha 2013). In this sense, discriminatory practices are inbuilt within the processes of class formation itself and this is reflected in the social characteristics of the domestic labour force. The second point to be noted about structural features forming the context of domestic labour is regarding the conversion of unpaid reproductive labour into wage labour through the domestic labour market (Federici 2012; Lutz 2011). Employment of wage labour for domestic work, in fact, commodifies the process of social reproduction of patriarchal relations without providing it adequate recognition. The importance of the politics of recognition also needs to be seen in this context. Another theme of significant debate has been the relationship between paid and unpaid labour in domestic work (Antonpoulos and Hirway 2010). While reproductive labour and the social reproduction of family relations have always been seen as unpaid and unaccounted for labour, the relationship between surplus labour accumulation and wage labour has received less attention. In fact, the process of the commodification of social reproduction into productive wage labour results in the accumulation of greater surpluses which have a high degree of unpaid element in them (Custers 2012; Ghosh 2012a). Therefore, the relationship between paid and unpaid labour needs to be revisited.

This essay deals with some of the aforementioned debates and questions by studying how the home as a workplace functions. It focuses on the labour relations that operate within the household and analyses the working conditions under which domestic labour is performed. This analysis is based on a survey conducted by the Delhi Committee of the All-India Democratic Women's Association (AIDWA) to understand the conditions of work of domestic workers in Delhi. This survey was conducted in the first half of 2014 with the aim of understanding the main problems and demands of the domestic workers in the city in order to build a consciousness that will enable further organisation and mobilisation amongst this class of workers. The questionnaire was thus created to enable area-level activists to do the survey on their own and both become aware and raise awareness of the issues concerning domestic workers in their own areas. Hence, the survey itself has been embedded in an area-level campaign to begin the organisation of domestic workers in Delhi. The focus of the survey was mainly on understanding the different dimensions of the conditions of work faced by live-out domestic workers.

Salient Features of the Domestic Workforce[1]

Where the Domestic Workers Live and Where They Work

The survey was conducted through different district- and local-level committees of the Delhi AIDWA. Its focus was not on the living conditions of the women, but on their working conditions. The total sample size of the survey was 1,128, of which consistent data for basic parameters was available for 1,077 domestic workers. The main areas of the survey in the place of residence of the domestic workers are given in Table 6.1.

As can be seen, the survey was conducted in all seven districts of Delhi where the women workers live in *jhuggi jhopdi* (shanties) or

Table 6.1: List of Survey Areas and Sample Size, 2014

S. No.	District	Areas Where Survey was Undertaken	Sample Size
1.	North Delhi	J. J. Colony Wazirpur, J. J. Camp Badli, Bawana, Kishore Nagar, Maharana Bagh, Mukundpur, Rohini, Civil Lines, Malka Ganj, Swaroop Nagar, Vijay Vihar, Jahangirpuri	321
2.	North East Delhi	Kabir Basti, Prathap Nagar, Balweer Nagar, Kabir Nagar	164
3.	North West Delhi	Sultanpuri, Mangolpuri, Aman Vihar	57
4.	New Delhi	Gole Market, Firoz Road, Peshwa Road, Talkatora Park, K. G. Marg, Rafi Marg, Rajendra Prasad Road	81
5.	South Delhi	Dakshinpuri, Subhash Camp, Sahid Camp, Govindpuri, Kalkaji, Greater Kailash, Tuglakabad, Bilaspur, Gaddha Colony, Ambedkar Nagar	275
6.	South West Delhi	Kusumpur Pahadi, Rangpuri Pahadi	126
7.	East Delhi	Sonia Vihar, Khajuri Khas, Chauhan Patty, Ghaziabad	23
	Total		**1,047**

Source: Delhi AIDWA Survey, 2014.

other working-class colonies. But this fact does not help us to test the hypothesis that the working conditions of the domestic workers are determined by the class position of their employers and the areas in which they go to work. For that, it is essential to classify the type of colonies in which the workers go to work.

Table 6.2 shows that about 42.6 per cent of the women went to work in middle-class areas and households, and 30.6 per cent of the women worked in upper-middle class areas. Together, more than two-thirds of the workforce is employed in these households. This may not be surprising since upper-middle and middle-class households are expected to have working women employing live-out 'part-time' domestic labour. In this sense, the erstwhile 'housewife'

Table 6.2: Classification of Sample by Place of Work, 2014[2]

Destination or Place of Work of Domestic Workers	Rate Per Square Metre (Rs)	Zone	Class Classification	Sample Size
Siri Nagar, Siri Fort, Vasant Vihar, Anand Niket, CBI Company	774,000	A	Upper-class	71
GK1, GK2, IIT Gate, Green Park, Hauz Khas, Panchsheel Enclave, Nehru Place, Kailash Colony, Krishi Vihar, JNU, Safdarjung	245,520	B	Upper-middle class	137
Civil Lines, Kamla Nagar, Underhill Road, Avantika, C. R. Park, Saket, Lajpat Nagar, Neelgiri, Malaviya Nagar, Alaknanda, Kalkaji, Sekh Sarai, Vasant Kunj, Munirka	159,840	C	Upper-middle class	160
Rajendra Nagar, Maharaja Lines, Shakthi Nagar, Ashok Vihar, Daryaganj, Rana Pratap Bagh, Model Town, Shalimar, Murwaji Nagar, Madhuban Chowk, Vijay Nagar, Ashil Vihal, Motira Road, Janakpuri, Tagore Park, Pitampura, Bhaira Enclave, Paschim Vihar, Kapil Vihar, Deepali Chowk, Sundar Vihar, Virat DDA Flats, Sainik Farms	127,680	D	Middle-class	289
Sabzi Mandi, Barath Nagar, Rohini, Ghanta Ghar, Matia Mahal, Chandni Chowk, Jain Colony, Paharganj, Sangam Park, Jama Masjid, Malkaganj, Moti Bagh, Kishangarh	70,080	E	Middle-class	125
Bhajanpura, Adarsh Nagar, Trinagar, Kanhaiya Nagar, Shastri Nagar, Mahendra Park, Hind Rao, Kabhir Nagar, Nehru Kutia, Satyawati, Shanti Nagar, LIG, Chirag Delhi, Govindpuri Extension, Air India Colony, Saraswati Colony	56,640	F	Lower-middle class	110

(*Contd*)

Table 6.2: (*Contd*)

Destination or Place of Work of Domestic Workers	Rate Per Square Metre (Rs)	Zone	Class Classification	Sample Size
Saroop Nagar, Sonia Vihar, J. J. Colony, Badli Village, Azadpur, Sultanpuri, Rihala, Keval Park, Laxmi Bai Colony, Aman Vihar, Kirti Nagar, Peeragari, Mongolpuri, Tuglaqabad Extension, Dakshinpuri, Madangir, Masjid Mod, Mehrauli, Khanpur, Amar Colony, South Extension, Ambedkar Nagar	46,200	G	Lower-middle class	73
Mukundpur, Molarband, Munirka Village	23,280	H	Lower-class	6
Total				**971**

Note: In this table, class is taken to correspond to the price of land where the employers' house is located. This means that if the employer is living in Zone A, then they must be able to afford ownership or rent of that house in that zone, which reflects their economic status.

Source: The zones have been taken as per the Delhi Municipal Corporation classification compiled from http://mcdonline.gov.in/tri/ndmc_mcdportal/colonylist.php, http://mcdonline.gov.in/tri/sdmc_mcdportal/colonylist.php, and http://mcdonline.gov.in/tri/edmc_mcdportal/colonylist.php (accessed 20 October 2014).

is also turned into a productive worker under the current relations of production. On the other hand, as far as the domestic worker is concerned, wage labour in non-capitalist salary-earning households becomes the main method of integration into the labour market, thus creating a primary contradiction between the employer and worker. This process is, however, structured by significant macroeconomic concerns and the relationship between class, caste and gender. A major macroeconomic factor that has affected the nature and work of the domestic workforce has been the changing trends in overall employment and, in particular, women's employment since the neo-liberal reforms in India in 1991–92.

Domestic Labour as Distress Employment

The process of informalisation and casualisation of labour has been rapid in the decades following neo-liberalisation in India. The new Modi government's promotion of increasing flexibility of labour and contract labour further decreases the bargaining power of the workers. This gives more space for the capitalist class to increase the accumulation of surplus at the cost of its lowest paid workers. The women workers in the domestic work sector face the harshest consequences of the neo-liberal regime, being at the bottom of the social and economic pyramid. They face multiple discriminations of caste, class and gender reinforcing each other in setting minimal wages and at the same time they suffer the worst due to the removal or decrease in social welfare schemes. The increase in domestic work in the last two decades (the late 1990s and the early 2000s) has to be seen in this context.

Studies using both government data sets (NSSO and NSSO employment-unemployment surveys) and field surveys show a significant increase of women engaged in domestic work in the decades since neo-liberalisation (Ghosh 2012b; Neetha and Palriwala 2011). Contemporary analysis shows that the rate of feminisation of domestic work has been increasing, particularly in urban India. For instance, over the decade of the 2000s, 75 per cent of the increase in the total number of domestic workers consisted of women workers. Domestic work also accounts for a growing share of the total employment of women. Of the total increase in the number of women workers in the decade from 1999–2000 to 2009–10, a massive 14.4 per cent was accounted for by domestic workers (Ghosh 2012b).

The survey data confirms this analysis and shows a spurt in domestic work in the last decade. In this survey, around 80.52 per cent of the domestic workers surveyed started doing this work within the last decade, and about 94.72 per cent of the sample started taking to domestic labour within the last two decades (1993/94–2013/14). It is interesting to note that the maximum number of people in the domestic workforce in the survey is between 30 to 44 years of age and has less than 10 years' experience in domestic work. At a time when jobless growth has resulted in declining employment of female workers in the workforce, women are still being forced into the labour market because of economic distress. This was reinforced during the primary survey which found that the rate of domestic workforce participation is highest among the Other Backward Classes (OBCs)—(67 per cent)—followed closely by the others (almost 65 per cent) in the last decade (2003/04–2013/14). These have traditionally been communities where families have been conservative about letting women out of the household, and women do not have a long contemporary history of being in the domestic workforce. This is borne out in conversation with domestic women workers. As Saraswati from Kusumpur Pahadi in South West Delhi says, 'We have to work because of our helplessness. Earlier there were lots of jobs and fewer people to do domestic work. But now there are many domestic workers in the market but little work. That is why we are forced to work for low wages.' Thus, the data indicates that the availability of surplus domestic workers in the labour market increases the vulnerability of these workers and reduces their bargaining power.

At another level, the bargaining power of the domestic workers is also limited by the employers' ability to pay. In this context, the relationship between the class character of the employer households and distress employment for domestic labour reveals interesting results. For example, 97.82 per cent of the domestic workers in lower-middle class employer households started working within the last two decades, whereas 86.34 per cent of them started working within the last 10 years. We can infer that this may mean that lower-middle class women employers were also entering employment to meet their economic needs. A similar situation is true of the middle-class employer households where about 82.29 per cent of the domestic workers only started working in the last decade (2003/04–2013/14). This, however, is not true of upper-middle class and upper-class houses where less than 75 per cent of the domestic women workers had started working in the last decade. Such a pattern clearly shows that the conversion of the home into a marketplace for labour is linked to the need for women's employment in middle and lower-middle class households. In this sense, the market for domestic labour is not only linked to cheap wage labour within the household but also the way in which women's labour is exploited within the larger economic system. Hence, we see a hierarchy within the process of exploitation, where the employer household is becoming a mediator in the extraction of super-surplus from the domestic labourer.

Class, Caste and the Domestic Workforce

The stigma theory of work suggests that social discrimination is one of the main factors that structures the distinct features of domestic work. It has also been suggested that the stigma theory of work stands in direct contrast to the labour theory of value (John 2013). While macroeconomic factors lead to labour market segmentation, discrimination within the labour market goes into the formation of the domestic labour workforce. The structure of the workforce suggests that the processes of de-skilling and devaluation are a result of the mediation of workforce formation by caste and gender factors. Hence, discriminatory processes are built into the structuring of the workforce.

The literature on domestic work shows that socially and economically deprived women form the majority of the domestic workers (Neetha 2004; Neetha and Palriwala 2011). The present survey confirms this hypothesis but also shows interesting area-wise differences. About 60 per cent of the sample belongs to social groups that are the economically deprived and socially marginalised sections of society, that is, SC, ST and women from the minorities. About 75 per cent of the sample can be categorised as 'socially and economically backward' in constitutional terms. In other words, the upper castes constitute less than 25 per cent of the total surveyed women (Figure 6.1). This clearly confirms the well-acknowledged fact that economically and socially weaker sections of the society form the majority of domestic workers.

Figure 6.1: Percentage Distribution of Women Domestic Workers by Caste, 2014

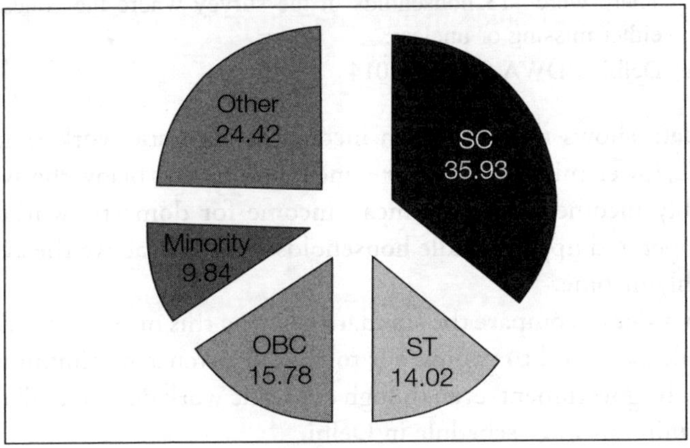

Source: Delhi AIDWA Survey, 2014.

While there is a difference in wages paid to SC women workers as against the others, the discrimination is brought out by the concentration of Dalits in occupations which, despite being strenuous and unpleasant, are extremely poorly paid.

Wages and the Accumulation of Surplus in Domestic Work

Domestic work is a low-wage employment where the element of unpaid labour is very high because it is unregulated, undervalued and de-skilled. The mean monthly wage is Rs 2,877.78 for the 1,048 women domestic workers surveyed across Delhi. This varies across the different class household zones as seen in Table 6.3.

Table 6.3: Mean Monthly Income by Zone of Work (Rs), 2014

Zone	Mean Monthly Income	No. of Workers
Lower	2,440	5
Lower-middle	2,567	178
Middle	2,724	389
Upper-middle	3,349	295
Upper	3,078	68
Total	**2,916**	**935**

Note: There were 113 households in the survey where the zones were either missing or unclear.

Source: Delhi AIDWA Survey, 2014.

The data shows that the mean income of domestic workers in the middle, lower-middle and lower-zone households is below the average monthly income, while the mean income for domestic workers in the upper and upper-middle households is slightly above the average monthly income.

In order to compare the standard of living this mean wage affords, it would be useful to compare it to the subsistence minimum wages set by the government, even though domestic work does not fall under the minimum wage schedule in Delhi.

Table 6.4 shows that the domestic workers earn barely one-third of even the inadequate subsistence 'minimum wages' recognised by the Delhi government. While this conclusion may be broadly true, it needs to be taken into consideration that the average number of hours worked in the surveyed sample is 6.69 hours (including travel time), whereas the minimum wage is calculated on the basis of eight hours of work. Hence, it is more accurate to compare the hourly income of domestic workers with the minimum hourly income derived from the minimum monthly wage set by the government, as it reveals the actual rate of exploitation faced by the domestic workers.

Patterns of Undervaluation and De-skilling

The comparison of hourly income points towards both an undervaluation and a de-skilling of domestic work which is shown here. If we look at the hourly wages, the results are as given in Table 6.5.

Table 6.4: Domestic Worker Monthly Wages as Percentage of Minimum Wage, 2014

District	Mean Monthly Income (Rs)	Minimum Wage (Rs) (From the Delhi Govt. Website)			Domestic Workers' Wages as Percentage of Minimum Wage		
		Unskilled	Semi-skilled	Skilled	Unskilled	Semi-skilled	Skilled
North Delhi	2,695.45	8,086	8,918	9,802	33.33	30.22	27.50
North East Delhi	2,527.13	8,086	8,918	9,802	31.25	28.34	25.78
North West Delhi	2,642.10	8,086	8,918	9,802	32.67	29.63	26.95
New Delhi	2,336.73	8,086	8,918	9,802	28.90	26.20	23.84
South Delhi	3,092.01	8,086	8,918	9,802	38.24	34.67	31.54
South West Delhi	3,247.06	8,086	8,918	9,802	40.16	36.41	33.13
East Delhi	4,679.16	8,086	8,918	9,802	57.87	52.47	47.74
Total	**2,877.53**	**8,086**	**8,918**	**9,802**	**35.59**	**32.27**	**29.36**

Source: Delhi AIDWA Survey, 2014.

Table 6.5: Domestic Worker Hourly Wages as Percentage of Minimum Wage, 2014

District	Hourly Income of Domestic Worker (Rs)	Hourly Income (Rs) (Calculated on the Minimum Wage from the Delhi Govt. Website)			Domestic Workers' Wages as Proportion of Minimum Wages		
		Unskilled	Semi-skilled	Skilled	Unskilled	Semi-skilled	Skilled
North Delhi	15.44	33.69	37.16	40.84	45.83	41.55	37.80
North East Delhi	15.88	33.69	37.16	40.84	47.13	42.74	38.88
North West Delhi	14.91	33.69	37.16	40.84	44.25	40.13	36.51
New Delhi	12.30	33.69	37.16	40.84	36.51	33.10	30.12
South Delhi	17.67	33.69	37.16	40.84	52.45	47.55	43.26
South West Delhi	17.35	33.69	37.16	40.84	51.50	46.69	42.48
East Delhi	15.95	33.69	37.16	40.84	47.34	42.92	39.05
Total	**16.27**	**33.69**	**37.16**	**40.84**	**48.29**	**43.79**	**39.84**

Source: Delhi AIDWA Survey, 2014.

This comparison points towards both an undervaluation and a de-skilling of domestic work. Table 6.5 shows that the wages earned through domestic work are more than 50–60 per cent less than what the domestic workers should be getting under a legally mandated, yet highly inadequate subsistence wage. This proportion may be considered an 'unpaid' part of paid domestic work in the city. It is also significant to note that the gap between actual wages and legally mandated minimum wages will depend on the level of skill at which domestic work is placed. In popular perception, domestic work is considered an 'unskilled' work because it is considered work that women perform naturally (as a part of the traditional social division of labour). It is considered part of reproductive labour and is placed within the household and hence undervalued. But considering that these women workers perform a task that only an 'unpaid housewife' has the time and the years of experience to perform, it is rather unfair to consider it unskilled work. In fact, the unpaid work of the housewife is getting transformed into paid domestic work through domestic wage labour, especially when women are going out to work and men are unwilling to perform that labour, either because of their patriarchal mindset or because they are unable to do so because of lack of training or time. Therefore, the wages should be compared with the wages for skilled work in accordance with a re-classification of occupations based on uniform labour standards. This requires that the domestic worker is recognised as a 'worker' and her skills are also recognised in this process.

It has also to be borne in mind that earning a low proportion of designated minimum wages is not true of only the domestic workers. It is well known that other casual and informal sector workers do not get minimum wages even though their work is included within the schedule of minimum wages. Hence, this comparison shows that the fight for the economic rights of domestic workers is closely linked to the larger struggle of all workers in the unorganised sector. The wages in the domestic work sector also need to be compared with the actual wages paid to casual workers in other sectors. But in terms of the rights of the worker, parity with even a notional legal minimum is the first step towards decreasing the rate of exploitation in domestic work.

Widening Gaps with Minimum Wages

In this context, it is also important to look at the trajectory of wages over time. Studies on the National Capital Region (NCR) that have mapped wages in different areas of the city provide some data for a weak comparison of average wage rates during three periods.

Table 6.6: Average Monthly Incomes of Live-out Workers, 2009–2011

Source	Sample Size	Year	Average Monthly Income (Rs)
ISST Survey	1,498	2008	1,874
Jagori Survey	691 (in one area of South Delhi)	2010	2,175
Delhi AIDWA (JMS) Survey	1,128	2014	2,878

The comparison in Table 6.6 shows that the average total monthly income of a domestic worker has increased by Rs 1,001 in six years. This constitutes an absolute increase of 51 per cent or an annual increase of 8.5 per cent. A comparison of the figures in South Delhi (between the Jagori Survey and Janwadi Mahila Samiti Survey) shows that the average income has risen by Rs 913.95 or 42.2 per cent in four years, an increase of 10.5 per cent per annum. A better understanding of the trends can be gauged from their comparison with the legal minimum wages of their times. For this, a comparison may be done of the Institute for Social Studies Trust (ISST) and the Janwadi Mahila Samiti (JMS) survey which are similar in sample size and character. Once again, the indicator used is hourly income, as it takes into account the differences in average working hours within regions and different time periods.

Table 6.7 clearly indicates the widening gap between the actual wages of the domestic worker and the minimum wages set by the government. Whereas the gap between the minimum wage and actual wage of the domestic worker ranged from 17 to 24 per cent depending on which skill level domestic work is identified with, the gap increased to 51–60 per cent in 2014. Within six years, the element of the unpaid

Table 6.7: Hourly Income of Domestic Workers as a Proportion of Minimum Wage-based Hourly Income, 2008 and 2014

Source	Hourly Income of Domestic Worker (Rs)	Hourly Income on Basis of Minimum Wages (Rs)			Domestic Workers' Wages as Proportion of Minimum Wages		
		Unskilled	Semi-skilled	Skilled	Unskilled	Semi-skilled	Skilled
ISST Survey, 2008	13.02	15.34	16.03	17.11	84.80	81.20	76.00
AIDWA Survey, 2014	16.30	33.70	37.20	40.80	48.20	43.70	39.80

proportion of paid domestic work (using the minimum wage standard) has increased by 34–36 per cent. This means that women have to work more than before to earn even their actual average income. Conversation with the workers brings this point out. As Jamna from Sultanpuri states, 'I have been working for 30 years. I have spent my life in this job, but neither my wages have gone up nor have I got any increment.' In another instance, Rajeshwari from Sonia Vihar stated that she got a salary raise of only Rs 100 in three years. The extra surplus generated is expropriated by the capitalist class through increasing prices and slower increases in income of the middle-class households that act as intermediator in this case between the domestic workers and the capitalist class.

Informal Labour Relations and Conditions of Work

It is well known that the relationship between the employer and domestic labourer have an extreme informality. This is reflected in the fact that wage determination is fairly arbitrary in character and it is difficult to identify the factors that go into wage determination of domestic labour. These factors may include the nature and characteristic of employer households, the nature of jobs, the number of hours of work, the role of experience, and the interrelationship between caste, class and work. The relationship between these factors provides the basic foundation of the structural informality influencing the exploitative working conditions of domestic labour.

Hierarchy of Work

Domestic work covers a wide range of jobs from sweeping, mopping, washing vessels, washing clothes to cooking, dusting, taking care of children, taking care of old people and other odd jobs. Domestic workers are involved in various combinations of these tasks in every household they work at. This adds flexibility to the labour force and at the same time leads to a spectrum of varying wages. The same domestic worker often gets different wages for the same job in different houses according to the list of jobs she performs. Without clearly delineated job descriptions, there are constant negotiations over what constitutes her job and the number of hours they involve. Within this range of jobs, there is a hierarchy in wages, with taking care of children and cooking falling as more prestigious and more skilled with higher wages, and the highly manual and menial jobs of sweeping, washing clothes or washing vessels getting lower wages.

Table 6.8 clearly shows this hierarchy in work according to wages. Taking care of children has the highest monthly and hourly average incomes, with workers working in one or two houses for longer periods of time (an average of 8.8 hours of work). Cooking food is next, with slightly lower monthly and hourly wages, and a lower average of 6.25 hours of work and working in about two houses on an average. Only washing vessels has the lowest wages with the removal of an extreme high-end value. Sweeping and washing clothes are also at the lower end of the spectrum with low monthly and hourly wages, just around the average hourly income. The workers who get lower wages have to work at more than one task in a house. This is seen clearly in that the mean hourly wages for workers in both sweeping and washing vessels and in sweeping, washing vessels and washing clothes is far below the average hourly wage. And these workers are the maximum in number, forming almost half the total domestic workers surveyed.

Within domestic work, therefore, there clearly exists a hierarchy of work with a caste bias. The survey finds that there are more SC women in the tasks considered more menial and demeaning like sweeping and cleaning bathrooms. In contrast, more women of the general category perform tasks like cooking food and taking care of children. This is shown in Table 6.9. For instance, in the sample, only around 66 women workers clean bathrooms, 32 of whom are of SC category and only 10 from the general category. Among women workers whose only task is sweeping, there are a total of 42, 45.24 per cent of whom are SC and only around 28.57 per cent general category. On the other hand, out of 45 workers in the sample whose only task is cooking, 44.44 per cent belong to the general category and only 28.89 per cent belong to the SCs. This implies discrimination in the way in which the domestic workers are recruited for specific jobs. The STs form a smaller sample in this survey, possibly because more of them are live-in domestic workers. Out of 152 ST women domestic

Table 6.8: Incomes by Type of Work (Rs), 2014

Work	Monthly Income	Per House Monthly Income	Hourly Income	Per House Hourly Income	Average Total Hours of Work	Average No. of Houses Worked in	No. of Workers
Only sweeping	2,573	1,410	16.5	9.9	5.7	2	41
Only washing vessels	2,108	794	15.0	7.4	5.1	3	12
Only washing clothes	2,387	801	16.8	7.3	5.5	4	15
Only cooking	3,094	1,597	19.4	10.8	6.2	2	36
Only taking care of children	4,375	3,493	19.5	13.3	8.8	2	12
Sweeping and washing vessels	2,354	974	14.9	6.7	6.0	3	233
Sweeping, washing vessels, washing clothes	2,956	1,061	15.5	6.0	6.8	3	290
Sweeping, washing clothes and vessels, cooking, odd jobs, taking care of children and cleaning bathroom	3,000	806	10.4	2.9	9.7	4	3
Including cleaning bathroom	3,231	1,638	18.4	10.1	6.9	3	58

Source: Delhi AIDWA Survey, 2014.

workers, 85 per cent work in sweeping and washing clothes, about 55 per cent wash clothes, only around 30 per cent (46 women) cook food and 10 per cent (16 women) take care of children. The minority workers also form a smaller sample of 104 women workers, where about 92 per cent of the women's work involves sweeping, around 80 per cent work in washing vessels, 60 per cent in washing clothes and only 19 work as cooks and six women take care of children.

Table 6.9: Mean Hourly Income by Type of Work and Caste of Domestic Worker (Rs), 2014

Work	SC	ST	OBC	Minority	Others	Total
Only sweeping	16.8 (18)	8.1 (4)	18.1 (2)	19.8 (5)	17.4 (11)	16.6 (40)
Only washing vessels	13.5 (3)	14.6 (2)	12.4 (4)	– (0)	20.6 (3)	15.1 (12)
Only washing clothes	11.4 (2)	14.3 (1)	10 (1)	– (0)	18.7 (11)	16.8 (15)
Only cooking	20.9 (12)	17.8 (3)	12.9 (4)	10.1 (2)	21.4 (15)	19.4 (36)
Only taking care of children	18.1 (2)	9.1 (1)	36.1 (2)	18.8 (2)	15.8 (5)	19.5 (12)
Sweeping and washing vessels	13.7 (93)	15.4 (29)	16.1 (36)	18.1 (21)	15.5 (45)	15.1 (224)
Sweeping, washing vessels, washing clothes	14.8 (100)	15.1 (33)	16.8 (45)	15.6 (36)	16.3 (71)	15.6 (285)
Sweeping, washing clothes and vessels, cooking, odd jobs, taking care of children and cleaning bathroom	– (0)	11.1 (1)	9.7 (1)	– (0)	– (0)	10.4 (2)
Including cleaning bathroom	18.1 (32)	10.3 (6)	10.2 (6)	48.5 (5)	14.5 (5)	18.8 (54)

Note: Frequencies in parentheses.
Source: Delhi AIDWA Survey, 2014

The analysis in Table 6.9 shows that absence of labour regulations and the informality of work lends to the presence of a range of wages. There are instances of very high wages which, for instance, lead to high average wages for minority women in cleaning bathrooms, and cases of very low wages, for instance, where one of the workers in washing vessels gets a paltry Rs 200 monthly income for every house in which she works. This also means that for frequencies below 10 households and particularly below five households, the vagaries in wages received prevail. The table clearly shows the lower incomes received by lower-caste and lower-class women workers and their higher concentration in lower paying jobs. The data shows that caste and class reinforce each other with low overall wages and particularly lower wages for the SC women in more menial work. The number of hours they need to work, the number of houses they need to work in and the number of jobs they need to take on to even earn the average monthly income is correspondingly higher.

This segmentation of SC women into lower paying jobs clearly indicates how class formation is mediated by both patriarchy and caste. As mentioned earlier, the performance of domestic labour results in the commodification of social reproduction and also makes the home into a marketplace for labour. It also shows the complex process of intermediation between social structures and the labour markets. The processes of social discrimination are also embedded in these processes and have an impact on the rates of exploitation of domestic labour.

Decreasing Rate of Returns to Increasing Work

The survey also highlights the patterns of diminishing returns with respect to longer hours of work. The data shows that the income earned per hour decreases substantially if a woman works for a longer number of hours. The story repeats itself if women perform a greater number of jobs and also work in a larger number of households. There is a threshold below and above which women workers get less than the average hourly income. The highest hourly income is achieved when women work 2–3 hours per day (or about Rs 18 per hour). They get Rs 1–1.7 less per hour for every hour they work after three hours. Hence, the average hourly income of 6–7 hours of work is about Rs 14.78 per hour and for more than seven hours is Rs 11–12 per hour. By this standard, only 33 per cent of the sample is able to achieve the mean wage. The same is the case with number of jobs. The best average hourly wage (Rs 15.84–17.44 per hour) is achieved when the women cumulatively perform up to four jobs in three houses. The data shows that only one-fourth of the women surveyed are able to achieve this standard which is required to make the average monthly income or more. By relating these three factors, it is possible to surmise that only half the women surveyed earn at least the average income of Rs 2,877 per month.

The number of hours worked includes the time to travel to the workplace. Participation in domestic work by live-out workers is generally considered a part-time job by the employers of the multiple houses in which they work. But for the woman worker it is a full-time occupation involving her whole day. In this survey, the total number of working hours was calculated from the time the worker left the home for work till the time she came back from work. Therefore, if a woman is doing morning and evening shifts, the time taken in both these shifts would be combined to calculate her total hours of work. As per this calculation, the total average hours of work for domestic workers covered by this survey are given in Table 6.10.

Table 6.10: Number of Hours Worked and Incomes by Area, 2014

District	Mean No. of Hours Worked	Mean Hourly Income (Rs)	No. of Observations
North Delhi	6.8	15.4	332
North East Delhi	6.5	15.9	158
North West Delhi	5.9	14.9	55
New Delhi	7.3	12.3	79
South Delhi	6.6	17.7	265
South West Delhi	6.1	17.7	153
East Delhi	9.8	15.9	24
Total	**6.7**	**16.3**	**1,066**

Source: Delhi AIDWA Survey, 2014.

Women domestic workers on an average work at least six hours a day. Table 6.10 shows that the district-wise variation in the hours of work is closely related to the distance travelled by women. About 70 per cent of the surveyed women take about a 30 minute walk to work.

If monetised, this would mean that a woman worker saved Rs 10–15 per day by walking to work as the distance to their place of work was about 1–2 km. But 30 per cent of them took the bus or Grameen Sewa to travel longer distances. This is especially true of Sonia Vihar (East Delhi) and Kabir Nagar (North East Delhi) which are both resettlement colonies. For these women, the daily travel time is 1–2 hours and in a couple of cases even 3–4 hours. This is seen in the total working hours of the women in East Delhi but gets hidden in the data of North East Delhi where Kabir Nagar forms only 3 per cent of the total sample. But the average transport cost of these women is Rs 900–1,200 per month. That this time and cost is not taken into account is reflected in the relationship between total hours of work and hourly income. Thus, neither East nor North West Delhi reaches the mean hourly income of the entire sample. In fact, in the case of New Delhi, women work from the vicinity and also work longer hours, but get one of the lowest hourly incomes. This has something to do with the age of the workforce where the total hourly income is the lowest, with a large section of the women belonging to the age group of 15–29 years.

Capacity to Pay and its Impact on Wages

The number of hours of work can also be analysed taking into consideration the class of the employer household. This determines their ability to pay the workers and to an extent the amount of work generated in the household (according to the size of the house).

It is very clear from Table 6.11 that the hourly wages for 0–4 hours of work is uniformly much greater than the mean hourly income in all categories of households. The hourly income for 4–8 hours of work is just around the mean and drops sharply for more than eight hours of work for all categories of households. This means that more than 80 per cent women domestic workers working in the lower-middle class households work for four or more hours and earn just around or below the mean wage. Around 85 per cent of domestic workers working in the middle-class households work for more than four hours in total and earn just around or less than the mean wage. And more than 90 per cent of domestic workers working

Table 6.11: Zone, Hourly Income and Total Hours of Work, 2014

	Average Hourly Income				
Zone	**0–4 Hours' Work**	**4–8 Hours' Work**	**8–12 Hours' Work**	**Over 12 Hours' Work**	**Total**
Lower	–	15.60	7.41	–	13.96
	(0)	(4)	(1)	(0)	(5)
Lower-middle	21.86	15.60	10.40	8.35	14.70
	(30)	(81)	(49)	(12)	(172)
Middle	26.49	15.63	11.14	11.85	15.80
	(53)	(194)	(88)	(31)	(366)
Upper-middle	29.49	18.65	14.03	13.20	17.99
	(24)	(170)	(87)	(9)	(290)
Upper	17.59	17.97	15.07	13.89	17.33
	(6)	(46)	(12)	(1)	(65)
Total	**25.43**	**16.88**	**12.23**	**11.33**	**16.40**
	(113)	**(495)**	**(237)**	**(53)**	**(898)**

Note: Frequencies in parentheses.
Source: Delhi AIDWA Survey, 2014.

in the upper-middle class households work for more than four hours and earn around or below the mean wage. It is important to note that despite higher hourly wages in the upper-middle households, this is because of fewer number of higher earners, with a large section earning below the mean wage.

Table 6.12 shows that the variation of average hourly incomes received by the domestic worker above the mean is minimal in the upper- and upper-middle class households with less than Rs 1.5 rise in mean hourly income and less than Rs 500 rise in mean monthly income of the domestic workers. If we look at the real estate prices as an indication of their income status, the upper-middle class households hold property worth almost thrice as much as the lower-middle class households, and the variation is even more on comparing the upper- and lower-class households. The small variation in the wage differentials the upper-class households pay the domestic workers shows a greater extraction of surplus from the domestic workers. Even this

Table 6.12: Hourly Income and Monthly Income by Zone (Rs), 2014

Zone	Hourly Income	Monthly Income
Lower	13.96 (5)	2,440.00 (5)
Lower-middle	14.70 (172)	2,567.14 (178)
Middle	15.80 (366)	2,723.96 (389)
Upper-middle	17.99 (290)	3,348.81 (295)
Upper	17.33 (65)	3,077.94 (68)
Total	**16.40** **(898)**	**2,915.48** **(935)**

Note: Frequencies in parentheses.
Source: Delhi AIDWA Survey, 2014.

small variation has to take into consideration that these houses are generally bigger and therefore involve more work. Thus, there appears to be a greater rate of exploitation of domestic labour in upper/upper-middle class households where they need to pay the domestic workers only the generally prevalent low wages. In such a situation, 46 per cent of the women surveyed earn a monthly income that is below the average monthly income of Rs 2,877 per month and 48.7 per cent of the domestic workers surveyed get an hourly wage that is below the average hourly wage of Rs 16.03 per hour.

Capacity to Earn and its Impact on Wages

The foregoing analysis shows that zoning has had a very limited role in the determination of wages. Therefore, the capacity to pay has little to do with provisioning of higher wages. On the other side, our data also shows that the capacity to earn also has a limited role to play in the determination of wages. The capacity to earn may be determined by a combination of age and experience. Only women workers between the age of 30 and 44 years get an hourly income (Rs 16.45) that is above the average hourly income of Rs 16.03. This constitutes about 48.9 per cent of the total sample surveyed. The average hourly income of children is Rs 12.77, whereas the women above the age of 45 get about Rs 14–15.5 per hour. Similarly, in terms of the experience in paid domestic work, workers who have been working for less than 10 years make an hourly income (Rs 15.67 per hour) which is lower than the mean hourly income. This constitutes about 62 per cent of the total sample. All workers with 10 and above years of experience make a higher hourly income. It is noteworthy that their higher hourly income has not driven up the wages received by new entrants to the workforce. A combination of the above two factors shows that about one-fourth of the women workers make much less than the average hourly income. Hence, like the capacity to pay, the capacity to earn also plays a minimal role in the determination of wages, once again reflecting a great deal of informality in relations.

Social Discrimination and Caste as a Mediating Factor

This essay has shown that economic factors usually governing the demand–supply relationships in the labour market have little role to play in the management of labour relations within the household. Rather, it is the surplus availability of domestic labour (that is, a reserve army of women labourers) that determines depressed wages, and structure the employer–employee relationships. But this structuring is mediated by practices of social and caste discrimination. This is clearly shown in the relationship between caste and income. The data shows that the proportion of women workers across all income ranges was proportionally distributed across castes. But the difference in the discrimination in wage payment is revealed in the distribution of hourly incomes.

Table 6.13 shows that SC and ST women have the lowest average hourly incomes, which are well below the average hourly income of Rs 16.03 per hour. It is surprising that women from the minorities group report the highest hourly income. This can be explained by the fact that, as seen in the table, a few of the women workers from the minorities have a high income, whereas 72.5 per cent of them

Table 6.13: Mean Hourly Income by Caste of Domestic Worker, 2014

	Mean Hourly Income (Rs)						
Caste	**0–9**	**10–19**	**20–29**	**30–39**	**40–49**	**50 and Above**	**Total**
Minority	7.36 (15)	15.07 (51)	24.20 (16)	33.12 (10)	44.44 (1)	58.33 (1)	18.09 (94)
OBC	7.23 (32)	13.66 (85)	23.93 (31)	33.33 (3)	40.00 (1)	78.70 (3)	16.19 (155)
Others	6.99 (34)	14.49 (137)	23.02 (40)	33.10 (12)	40.00 (1)	66.66 (1)	16.21 (225)
SC	6.812 (77)	14.50 (190)	22.95 (78)	33.67 (14)	44.25 (3)	51.66 (2)	15.88 (364)
ST	7.20 (31)	14.02 (75)	22.73 (23)	33.33 (2)	44.44 (1)	– (0)	14.45 (132)
Total	**7.03 (189)**	**14.36 (538)**	**23.21 (188)**	**33.33 (41)**	**43.10 (7)**	**66.35 (7)**	**16.03 (970)**

Note: Frequencies in parentheses.
Source: Delhi AIDWA Survey, 2014.

earn well below the hourly income of Rs 18.09. Though a majority of the women workers from 'other' upper castes fall well below their own average hourly income, the proportion of people earning higher incomes is also greater. Hence, we reiterate that class formation is mediated by caste factors especially because the non-upper castes form more than two-thirds of the domestic workforce. An important reason for lower average hourly incomes among SC and ST workers is their concentration in the lower-paying tasks within domestic work, as shown in the earlier discussion on the hierarchy of work.

This intermediation is reflected in the general conditions of work of domestic labourers. There is no concept of overtime wages. Not only are there no overtime or holiday wages, around 44 per cent do not even get any scheduled holidays in a month. According to employer preferences, a large section of them get their pay cut if they have to take leave for any reason. At the same time, there are not only no benefits for festivals, many do not get any leave for them either.

There is no job security or sick leave, with 46 per cent having lost a job due to illness, and no health benefits with only around 12 per cent employers helping the workers in case of illness. The data shows that around 44 per cent of the women have no holidays, 33 per cent have two monthly holidays, 11.22 per cent of women have one monthly holiday, 2.74 per cent have holidays twice a week and 4.74 per cent have holidays once a week. These trends also have regional variations. About 84.52 per cent have no holidays in North East Delhi and around 70 per cent do not have any holidays in New Delhi. Around 53.85 per cent in South West Delhi and 47.04 per cent in North Delhi do not have any holidays. In East Delhi, North West Delhi and South Delhi, the highest percentage of total women get two monthly holidays. About 88 per cent of women report that they regularly get wage cuts for taking time off. The zone-based holidays vary with only upper-middle class households giving about 50 per cent of the workers holidays twice a month. More than 50 per cent workers in all the other households get no holidays.

About 46 per cent of the women have lost a job due to illness. Pregnancy, accident injuries and leave to go to their hometowns seem to be the other frequent reasons for job loss. Job loss due to illness is highest in North West Delhi, with 55 out of 57 women having lost a job due to illness. Around 60 per cent women in South Delhi and 57 per cent in East Delhi have also lost a job due to illness. On the other hand, only 11 per cent women in New Delhi and 27 per cent in South Delhi have lost a job due to illness. Job loss due to illness is highest in the upper-middle and middle-class households, and slightly less for women working in the lower or lower-middle class households. Employers in these households seem to be less likely to fire workers absent due to illness.

The miserable conditions of work become even clearer on talking to the workers. For instance, Rekha from Mangolpuri states, 'There is no rule and regulation in the manner in which we are paid our wages. If we take one holiday, the lady employing us cuts pay for three days instead of one. If we do extra work, we are not paid overtime as our employers state that we have taken too many leaves. This month I was paid my monthly wage after one week and that too Rs 900 less on the pretext of taking leave. What should we do? We have to work, otherwise who would accept this situation.' Sunita from VP House has the same story to tell. She says that her employer cut her wages by telling lies about how many holidays she had taken. When she protested, she lost her job.

It is, therefore, clear that most women are forced to put up with the harassment of their employers because they need the work. The vulnerability of the worker and the absence of labour regulations act as a means for the employer households to extract extra work and surplus from the domestic workers. This is a major point of conflict within the household labour relation with a constant struggle for and against holidays and the determination of wages.

The data shows that the domestic workers also face social discrimination in their place of work. The most prominent form of this discrimination is the refusal to let women workers use bathrooms. About 45 per cent of all the women do not have access to a bathroom in the workplace. Again, patterns vary a lot across the districts but do not seem to vary greatly across castes. Around 93 per cent women in North West Delhi, 78 per cent in East Delhi and 60 per cent women in South Delhi have access to bathrooms. Conversely about 94 per cent women in New Delhi, 74 per cent women in South West Delhi, 60 per cent women in North Delhi and 56 per cent women in North East Delhi do not have any access to bathrooms in the workplace. There is no specific trend in the use of bathrooms according to household zones. It may be dependent on the type of housing, flats, etc. The only thing noticeable is that almost 80 per cent workers in the upper households have no access to bathrooms.

The third facet of social discrimination is violence against domestic workers in the workplace. While a large number of women do not report any complaints, verbal abuse seems to be the most frequent problem that is faced by the domestic workers. A large part of this may also go unreported. Apart from this, five women workers also reported other types of abuse. Of these, one was a case of sexual assault. The other four cases were that of blaming the domestic worker of theft. No particular caste pattern was noticed in these cases. Hence, it may be concluded that non-economic forms of discrimination in working conditions are rampant in domestic labour.

Conclusion

In the context of this analysis it is possible to reach some general conclusions with respect to the processes of accumulation through productive domestic work. First, the high degree of informality in work relations is structured through the integration of household into the labour market. The invisibility of work created by this process has propelled and, in fact, perpetuated the lack of regulation of this sector, thus highlighting why it is virtually impossible to identify the processes of determination of fair wages. Second, labour relations within the household are structured by the commodification of the processes of social reproduction. The conversion of the 'housewife's' labour into wage labour ensures that the household becomes the first mediator in the accumulation of surplus from the domestic worker. In cases where the employers themselves work for others, they become the vehicles of transfer of the surplus from the domestic workers to their own employers. In this sense, a hierarchy of accumulation is established between the domestic workers and the ruling classes. Third, the relationship between paid and unpaid labour has to also be seen in this context. Conventionally socially reproductive labour like domestic duties by the housewife has been considered unpaid and unaccounted for work. But the analysis of this essay also shows that a large portion of the paid wage labour of a domestic worker can be perceived as 'unpaid' or unaccounted for work. In this sense, domestic labour provides an opportunity for understanding the complex interlinkages between paid and unpaid work. Fourth, it has also shown that the stigma theory of work can be explained through the labour theory of value if the complex interrelationship between class formation and social structures is adequately analysed. It shows that the formation of a class of domestic labourers in Delhi is mediated by both caste and patriarchal institutions. In this sense, practices of social discrimination are structured into the composition of the workforce itself. This is shown by the lack of significant caste specificity in discriminatory practices. By the same measure it may also be argued that discriminatory practices have class specificity in that they are spread across different social groups. This shows that the class factor is more pronounced than the 'social group factor' in analysing the character of domestic work. Finally, the analysis of this essay highlights the impact of the lack of recognition and regulation of domestic labour on the lives of women workers. The politics of recognition practised by women's organisations and workers movements has to be seen in this context.

Notes

1. This is based on the sample based on the survey by JMS (2013–14).
2. The localities where they work have been classified according to the real estate property rates with Category A colonies at Rs 774,000 per square metre as upper-class households; Category B colonies at Rs 245,520 per square metre and Category C colonies at Rs 159,840 per square metre as upper-middle class households; Category D colonies at Rs 127,680 per square metre and Category E colonies at Rs 70,080 per square metre as middle-class households; Category F colonies at Rs 56,640 per square metre and Category G colonies at Rs 46,200 per square metre as lower-middle class households; and finally Category H colonies at Rs 23,280 per square metre as lower-class households.

References

Antonpoulos, R., and I. Hirway. 2010. *Unpaid Work and the Economy: Gender, Time Use and Poverty in Developing Countries.* Hampshire: Palgrave Macmillan.

Custers, P. 2012. *Capital Accumulation and Women's Labor in Asian Economies.* New York: Monthly Review Press.

Federici, S. 2012. 'Theorising and Politicising Housework'. In *Revolution at Point Zero Housework, Reproduction and Feminist Struggle,* 1–60. Oakland: PM Press.

Ghosh, J. 2009. *Never Done and Poorly Paid.* Delhi: Women Unlimited.

———. 2012a. 'Women, Labor and Capital Accumulation in Asia'. *Monthly Review* 63 (8): 1.

———. 2012b. 'Women and Domestic Work: Creating Conditions for Decent Work'. Report for UN Women. Available at http://www.undp.org/content/dam/india/docs/Women-and-domestic-work.pdf (accessed 10 October 2014).

Institute of Social Studies Trust. 2009. 'Urban Livelihoods in India: Domestic Workers of Delhi'. Unpublished Report submitted to Sri Dorabji Tata Trust, Mumbai.

Jagori. 2010. *A Report on Domestic Workers: Conditions, Rights and Responsibilities—A Study of Part-time Domestic Workers in Delhi*. Delhi: Jagori.

Jain, D., and N. Banerjee. 1985. *Tyranny of the Household: Investigative Essays on Women's Work*. New Delhi: Shakti Books.

John, M. 2013. 'The Problem of Women's Labour: Some Autobiographical Perspectives'. *Indian Journal of Gender Studies* 20 (2): 177–212.

Lutz, H. 2011. *The New Maids: Transnational Women and the Care Economy*. London: Zed Books.

Mazumdar, I., and Neetha N. 2011. *Gender Dimensions: Employment Trends in India, 1993–94 to 2009–10*. Delhi: Centre for Women's Development Studies (CWDS).

Neetha N. 2004. 'Making of Female Breadwinners: Migration and Social Networking of Women Domestics in Delhi'. *Economic and Political Weekly* 39 (17): 1681–88.

———. 2009. 'Contours of Domestic Service: Characteristics, Work Relations and Regulation'. *Indian Journal of Labour Economics* 52 (3).

———. 2013. *Inequalities Reinforced?: Social Groups, Gender and Employment*. CWDS.

Neetha N., and R. Palriwala. 2011. 'The Absence of State Law: Domestic Workers in India'. *Canadian Journal of Women and the Law* 23 (1): 97–119.

Palriwala, R., and N. Pillai. 2009. 'Paid Care Workers in India: Domestic Workers and Anganwadi Workers'. Unpublished report, United Nations Research Institute for Social Development (UNRISD), Geneva.

Ray, R., and S. Qayum. 2009. *The Cultures of Servitude: Modernity, Domesticity and Class in Kolkatta*. Stanford, California: Stanford University Press.

7

Labouring Livelihoods

Vulnerabilities and Visibilities in Women's Labour and Livelihoods

Ritu Dewan

The past three decades (particularly since the formal implementation of the neo-liberal model of growth) have witnessed rather dramatic changes in the nature of vulnerabilities characterising the livelihoods and also the labour of poorer women, particularly in rural India. While there is no attempt either to romanticise the past or to demonise the present, there can be little doubt that these transformations need to be examined in the context of several decisive and defining processes that have come to characterise the neo-liberal phase. One, the withdrawal of the State from the public sphere, especially that pertaining to where the majority of Indians and especially women live and labour. Two, the altered equation between capital and labour as well as the forms of surplus extraction, with appropriation extending beyond individually 'owned' property to that which is 'collectively owned' and accessed. Three, that of visibilisation and de-visibilisation of women's work in the context of their perceived decline in contributing to the nation's economy.

The fundamental character of the relationship between women's labour and women's livelihoods is not only complex but also complicated, in that both their sources of sustenance and their strategies of survival are primarily non-linear in the context of the agrarian realities in India. This holds true for both landed and landless women; in actuality, of course, women are yet to be recognised officially as farmers, the majority not holding ownership rights over the chief means of production, whether of goods or services. We thus have a rather absurd situation where women who are engaged in agricultural activities—as over four-fifths of them are—have no formal title as they do not own land, while simultaneously, women workers in non-rural sectors are termed legally, as per labour laws, as 'female workmen' (see Government of India 1947 and thereafter).

Based on extensive field experience in several regions of India, the focus is on various unrecognised and hence unquantified forms of livelihood-generating activities that are being resorted to especially and exclusively by poorer women, a not insignificant proportion of them single. These forms of labour bring into focus the changing role of women in production and reproduction, as well as the dangers of ignoring the existing and also emergent conceptual and methodological biases that do not recognise these 'unrecognisable' and hence 'unquantifiable' strategies of survival. Non-inclusion would imply not only reinforcement of perceptions of women's secondary status and non-contribution to the economy but also become a justification for keeping them out of policy benefits and the developmental framework.

Beginning with identifying three forms of labouring livelihoods that we came across in our field experience and that which compelled the re-questioning of several interpretations of the very basis of 'economic existence', the analysis focuses on interrelated issues at debate, including the criteria of quantification and 'visibility' that are generally utilised, and the conceptual and methodological consequences of labouring livelihoods that are based on ownership of and access to privately and commonly-owned resources, as well as that based on alienation from all forms of resources both economic and extra-economic. Each illustration is dealt with individually, incorporating the resultant identification of issues, questions and inquiries.

Illustrations from Fieldwork

Sea Buckthorn (*Shalulu*): Nubra Valley and Siachen, Ladakh Region, Jammu and Kashmir

Sea buckthorn (*Hippophaerhamnoides L.*) is found mainly in Central Asia, including Nepal, Bhutan, Pakistan, Afghanistan and Kazakhstan.

Known as a wonder-plant (*tasru*), the fruits of this thorny bush are rich in carbohydrates, protein, organic acids, amino acids and vitamins, thereby making it an important raw material for health and pharmaceutical products as well as cosmetics. In India, the sea buckthorn (known locally as shalulu) grows mostly in the Himalayan region, with only Ladakh berries containing Omega 7, while those from other regions have the standard Omega 3, 6 and 9.

Growing primarily on forest and 'uncultivable' wastelands which are essentially common property resources, the uses of the sea buckthorn tree even in an unprocessed state are numerous: the leaf for tea, animal feed and fodder; the stem and root for firewood, charcoal, and wood for handles of agricultural implements; the berry for herbal medicines, nutritional supplements and oil for household lighting; twigs and branches for shed-roofs, tree guards and fencing of fields. The plant itself plays an extremely crucial role as a protection against water and soil erosion, a major issue in cold desert conditions. Its extensive root system is ideal not only for containing erosion but also for land reclamation, habitat enhancement and farm protection. Flowering in June and ripening in late August, harvesting of the berries has to be completed within a short period of three weeks, plucking being carried out either early in the morning before sunrise or late in the evening after sunset; this is because the strong sunrays cause the fruit to develop turgidity. Post-harvest processing and marketing is done almost exclusively by the three Government Departments of Cooperatives, Horticulture, and Forests; a common date for commencement of harvesting as well as the rate per kg is publicly announced in all villages.

The illustration of the sea buckthorn integrates two fundamental and interlinked issues. One, the strongly gendered context in that the berry-collectors are invariably and exclusively women, this harvesting not being considered as 'work' and hence not quantified. Two, the issue of what should be the basis of distribution of benefits from what is primarily a collectively owned and accessed resource.

The issue of recognition of berry-plucking as work and hence 'capturable' in data sources is central to our analysis; this is particularly crucial in order to unravel the vexed issues of unrecognised and hence uncalculated contribution of women to development both nationally and internationally. In this context, it would be extremely interesting to calculate and compare WPRs as per what is recorded, and what the reality emerging from our fieldwork reports is. Our contention is that female work participation rates (FWPRs) are much higher than those reported in secondary data; women's contribution to economic growth is heavily unrecognised and uncalculated in the absence of incorporation of harvesting of the sea buckthorn. Eight villages were surveyed in the vastly different regions of Ladakh—Changthang Valley and Nubra Valley—Skuru, Chamshan-Charasa, Diskit, Hunder, Panamic, Sumoor, Turtuk and Chemrey. All of these already report quite high FWPRs as per the 2011 Census, exceeding 45 per cent in the first five, that is, Chamshan-Charasa, Diskit, Hunder, Panamic and Skuru. We found even these high proportions to be under-representative of the reality.

As per the 2011 Census, the WPR in Hunder is a rather high 61.5 per cent for women, just a percentage point less than that of men. We, however, found that the FWPR would in fact be even more, at a massive 90 per cent, with almost all able-bodied women and also girls involved in agriculture and berry collection; 80 per cent of village women are 'officially' involved in cultivation. All 56 households in Skuru village are agriculturists, and all women from all households are engaged in berry-plucking; we would add at least another 20 per cent to the 66.2 per cent recorded in the 2011 Census. In Diskit, the FWPR, which was reported to be 47 per cent, is about 80 per cent once the sea buckthorn activity is included. The FWPR of 52.2 per cent as recorded in the 2011 Census for Panamic is heavily underestimated, the actual, as women insisted during our field interviews, being 'at least 90 per cent'. Female and also male residents of the large village of Sumoor which reported a ridiculously low 20.2 per cent FWPR in the Census insisted vociferously that at least three-fourths of its women were involved in berry-collection.

Similarly, women in the famous village of Chemrey, which lies outside the Nubra region in Changthang Valley and is located on the main road leading to the famous Pangong Lake, insisted that at least 90 per cent of them work if sea buckthorn harvesting is counted as work—that is, a WPR three times higher than 2011 Census data, and matching the rural male WPR of an astounding 95 per cent.

Additionally, apart from the fact that most women participate in berry-plucking—an activity that is neither perceived nor recognised as work and hence not recorded in data systems—is the issue of the very basis of what is called as 'criterion' of work. In terms of time-based criterion, berry-plucking takes up less than 20 days in the year, while if the income-criterion is used, the approximate earning per woman per year for harvesting sea buckthorn ranges between Rs 20,000 to Rs 35,000 which constitutes a rather substantial component of annual income from all other sources of livelihood.

The second point of discussion in this case study cum illustration relates to the ethics and hence also the institutional mechanisms necessary to ensure that benefits from commonly owned and accessed resources enhance the rights of the community and communities, and also result in better and more sustainable livelihoods.

Harvesting of the sea buckthorn is carried out collectively by the women, almost all of them constituted into SHGs. These groups, each with about 8–10 women and teenage girls, work collectively, the earnings going again collectively to groups rather than individuals.

While certainly not claiming that their functioning is ideal and efficient, marketing and processing by cooperatives fulfils the fundamental ethic that public benefits should accrue to people while appropriating the produce of what is essentially a common property resource. As of today, the profits accruing to these cooperatives are shared in a rather remarkable manner. Membership fees that are collected are used for maintenance, and for paying wages to those employed—Rs 500 per day to skilled workers and Rs 300 to unskilled workers, these rates being significantly higher than the stipulated minimum wages pertaining to the region, and in some places even higher than the prevailing market rates. What is most impressive is that dividends to shareholders are not paid in cash but in kind—environmentally friendly lamps, bulbs, solar equipment. There has not been in my fieldwork experience of over three decades a better illustration of collective people-oriented and people-centred environmental responsibility linked to processes of production and sale, with no concern for individual profit or gain.

However, it is extremely disquieting that recent political and economic decisions that have been taken will deny these women their collective benefits from their collectively owned and accessed resources. The rights to technology in the form of research and development (R&D) as well as marketing of the produce are reportedly in the process of being handed over to the largest emerging indigenous corporate entity in India today that is based on purportedly ancient techniques of medical healing and holistic wellbeing. The consequences would be rather disastrous, to say the least—the conversion of a 'collective' to a 'corporate'; the appropriation of what is essentially and primarily a resource owned by all and accessed almost exclusively by women; the emergence of private appropriation of what has always been a publicly owned property; the denial to women and their households what is probably the single most crucial component of their cash earnings; the enclosure of what has historically always been a common resource, with laws and legislations denying entry to the local residents; with 'accessors' being now termed as trespassers; with one of the most important methods of controlling erosion in the cold desert that characterises the region shifting from the 'open and free' category to one that would be not only controlled but also priced and converted into a commodity; a possibly non-recoverable blow to sustainability of agriculture as well as livelihoods.

'Foot Fishing'/Mud Fishing (*Zol Takane*): Konkan Coast, Maharashtra

One of the most important sources of livelihood in the monetised as well as the non-monetised markets is that of fishing in both coastal and interior regions. Various levels of fishing exist in coastal zones—deep-sea fishing with mechanised or non-mechanised trawlers that stay out for over a week; smaller boats that fish in relatively shallower waters and return within a day or two; two-person boats that fish in brackish waters and in creeks—all these activities are conducted by men. While women do not go fishing into water at all, they are generally exclusively responsible for the catch once it is brought to the shore—unloading, sorting, storing, drying and marketing. All these activities are of course defined and hence also recorded as 'work' in data sources; underestimation is possible, but not non-acceptance and non-recognition of women's participation in this important economic activity.

There is, however, a form of fishing that is not only neither reported nor recorded, but not even publicly acknowledged—that of what we have termed as foot fishing or mud fishing. We came across this type of fishing during the course of two extensive field studies across the western coast of Maharashtra—one, a survey of 16 villages in Rewas-Mandwa located off the coast of the mega-city of Mumbai, which were to be displaced for the construction of a new international airport and now for the Reliance Special Economic Zone (SEZ); two, the societal-environmental cost–benefit analysis of the 47 villages in Dahanu taluka of Thane district which would have been displaced if the Vadhavan port of the multinational P&O (Peninsular and Oriental Ports Private Ltd, Australia) had been allowed to be built, and which are now being re-threatened out of existence with the recent declaration of the construction of the port by Adani Ports and Special Economic Zone Ltd.

Mud fishing is referred to as '*zol takane*' in Marathi, the literal meaning being 'to throw a net'. The net that is used represents one of the lowest forms of technology—a rough, hand-hewn zol (*jhole*) often made of leftover twine and plastic, attached to a rounded twig. This net is literally thrown on the mud portion of the beach after the tide recedes; this is the only part of the sea that women are permitted to fish in, as 'culture' does not permit the entry of women into the actual waters, restricting them to muddy marshes, yet another literal form of marginalisation, off the major source of livelihood in coastal regions. That is why I have additionally termed this form of fishing as 'foot fishing'. The main types of fish include mud-lizards, newts, tiny crabs and shrimps, *kalwae*—the smallest, the least nutritious and the least marketable of varieties. These fish are either sold in the local market at absurdly low prices in order to fulfil at least partial cash needs or used primarily for home consumption. Fish thus comprise an important priced and also non-priced component of the nutrition of the people.

We interviewed several such women selling fish in the local market, and found that the majority are single, deserted, aged and disabled, and are often the main earners in their families. Every evening one can witness a line of these women stretched out over a few hundred metres on the roadside, on the dusty footpath that runs along the tarred road. The location of their marketplace reflects their location in society, literally off the page, almost fully marginalised, keeping in sync with the very nature of this unacknowledged economic activity.

Predictably, the majority belongs to the 'lower' and 'backward' castes and communities, with a handful of destitute women from the 'middle' social groups. Several sit with their faces covered, especially those who may be 'newly' deserted, or from non-lower classes and non-lower castes; there is, after all, a 'shame' attached to being reduced to foraging for nutrition. However, catching fish on foot along the coastal regions does provide women who are out of the patriarchal slot not only a source of livelihood, but also some economic independence if not dignity. None of these women are hence 'unproductive' in the strict economic sense of the term, nor are they non-earners; they do contribute—however little it may be in cash terms—to the national economy. To perceive them as non-workers and dependents is to deny the reality of the nature of labouring livelihoods that these women have been compelled to create in the actuality of their economic and extra-economic existence and survival.

Scarecrow (*Bujgavne/Gophan Firawne*): Partur Taluka, Jalna District, Maharashtra

The concept of livelihoods is among the most textured and diverse, the most simplistic working definition comprising the capabilities, assets and activities required for a means of living. Concomitantly, a livelihood becomes sustainable when it can combine at the very least two essential components—the development of the capacity to manage 'stresses' and 'shocks', and when it can at the very least maintain its assets including labour power.

In the fieldwork undertaken to identify and assess the prevailing strategies of survival in the three districts comprising 19 tehsils in rural Maharashtra, a special focus was given to the situation of single women. The region of Marathwada has historically recorded a huge number of deserted women, the maximum apparently in the entire country. The taluka of Partur located in the Jalna district of this region was deliberately selected as it reportedly has a rather large proportion of such women, apart from the maximum number of women agricultural labourers and the highest houseless population in the entire area under study. We called for a meeting soon as we reached the taluka headquarters, without specifically mentioning that single women were the focus. Automatically, at least one-third of those who turned up for the impromptu meeting held in the late evening were single women.

The majority of single women in this area is primarily landless labourers. Most widows who had held some small pieces of land after their husbands' deaths were rendered 'illegally' landless after their 'in-laws' had taken the plots away; some became non-cultivators after being deserted, illegal desertion being perceived as a 'cultural tradition' in the region. All are consequently dependent almost solely upon the sale of labour power, both their own and that of their children.

The bias against single women workers, of course, not unusual at all, manifests itself in several ways, each one reinforcing gender-based division of labour as well as wage differentiation, apart, of course, from the predictable misogynistic attitudes. We mention each one along with the 'excuse' given by the employer.

> Not being given wages on time: 'Come again; you have enough time now—no husband to look after, do you?'
>
> Being employed for few number of days and being paid low wages: 'Who do you want to earn and save for? Will you have any more children now?'
>
> Undignified work: 'Be grateful that I am giving you some work at least!'
>
> Undefined hours of work: 'Why do you want to rush back? Who is waiting for you?'

While all gender-specific agricultural tasks are, of course, performed by both single and married women, there is one utterly humiliating 'job' which only single and erstwhile married women are employed for—as scarecrows, as *bujgavna*. There is no word for this economic activity in the local language; I had to discuss this source of sustenance at length with several villagers who could not come up with a 'satisfactory' term, and consequently was compelled to take the suggestion of several litterateurs and 'language' experts. The nature and conditions of this work, as described to us by the women we interviewed, apart from the 'employers', was traumatising to hear and is even more painful to record.

The job description is simple—to stand in the fields and 'perform' the task of *bujgavne*—the act of scaring away birds. The 'skills' required are simple—the ability to shout, to flap one's hands, to throw *gophan firawne* (stones), to keep constantly moving, and, of course, the strength to stand for hours under the blazing sun. She can cover her head, and is generally permitted to keep water with her, both for drinking and for splashing on her face. 'Breaks' of about 10 minutes each are not too limited, during which she generally rushes back to check on her children and complete her household chores.

The daily hours of work average between six to eight, extendable by two hours when the sun sets late and daylight hours are longer. Wages do not depend on the number of hours but the number of days, that is, a higher level of appropriation of surplus labour via the 'absolute' route. The wages are mainly in kind: one meal for the woman and her children, the meal consisting of the inevitable *paez*—a thin gruel of rice and water, cooked and generally fermented both to increase the quantity and to kill hunger. On rare occasions, a handful of lentils are thrown in so that the meal now gets converted to the more 'nutritious' *khichdi*.[1] Milk-less tea can be collected from the landowner's house twice a day, along with a few slices of bread or leftover *bhakri*.[2] However, the bujgavna is permitted to collect from the farm she is working on the vegetables, roots and herbs that she requires for cooking for her family.

Additionally, two or three sets of old clothes are sometimes given for her and the children. The cash component of wages are a few 'twenties', given once in four or six weeks. Education, health, nutrition, electricity, protection from the heat and the cold—all these have no role to play in the lives of these bujgavne families.

The calculation of imputed wages paid for gophan firawne would include housing. The female-headed household is provided shelter, a place to sleep in, almost invariably in the outhouse where cattle are kept. This rather ingenious resolution of 'homelessness' incorporates, of course, the utilisation of the labour power of both the woman and her children for the tending of livestock—feeding, cleaning, washing, milking, collection of cow dung, making of dung cakes for fuel both for the landowner's family and her own, etc., the list of productive activities related to livestock is quite long.

The linking of the wage/non-wage components in an ingenious and insidious manner ensures almost total control over the labour-power and also the labouring capacity of these 'scarecrow' women. While her labour on the fields is grossly underpaid, her labouring hours are extended from the field to the 'house' where she is compelled to look after those she shares her home with. And when there are no crops to protect, she is 'requested' to help out with the employer's housework by assisting in washing vessels and clothes in order to 'earn' her rent. This almost complete control is reinforced by her pathetically low nutritional levels, thus maintaining her in a state of too low a capacity to undertake arduous physical work under available employment schemes. The only saving grace, if one can use such a term, is that no cases or incidents of sexual exploitation of these women were reported.

In the context of a perennially drought-impacted economy with little and in fact declining State investment in irrigation, the generally one-crop cultivation resorted to by most farmers in this region implies obviously that becoming a scarecrow to source a livelihood as a source of sustenance cannot be an economic activity that can provide employment throughout the year. The issue, therefore, is that, in the absence of effective State support systems and structures, especially those designed for the 'extremely vulnerable', deserted single women and widows are compelled to accept whatever form of livelihood is offered to them, sometimes even created for them in the name of 'community' support; several landowners and employers of bujgavne women asserted rather proudly that they were in fact extending support to these 'poor' women who did not have any schemes to assist them.

Gophan firawne is not recorded in any data system as an economic activity, or a form of 'work' that is definable, or recognisable, or quantifiable; in fact, not even acknowledged as 'work'. In any case, how does one then answer the many issues that arise? Should the definition of labour include inanimate objects such as scarecrows? When we ask the ubiquitous question 'do you work', should we also ask 'what do you work as'? Under which sub-sector would this activity be slotted—agricultural, allied agricultural, rural non-farm, livestock? What skills need to be upgraded? Which vocational training can be provided to a bujgavne? What indicators could be used to measure her abilities and capabilities? What is the contribution of a scarecrow to production and productivity? And the valuation of the cost of production? What are the imputed wages? Can the kind component of wages be equated to the operative rent of a cowshed? Should the imputed value of work include non-living inanimate hours equal to the cost of building a scarecrow? Is the work substitutable? By whom or what?

In Lieu of a Conclusion

The several issues of visibilities and vulnerabilities in the labour and livelihoods of particularly rural women are closely interlinked and depend fundamentally and primarily on the patriarchal construct of gender. These interconnections are located within a specific developmental and macroeconomic framework that not only merely denies women their 'rightful' role in society, but in fact whose very existence depends on this denial and the perpetuation, if not reinforcement, of this denegation. This disaffirmation extends to all economic and extra-economic aspects, including that of not recognising and hence not incorporating their contribution to production or even to mere survival whether on an individual basis or collectively.

There can be no debate on the oft-asserted need to clarify and differentiate the concepts of work, employment and livelihood, accompanied by identifying and isolating methodological data biases so inherent in information systems and sources at all levels of macro, meso and micro. This is so particularly in the context of rural women whose sources of livelihood and strategies of survival are not only non-linear, but fundamentally and almost always characterised by synchronicity, multiplicity, unevenness, intermittency and instability.

Understanding the nature of the dynamically dialectical relationship between women's labour and livelihoods is consequently perceived as being, to say the least, rather problematic—the questions are many. Even if the work is included in data systems, does the technique of measurement adopted incorporate the nuances? Is the work recognisable and hence is it definable and quantifiable? Would those performing these forms of activity for purposes of sheer survival still be considered a burden on the economy as well as the society? What if it is unrecognisable and hence unquantifiable and indefinable? Is this form of work at all acknowledgeable? Can a scarecrow be employable? On what basis would payment be made; is her labour payable? How can mud fishing or foot fishing even be called fishing?; it is out of water and hence not categorisable. Should not then the very concept of work be reconceptualised and redefined? Or should there be a demarcated divide between work, employment, livelihood and so on? Will this disassociation then extend to a forcible and facile differentiation between the multiple and myriad contributions of marginalised women and also men? Can de-association and re-association incorporate the concepts of exchange-value and use-value? Can measurement and quantification of work in all its forms and manifestations prove to be reductionist of a marginalised person's contribution to the economy and the society?

The appropriation of the labour power of single and especially deserted women extends across several 'analytical' categories—paid, underpaid, unpaid—each of them connected and sometimes disconnected, the underlying substructure essentially that of being within a strongly patriarchal production system and simultaneously being out of not merely a patriarchal slot but, almost as important, an acceptable patriarchal slot. This is particularly true of the strongly stylised nature of the economy, particularly when perceived even in the minimalist sense as well as context of market/non-market, formal/informal, organised/unorganised.

The de-construction and re-construction of the fundamentals of the wage/non-wage components assures the employer an almost total control over a single woman's labour power, cutting through the public–private dichotomy. Her capacity to work—in this instance, as a scarecrow—is not only de-visibilised and derecognised, but, much worse, is de-dignified and dehumanised. This is almost equally true of those 'reduced' to fishing by foot.

When production takes place on common property resources, the urgent need is to protect these areas in the form of environmental protection and regeneration, and control the possibilities of private appropriation of the land as well as the produce of that land; central to this is the role of the State that must protect people's rights to both individual and commonly owned land and resources. The issue of control over resources is fundamental to the relationship that exists between gender, labour and livelihoods. It is in this context that several major factors emerge—environmental degradation, deforestation, appropriation of land for non-agricultural purposes and, of course, the legal rights of women over not only the chief means of production but also their legal rights over land as inherited property as articulated in succession laws. Related to women's role in production that is outside the private property domain is the democratic definition of common rights; what are the collective rights that individuals must be either guaranteed or denied; to what extent are these rights articulated in law; are these rights implementable and how best can they be protected. This aspect goes beyond that of our illustrations of sea buckthorn and fishing by foot, and links with the broader canvas of non-farm forest produce, and other related commodities. In fact, they extend even further to cover every aspect of the very lives and lifestyles of the rural marginalised and vulnerable communities. This would also imply a re-questioning and re-structuring of the exact economic and ethical role of all the different private and public entities that have rights over resources.

'Work'—fully demystified and demythified—is an activity all persons in a poor country are involved in, involuntarily, with no choice. In an economy where the motive force for the overwhelming majority is subsistence and survival, and where the unit of livelihood is the household, there can be no family that is non-'working', there can be no family member who is non-producing, there can be no woman who is non-productive and non-'working'.

The debate therefore centres on several interdependent connects: one, the location of women in the systems of production and reproduction; two, the changing relations between capital and labour; three, the dynamics that operate between the market and non-market sectors; four, the extension of the 'work' and 'employment' debate to 'livelihoods' especially in the non-linear rural context, and ultimately the current processes and forces that not only re-intensify but also in fact depend upon the subordination of women and their labour in the context of an underdeveloped as well as a developing nation, a nation that functions via highly patriarchal production systems characterised by a rigid meshing of 'modern' yet strongly feudal remnants.

Notes

1. A watery gruel of cereals and pulses cooked together.
2. Millet bread.

References

Dewan, Ritu. 2003. *Strategies for Survival in Underdeveloped Maharashtra: Sustainable Livelihoods in Districts of Yawatmal, Jalna and Nandurbar.* New Delhi: UNDP-India and Maharashtra Human Development Action Research Study, Maharashtra State Planning Board.

———. 2008. 'Identifying Gendered Displacement Issues: A Conceptual and Empirical Overview'. In *Social Development Report 2008*. New Delhi: Oxford University Press.

———. 2014. *Gendering Green Growth: A Dialectical Analysis of Gender, Trade and Development in India, Volumes I and II*. Manila, Philippines: Asian Development Bank and United Nations Women.

Dewan, Ritu and Michelle Chawla. 1999. *Of Development Amidst Fragility: A Societal and Environmental Perspective on Vadhavan Port*. Mumbai: Popular Prakashan.

Dewan, Ritu and Sandhya Mhatre. 1997. *Runways across Villages: Critique of the Proposed New International Airport for the City of Mumbai*. Mumbai: Himalaya Publishing House.

Government of India (1947 and thereafter). Industrial Disputes Act.

8

Back to the Barracks

Changing Pattern of Women's Work Participation in India

Nisha Srivastava and *Anjor Bhaskar*

Women's relation with work is complex and mediated by many factors. The results of the NSS (2011–12) show that women's workforce participation rates (WPR) are at an all-time low. Globally, female WPR has been rising because of economic development, rising education and declining fertility. Economic progress has led to enhanced demand for female labour, and better family support infrastructure. Improvements in education have promoted women's access to jobs (increase in education explains 42 per cent of the increase in female WPR in Latin America). Increase in age of marriage and decline in fertility have contributed to higher WPR in most countries. This has been the global experience, but the experience in India has been the obverse of this. Economic growth has failed to boost women's work participation.

This essay is a contribution to the ongoing debate on the falling WPRs of women in India. While jobs and earnings are important to both men and women, for women, a job has added significance. Women, particularly in rural areas, are frequently victims of violence inside and outside the household, and are still circumscribed by rigid norms that dictate almost every aspect of their life. Employment has the potential to enhance her status both in the household and in society, increase her autonomy and self-confidence and improve her own wellbeing and that of her family. On the other hand, a job, if it is low-paying and exploitative will only increase her drudgery. Only decent work that not only pays well but also upholds her dignity as a worker can improve the subordinate status that women suffer in our society.

It is imperative, therefore, that employment opportunities for women should grow. Actual trends, however, show that women's participation in work has been falling. Table 8.1 shows the trends in the work participation of women over the different survey rounds conducted by the NSSO. Thus, in 2011–12, the WPR in rural areas had fallen to 24.8 per 100 women from 32.8 in 1993–94.

Several authors have noted this decline and subjected it to careful scrutiny (Abraham 2013; Kannan and Raveendran 2012; Mazumdar and Neetha 2011; Rangarajan et al. 2011). Some authors conclude that this decline is a positive development caused mainly by women and girls moving out of jobs to get education; others see it as a manifestation of an 'income effect': that is, a withdrawal of women from the workforce as a result of rising incomes. Himanshu (2011) examines the shorter-term period and suggests that women who had come out to work in the period 1999–2000 to 2004 because of economic distress, withdrew in the next period when conditions were better, hence the fall in female participation rates (see also Neff et al. 2012).

This essay, however, argues that while there are several socio-economic and cultural factors that may explain the decline in women's WPR, the most important factor is the stagnation and lack of job opportunities in most of the sectors that women were traditionally employed in. The essay is based on an analysis of unit record results from the NSSO surveys. It pertains mainly to rural areas and the period 1992–93 to 2011–12, the latest year for which data is available. According to the NSSO, a person is defined as being employed in the 'principal status' if he/she is employed for a major part of the year, and in the 'subsidiary status' if employed for only a part of the year. A person employed either in Usual Principal Status (UPS) or Usual Subsidiary Status (SS) is enumerated as being employed in the Usual Status (also known as UPSS). This essay uses the concept of UPSS throughout unless otherwise stated. This study does not

Table 8.1: WPRs in UPSS during Different Rounds of the NSSO, 1993–94 to 2011–12

	Rural			Urban			All		
	Male	**Female**	**Total**	**Male**	**Female**	**Total**	**Male**	**Female**	**Total**
68th Round (2011–12)	543	248	399	546	147	355	544	219	386
66th Round (2009–10)	547	261	408	543	138	350	546	228	392
61st Round 2004–05	546	327	439	549	166	365	547	287	420
55th Round (1999–2000)	531	299	417	518	139	337	527	259	397
50th Round (1993–94)	553	328	444	521	155	347	545	286	420

Source: NSSO, 68th Round.[1]

examine women's work by social group, which has been analysed elsewhere by the authors (Srivastava and Bhaskar 2016)

Activity Profile

The decline in women's work participation is often attributed to larger numbers of women leaving the labour force to take up education. This is true only for a segment of women. This can be seen by analysing WPRs by age group (Table 8.2).

Table 8.2: WPRs (UPSS) by Age Group (Rural), 1993–94 to 2011–12

		WPR				
		<15 Years	**15–24 Years**	**25–59 Years**	**>60 Years**	**Total**
1993–94	Male	4.71	69.81	97.49	70.24	55.14
	Female	4.59	40.43	56.01	24.00	32.40
2011–12	Male	1.04	49.16	97.25	65.27	54.19
	Female	1.06	21.30	43.47	21.24	24.65
Change in WPR	Male	–3.67	–20.66	–0.23	–4.97	–0.95
($WPR_{2011–12}$ minus $WPR_{1993–94}$)	Female	–3.53	–19.13	–12.54	–2.76	–7.74

Source: Calculated from unit record data of the NSSO.

In the first age group (less than 15 years), WPRs are already low, with most children in schools, and hence the decline is insignificant. In the second age group (15–24 years), there is a sharp decline in WPRs reflecting the transition to education. It is the WPRs of the third age group (25–59 years) that is of interest to us and is the subject of our scrutiny.

Table 8.3 shows the activity profile of women in the working age group in the two periods under study. The proportion of women in education is the same in both years, thereby establishing that the decline in WPR—at least in this age group—is not the result of a shift to education. It shows a dramatic decline from 56 per cent to 43.5 per cent in the proportion of workers in the overall female population. The proportion of the self-employed as well as casual workers shows a

Table 8.3: Activity Profile of Rural Women by UPSS (25–59 Years), 1993–94 to 2011–12

	1993–94	**2011–12**
Self-employed	33.0	25.8
Regular wage employee	1.6	2.4
Casual labour	21.5	15.3
All workers	**56.0**	**43.5**
Available for work	0.2	0.3
Student	0.1	0.1
Domestic duties only	22.0	23.6
Other domestic duties	20.3	31.0
Other non-work	1.4	1.4
Total	**100.0**	**100.0**

Source: Calculated from unit record data of the NSSO.

decline, with a marginal increase in the regular employed. The decline in the proportion of workers is offset by an increase in the category of women in domestic duties. What is the significance of this? What do women who are engaged in domestic duties do? Do they simply substitute leisure for work, as is often assumed?

The NSS distinguishes between a person who 'attended domestic duties only' (code 92) and one who 'attended domestic duties and was also engaged in free collection of goods (fish, wild fruits, firewood, cow dung, cattle feed, etc.)' for household consumption, maintenance of kitchen garden, orchards, etc., work in household poultry, dairy, etc., sewing, tailoring, weaving, etc., for household use and tutoring children (code 93). Codes 92 and 93 together include all women whose usual work is domestic. It has sometimes been argued that the shift to domestic duties under code 93 is simply a shift from paid work to unpaid work. If the activities that come under code 93 were to be acknowledged to be economic, then the overall rate of female labour force participation would rise.

As we can see from Table 8.3, there has been a small increase in the proportion of women who reported doing domestic duties only (from 22 per cent in 1992–93 to 23.6 per cent in 2011–12). The greater increase has been in those women who reported being engaged in 'other domestic duties', to whit from 20.3 to 31 per cent. If this was indeed a positive development, and women have withdrawn from the workforce because incomes have gone up, women would have shifted away from the workforce to stay at home, that is, to domestic duties only (code 92). This is not the case; the shift has largely been to code 93 (attended domestic duties and also engaged in free collection of vegetables, roots, firewood, fodder, etc.). These activities are most likely undertaken by the poor. It does not stand to reason, therefore, that women would increase their engagement in these activities if their household's economic situation had improved.

We argue that the falling women's work participation is largely because of falling opportunities for remunerative work in rural areas. Women withdraw from the labour force because work is not available. However, they do not report themselves as unemployed, but shift instead to activities that augment real household incomes, such as foraging for food, fuel or fodder and care for domestic poultry and animals. In fact, lack of money incomes is being made up by augmenting real incomes.

Work Participation and Monthly Per Capita Expenditure (MPCE) Class

The relation between women's WPR and economic status is hypothesised as being U-shaped, which means that women from the poorest economic strata have a higher WPR because they are compelled by economic distress to work and earn to make ends meet. However, as the household's economic situation improves, many women may withdraw from the labour market. At the highest economic levels, women may once again go back to the labour market, this time from a less vulnerable position and most likely to better jobs. We take MPCE quartiles to proxy for economic status. Table 8.4 shows the shift from the workforce to domestic duties differentiated across the quartiles. The distribution for 1993–94 follows the expected pattern: the proportion of casual labour is high and that of self-employed is low in the poorer MPCE quartile, and the converse is true for the higher quartile.

Table 8.4: Activity Status of Women (25–59 Years) by MPCE Quartile, 1993–94 to 2011–12

	1993–94					2011–12				
	MPCE Quartile					MPCE Quartile				
	1st	**2nd**	**3rd**	**4th**	**Total**	**1st**	**2nd**	**3rd**	**4th**	**Total**
Self-employed	27.8	33.9	36.6	39.5	33.0	23.2	25.8	28.8	28.4	25.8
Regular wage employee	1.1	1.4	1.6	3.5	1.6	1.4	1.7	3.0	6.5	2.4
Casual labour	32.3	19.9	13.3	7.5	21.5	17.9	15.8	14.0	7.8	15.3
All workers	**61.2**	**55.2**	**51.5**	**50.5**	**56.0**	**42.5**	**43.3**	**45.8**	**42.7**	**43.5**
Domestic duties only	17.5	21.7	26.6	28.2	22.0	20.6	22.3	26.1	32.8	23.6
Other domestic duties	19.6	21.5	20.2	19.6	20.3	35.2	32.8	26.2	21.5	31.0
All domestic duties	**37.1**	**43.2**	**46.8**	**47.8**	**42.3**	**55.8**	**55.0**	**52.3**	**54.3**	**54.6**
All others	1.7	1.6	1.7	1.7	1.7	1.8	1.7	1.9	2.9	1.9
Total	**100.0**	**100.0**	**100.0**	**100.0**	**100.0**	**100.0**	**100.0**	**100.0**	**100.0**	**100.0**

Source: Calculated from unit record data of the NSSO.

Participation in domestic activities—code 92—is lower in the poorer quartiles and higher among the better-off quartiles. Conversely, there is a larger proportion of women engaged in code 93 activities in the poorer MPCE groups, and this goes down with higher MPCE class, showing that most of the extra-domestic activities undertaken by women in this category are taken up under conditions of economic distress.

Work Participation by Industry and Operation

Rapid farm mechanisation has contributed to the massive displacement of labour and reduced opportunities for work. Data from the Ministry of Agriculture shows that in 2011–12, India had 5.352 million tractors, as against 1.063 million in 1991. Between 1991 and 2007, combine harvesters increased from 0.122 million to 0.477 million. India is the largest manufacturer of tractors in the world, accounting for one-third of the global production. Power tillers are being increasingly used and there has been rapid increase in the use of other mechanical and electrical equipment. Liberalisation gave a big boost to the production of agricultural machinery, particularly in states such as Haryana, Punjab, Rajasthan and Uttar Pradesh.

In a labour-surplus economy, there is always a threat of a potential conflict between mechanisation and employment. This conflict does not surface so long as mechanisation helps in increasing production and generates employment. This is what happened in Punjab in the 1980s, or what has been called the 'golden period' for the agricultural economy, when production, incomes and employment all improved. Though tractors and combine harvesters replaced human and animal labour, yet the negative impacts were offset by the increase in employment as a consequence of cropping intensity spurred by the adoption of new varieties of wheat and rice, expansion in irrigation, and shift to labour-intensive crops (Sidhu et al. 2005). Thereafter, however, the demand for labour declined because of the excessive use of herbicides and agricultural machinery, especially combine harvesters. According to the authors, the use of labour in wheat declined from

52.35 person-days per hectare in 1985–88 to 38.9 person-days in 1998–2000, and in paddy cultivation it came down from 102.4 to 56.3 person-days in the same period. The positive employment effects of cropping intensity and production growth slowed down and failed to counterbalance the negative employment effects of mechanisation and herbicide use.

Are the impacts of mechanisation any different for women? Mechanisation may lead to loss of jobs for both men and women: how each will be impacted will depend on the nature of tasks that are mechanised. There may be some occupations that are traditionally done by women and therefore have a high female intensity or a large proportion of women to all workers. Mechanisation will adversely affect women more in such a context.

Again, while lack of employment opportunities may impact both men and women, their responses are different. Women tend to withdraw from the labour force, but do not report themselves as unemployed and shift instead to work in household poultry, dairy, sewing, tailoring, weaving for household use, etc. (code 93 activities). Some women shift to domestic duties (code 92). Women's burden of work in the domestic sphere has increased because elder siblings who used to take care of younger children have started going to school, life expectancy has gone up and there are larger numbers of older people but there are no crèches, or other support structures to take care of old persons and children.

On the other hand, men scrounge for any work and take up whatever they can find. In traditional societies, there is still the mindset that men are the chief breadwinners, hence they have greater claim to whatever jobs are available. Non-farm sector jobs have grown but not enough to absorb all the labour rendered surplus in the agriculture sector.

Distribution of Workforce by Industry

In terms of industrial distribution, in 1993–94 the largest concentration of women workers was in agriculture, followed by manufacturing, trade, community services, education and construction (Table 8.5).

Table 8.5: Percentage Distribution of Workers (25–59 Years) by Industry (UPSS Rural), 1993–94 to 2011–12

	1993–94		2011–12	
	Male	**Female**	**Male**	**Female**
Agriculture	71.39	86.73	58.26	76.44
Mining	0.81	0.32	0.56	0.30
Manufacturing	7.38	6.47	7.77	8.05
Electricity	0.39	0.04	0.33	0.01
Construction	3.42	0.84	12.84	6.77
Trade	5.91	2.00	7.77	2.47
Hotels	0.53	0.30	1.02	0.44
Transport	2.58	0.04	4.59	0.11
Finance	0.37	0.05	0.48	0.10
Real estate	0.18	0.01	0.66	0.09
Administration	2.49	0.34	1.27	0.33
Education	1.86	0.88	2.28	2.80
Health	0.42	0.22	0.48	0.74
Community	1.82	0.91	1.48	0.84
Household	0.06	0.44	0.22	0.51
Missing	0.36	0.40	0.00	0.00
Total	**100.00**	**100.00**	**100.00**	**100.00**

Source: Calculated from unit record data of the NSSO.

This pattern changed by 2011–12. There was an absolute decline of 1.61 million in the number of women workers in agriculture. Despite that, agriculture was still the largest employer of women, followed by manufacturing. Construction and education moved up to third and fourth spots.

For male workers in 1993–94, agriculture and manufacturing were the biggest source of employment, followed by trade, construction and transport. In 2011–12, agriculture was still the largest employer with an absolute increase in number of male workers, but this was now followed in importance by construction, manufacturing, trade and transport.

Table 8.6 shows that the highest growth rates in employment have been in construction, with employment for men growing by 9.6 per cent per annum, while for women it grew by 12.9 per cent. The other rapidly growing sectors for men were real estate (9.4 per cent) and household services (9.2 per cent). For women, these were real estate (11 per cent), health (7.4 per cent) and education (7.2 per cent).

Overall, the number of male workers increased by 1.9 per cent per annum, while the number of women workers increased by 0.6 per cent per annum over the period under study.

Table 8.6: Compound Annual Growth Rate of Employment (UPSS Rural, 25–59 Years), 2011–12 over 1993–94

	Male	Female
Agriculture	0.7	–0.2
Mining	–0.2	0.3
Manufacturing	2.2	1.8
Electricity	0.9	–5.2
Construction	9.6	12.9
Trade	3.4	1.8
Hotels	5.6	2.8
Transport	5.2	5.5
Finance	3.3	4.2
Real estate	9.4	11.0
Administration	–1.9	0.4
Education	3.1	7.2
Health	2.7	7.4
Community	0.7	0.1
Household	9.2	1.4
Total	**1.9**	**0.6**

Source: Calculated from unit record data of the NSSO.

Distribution of Person-days of Work by Type of Operation

NSSO gives data on person-days of work by type of operation. An analysis of this provides important insights into the changes taking place in the division of labour by gender and the nature of work.

It is instructive to segregate work in rural areas by agriculture and non-agriculture to see where job opportunities are growing. Within agriculture, we further classify work by employment in crop agriculture and non-crop agriculture. The different operations and the percentage distribution of workers are given in Tables 8.7 and 8.8. What is most noteworthy is the relatively larger importance of non-crop agriculture in women's work as compared to men, and the sharp decline in this sector (drop from 25 per cent of all person-days to 17 per cent).

Table 8.7: Distribution of Annual Person-days (25–59 Years) by Type of Operation (Rural), 1993–94 to 2011–12

	1993–94		2011–12	
	Male	**Female**	**Male**	**Female**
Ploughing	6.2	0.8	4.2	1.4
Sowing	2.4	2.2	2.4	2.6
Transplanting	1.3	2.5	2.5	3.2
Weeding	5.2	11.8	5.6	12.0
Harvesting	10.7	15.8	11.1	14.2
Other cultivation activities	26.7	26.5	22.1	22.6
Forestry	0.4	0.5	0.1	0.1
Plantation	1.4	1.4	0.8	1.2
Animal husbandry	2.6	10.0	1.5	8.7
Fisheries	0.6	0.2	0.3	0.2
Other agricultural activities	11.2	11.7	5.3	6.7
Non-manual work in cultivation	2.0	1.1	0.8	0.3
Manual work in non-agricultural activities	14.9	9.1	25.2	16.9
Activities other than cultivation	14.3	6.2	18.0	9.9
Total	**100.0**	**100.0**	**100.0**	**100.0**

Source: Calculated from unit record data of the NSSO.

If we compare growth rates, Table 8.9 shows a slow growth in person-days of work per annum in crop agriculture, at 1.38 per cent for

Table 8.8: Distribution of Annual Person-days (25–59 Years) of Employment by Type of Operation (Rural), 1993–94 to 2011–12

	1993–94		2011–12		Change: 2011–12 minus 1993–94	
	Male	**Female**	**Male**	**Female**	**Male**	**Female**
Total crop agriculture	52.5	59.7	47.9	56.0	–4.6	–3.7
Total non-crop agriculture	18.2	25.0	8.8	17.2	–9.4	–7.8
Total agriculture	**70.7**	**84.6**	**56.8**	**73.2**	**–14.0**	**–11.5**
Total non-agriculture	**29.3**	**15.4**	**43.2**	**26.8**	**14.0**	**11.5**
Total	**100.0**	**100.0**	**100.0**	**100.0**	–	–

Source: Calculated from unit record data of the NSSO.

Table 8.9: Compound Annual Growth Rate of Annual Person-days of Employment by Operation (Rural), 25–59 Years, 1993–94 to 2011–12

	Male	Female	Total
Ploughing	–0.28	3.98	0.03
Sowing	1.93	1.49	1.81
Transplanting	5.66	1.91	4.25
Weeding	2.31	0.75	1.60
Harvesting	2.12	0.06	1.42
Other cultivation activities	0.84	–0.23	0.54
Total crop agriculture	**1.38**	**0.30**	**1.06**
Forestry	–5.35	–7.26	–5.93
Plantation	–1.21	–0.58	–1.02
Animal husbandry	–1.38	–0.11	–0.57
Fisheries	–1.55	0.12	–1.35
Other agricultural activities	–2.24	–2.46	–2.31
Non-manual work in cultivation	–2.87	–5.75	–3.31
Total non-crop agriculture	**–2.11**	**–1.42**	**–1.86**
Total agriculture	**0.66**	**–0.16**	**0.40**

(*Contd*)

Table 8.9: (*Contd*)

	Male	Female	Total
Manual work in non-agricultural activities	4.90	4.16	4.76
Activities other than cultivation	3.22	3.27	3.22
Total non-agriculture	**11.49**	**3.82**	**4.08**
Total	**1.90**	**0.65**	**1.56**

Source: Calculated from unit record data of the NSSO.

men and a negligible 0.3 per cent for women. Non-crop agriculture fares worse. There have been negative growth rates in non-crop agriculture for both men and women: it was –1.42 per cent per annum for women and –2.11 per cent for men.

The sectors where the decline in women's work has been most sharp are forestry (–7.26 per cent), plantations (–0.58 per cent) and animal husbandry (–0.11 per cent), apart from other unspecified non-crop agricultural operations. For males, the negative growth rates can be seen across all activities.

The only bright spot is offered by the non-agricultural sector: for males, the growth in person-days of work has been 11.5 per cent per annum; for women, it has been more modest at 3.82 per cent per annum.

It is well known that there are always some jobs which are traditionally performed by women, and others that are done by men. In order to understand this 'gender stereotyping' and how it is changing, if at all, we have looked at the proportion of person-days of work done by women workers as a proportion of the total; that is, we look at the 'female-intensity' of the operations in rural areas (Table 8.10).

Weeding and transplanting have a high female intensity: the ratio of women person-days to total was 48.3 per cent in weeding and 44.9 per cent in transplanting in 1993–94, but this came down to 41.5 per cent and 29 per cent, respectively, in 2011–12. Growth rates in person-days of work for women were very low at just 0.75 per cent and 1.91 per cent per annum for these two sectors. For men, the growth rates were higher, leading to a decline in female intensity.

Table 8.10: Proportion of Female to Total Annual Person-days (25–59 Years) of Work by Type of Operation (Rural), 1993–94 to 2011–12

	1993–94	**2011–12**	**2011–12 minus 1993–94**
Ploughing	5.0	10.1	5.1
Sowing	28.0	26.4	–1.5
Transplanting	44.9	29.8	–15.1
Weeding	48.3	41.5	–6.8
Harvesting	37.9	29.7	–8.2
Other cultivation activities	29.2	25.4	–3.8
Total crop agriculture	**32.0**	**27.9**	**–4.1**
Forestry	34.0	26.3	–7.7
Plantation	30.1	32.6	2.5
Animal husbandry	61.2	66.6	5.3
Fisheries	10.7	13.9	3.2
Other agricultural activities	30.1	29.3	–0.9
Non-manual work in cultivation	18.8	11.9	–6.9
Total non-crop agriculture	**36.1**	**39.1**	**3.0**
Total agriculture	**33.1**	**29.9**	**–3.2**
Manual work in non-agricultural activities	20.2	18.2	–2.0
Activities other than cultivation	15.2	15.3	0.1
Total non-agriculture	**17.8**	**27.1**	**9.3**
Total	**29.3**	**24.9**	**–4.4**

Source: Calculated from unit record data of the NSSO.

For a long time, women have had a dominant presence in the farming and animal husbandry sectors. This sector was the source of a large number of jobs for women. Among all the operations in rural areas, animal husbandry has the highest female intensity: in 1993–94, 61.2 per cent of all workers in this sector were women, this increased to 66.6 per cent in 2011–12. However, there was a huge decline in the person-days of employment in this sector, with work availability declining for both men and women. Animal husbandry was the third largest employer of women, but the person-days of work declined by 0.11 per cent per annum for women, and 1.38 per cent annually for men.

Table 8.11: Per '000 Distribution of Workers (UPSS) in Farming of Animal (012) and Agricultural and Animal Husbandry Service Activities (014), 1999–2000 to 2011–12*

	Male				Female			
	1999–2000	**2004–05**	**2009–10**	**2011–12**	**1999–2000**	**2004–05**	**2009–10**	**2011–12**
Farming of animals	22	23	16	10	98	132	95	89
Agricultural and animal husbandry services	11	4	3	6	13	4	6	10

Note: * National Industrial Classification code 012: farming of animal; code 014: agricultural and animal husbandry service activities except veterinary activities.

Source: NSSO, various rounds.

Analysis of NSSO data at the two-digit industry level shows that women are engaged both in upkeep of farm animals (8.9 per cent) as well as in animal husbandry activities (1.0 per cent), but a far greater percentage are in the former. Except for an increase in 2004–05, there appears to be a long-term downward trend in employment of both men and women in these tasks (Table 8.11).

The decline in employment in the livestock sector is accompanied by a decline in the number of livestock. There has also been a decline in the number of livestock per holding across all sizes of landholdings. This shows not only a decline of work relating to animal husbandry for women of the house, but also for casual labour that was hired for the purpose. Thus, the number of cattle and buffalo decreased from 3.9 per household in 2010 to 1.9 in 2013. Similarly, the number of sheep and goat reduced from 1.6 to 1.2 per household (Table 8.12).

Table 8.12: Percentage Distribution of Livestock by Size of Holding and Livestock Per Holding, 2010–13

Category of Landholding (Hectare)	2010			2013		
	Distribution of Livestock (%)	Livestock Per Holding		Distribution of Livestock (%)	Livestock Per Holding	
		Cattle and Buffalo	Sheep and Goat		Cattle and Buffalo	Sheep and Goat
Marginal (below 1 hectare)	46.5	2.9	1.3	50.1	1.5	0.8
Small (1.0–1.99 hectare)	22.5	4.4	1.7	21.6	2.3	1.4
Semi-medium (2.0–3.99 hectare)	17.5	5.7	2.1	15.9	3.0	1.9
Sub-total	**86.5**	**3.6**	**1.5**	**87.7**	**1.8**	**1.1**
Medium (4.0–9.99 hectare)	10.6	7.1	2.7	9.6	4.1	2.7
Large (10 hectare and above)	2.9	8.9	5.0	2.8	5.5	4.6
Sub-total	**13.5**	**7.4**	**3.0**	**12.3**	**4.3**	**2.9**
All size classes	**100.0**	**3.9**	**1.6**	**100.0**	**1.9**	**1.2**

Source: Government of India, various issues.

Wages

The movement of rural wages over the last two decades (1990s and 2000s) is of interest when one is trying to understand women's work participation. Among the many developments that would have had an impact on wages are the dramatic changes in policy in terms of liberalisation and economic reforms in the early 1990s, and the implementation of the Mahatma Gandhi National Rural Employment Guarantee Act (MGNREGA) in the latter part of this period. In a study on farm wages covering 16 major states from 1990–91 to 2011–12, Gulati et al. (2013) found that real farm wages increased by 3.7 per cent per annum during the 1990s compared to only 2 per cent per annum during the 2000s. They found that in the 2000s, there was a V-shape in real farm wages declining by 1.8 per cent per annum during 2000–01 to 2006–07, and then rapidly rising by 6.8 per cent per annum during 2007–08 to 2011–12. This seems to be the result of the implementation of MGNREGA, the rights-based employment guarantee programme.

Table 8.13: Average Wage Earnings Per Day Received by Casual Wage Labour in Other Types of Works, 1993–94 to 2011–12

	Male Wages		Female Wages	
Year	Nominal Wages	Real Wages	Nominal Wages	Real Wages
68th Round (2011–12)	149.32	45.31	103.28	31.34
66th Round (2009–10)	101.53	36.17	68.94	24.56
61st Round (2004–05)	55.03	30.36	34.94	19.28
55th Round (1999–2000)	45.48	29.54	29.39	19.09
50th Round (1993–94)	23.18	23.18	15.33	15.33

Source: NSSO, various rounds.

How do wages impact women's work participation? The relationship is not linear or unambiguous. On the one hand, economic theory postulates that the supply of labour will go up with higher wages. On the other, there is a view that if wages are high, input costs will rise. The increase in labour costs will lead to greater mechanisation and substitution of capital for labour. This may have the effect of reducing employment. We have calculated real wages of casual workers in other than public works for the period 1993–94 to 2011–12 based on data from the various rounds of the NSSO. These are given in Table 8.13. An increase in real wages from Rs 15.33 in 1993–94 to Rs 31.34 is not remarkable at all. Even nominal wages at Rs 103 is abysmally low. There is little possibility that with these wages, women's economic condition or that of their households would have improved so much that they would voluntarily quit the workforce.

CONCLUSION

The long-term decline in women's work participation in rural areas of the country has spurred a great deal of research and interest. Globally, women's participation in work has been rising and the gender gap has been closing; in India it is the obverse. It is being asserted by some that with rising incomes, women are withdrawing from the labour force and therefore, in some sense, it is a positive development. This essay contributes to this discourse and analyses women's work and the changes over time across economic classes, industries and activities in rural areas. It shows the industries and operations where women's work is declining and where it is increasing.

The trends reflect declining participation in many of the sectors that are generally considered 'women's work'. Agriculture is the biggest employer of women, but employment has come down by 1.6 million in the period between 1993–94 and 2011–12. Within agriculture, weeding, harvesting and transplanting are female-intensive tasks, but even here, work-days have grown very slowly, almost negligibly. Non-crop agriculture presents an interesting and curious study. Female intensity is high, particularly in animal husbandry, plantation, forestry and fisheries. It is striking that all these sectors posted negative growth rates in work-days, and women's work-days declined by 33.6 million in animal husbandry alone. In fact, in a country that boasts of highest production of milk, there was an absolute decline in livestock per household even as the sector was beset with problems such as increasing fodder prices and shrinking grazing lands. Policy-makers need to closely monitor the reasons for decline in the opportunities in these sectors.

The declining work opportunities in the agriculture and allied sectors were, to some extent, offset by the non-agricultural sector, in particular the construction sector, where the largest increase is recorded. In many of these occupations, work is deeply gender-segregated to the disadvantage of women. A woman may have years of experience in construction work, but she will always remain an unskilled labourer, while a man with little experience can quickly rise to become a mason and earn much more.

The analysis of wage rates may well demolish the view that women have withdrawn to the confines of domesticity because economic conditions have improved and they do not need to work anymore. Our results, as reported earlier, show extremely low real wages and a very subdued growth in real wages over this period.

It appears that neglect and sluggish growth of agriculture, rapid mechanisation and lack of development of new industries have pushed women out of the workforce in rural areas. When jobs are scarce, pervasive patriarchal mindsets dictate that men are the breadwinners and have the first claim on scarce jobs. As a consequence, women leave the labour force. Urgent initiatives are needed to revive the rural economy, create more productive jobs for women, as well as to put in place the infrastructure to take care of young children and older people so as to arrest the decline of female work participation.

Note

1. All tables are based on the authors' calculations from unit record data from the NSSO unless otherwise stated.

References

Abraham, Vinoj. 2013. 'Missing Labour or Consistent "De-feminisation"?'. *Economic and Political Weekly* 48 (31): 98–101.

Government of India (various years). 'Basic Animal Husbandry Statistics'. Delhi: Ministry of Agriculture, Department of Animal Husbandry, Dairying and Fisheries.

Gulati, A., Surbhi Jain and Nidhi Satija. 2013. 'Rising Farm Wages in India: The "Pull" and "Push" Factors'. *Commission for Agricultural Costs and Prices*. New Delhi: Department of Agriculture and Cooperation, Ministry of Agriculture, Government of India.

Himanshu. 2011. 'Employment Trends in India: A Re-examination'. *Economic and Political Weekly* 46 (37): 43–59.

Kannan, K. P., and G. Raveendran. 2012. 'Counting and Profiling the Missing Labour Force'. *Economic and Political Weekly* 47 (6): 77–80.

Mazumdar, Indrani and Neetha N. 2011. 'Gender Dimensions: Employment Trends in India, 1993–94 to 2009–10'. *Economic and Political Weekly* 46 (43): 118–126.

Neff, D., K. Sen and V. Kling. 2012. 'The Puzzling Decline in Rural Women's Labour Force Participation in India: A Re-examination'. *Working Paper No. 196*. German Institute of Global and Area Studies.

National Sample Survey Office. 2011. 'Employment and Unemployment Situation in India (July 2011–June 2012)'. NSS Report No. 554 (68/10/1), NSS 68th Round, National Sample Survey Office, Ministry of Statistics and Programme Implementation, New Delhi.

Rangarajan, C., P. I. Kaul and Seema. 2011. 'Where Is the Missing Labour Force?'. *Economic and Political Weekly* 46 (39): 68–72.

Sidhu, R. S., A. S. Bhullar and A. S. Joshi. 2005. 'Income, Employment and Productivity Growth in the Farming Sector of Punjab: Some Issues'. *Journal of Indian School of Political Economy*, January–June.

Srivastava, N., and Anjor Bhaskar. 2016. 'Dalit and Adivasi Women Workers in a "Resurgent India"'. Paper presented at the European Conference of South Asian Studies, Warsaw, 27–31 July.

9

Public Investment towards Promoting Women's Livelihoods

An Assessment

Kanika Kaul and *Saumya Shrivastava*

Creation of employment and livelihood opportunities has been recognised in national policies and programmes as an important instrument to promote gender equality. Consequently, efforts towards strengthening women's participation in the economy have focused on ensuring equal remuneration for women, creation of livelihood opportunities through wage employment programmes, ensuring conducive working conditions and promoting entrepreneurship development. However, despite these efforts, women's participation in the sphere of livelihoods is marked by sharp gender-based inequities, reflected in gaps in male and female labour force participation and economic participation rates in the country. Additionally, gender-based disparities in employment are also reflected in the wage differentials; female wages constitute only 61 and 69 per cent of male wages, in urban and rural areas, respectively, for casual employment (Mitra 2014). Moreover, over 90 per cent of women are engaged in informal sector activities that pay poorly, are not protected by labour laws, often have dismal working conditions and are vulnerable to insecurity of employment.

An important dimension of women's labour is also the invisibilisation of the unpaid work of women, which includes both subsistence activities, as well as care work. This labour of women, which does not receive any monetary rewards, is not accounted for in statistics on income and labour force. Despite most women being engaged in some kind of productive or reproductive work, it is possible that women could be fully employed and yet be poor in absolute terms. Hence, it is not simply creating access to employment or livelihoods but also the quality, recognition, remuneration of women's work as well as the conditions facilitating it that determine the economic circumstances of women; these, in turn, are influenced by broader economic policies and government interventions (Ghosh 2007).

It follows, then, that a gender-neutral macroeconomic framework, and the resultant monetary and fiscal policies, would fail to account for their differential impact on gender relations in society. In this essay, we have attempted to analyse the gender responsiveness of fiscal policy and the manner in which the fiscal policy has impacted government interventions in sectors and programmes that have a bearing on women's livelihoods and employment. More specifically, the essay analyses the implementation of the strategy of gender-responsive budgeting (GRB) in some of the programmes in this domain. An important dimension of women's employment pertains to their engagement as service providers in government schemes. Accordingly, the essay also outlines key concerns with women's engagement as service providers in some flagship programmes of the government of India.

The essay is structured in three sections. It begins with a discussion on the magnitude of overall public spending in India, arguing that the fiscal policy in the country has been rather constrained, owing primarily to a low tax–GDP ratio. It argues that women's higher dependence on public provisioning of essential services, limited government spending, especially on social sectors, is likely to have a disproportionately adverse impact on them. This also has implications for the employment opportunities and unpaid care work performed by women. The second section discusses the need for GRB and highlights the efforts at GRB by the Union government in two important sectors pertaining to women's livelihoods, that is, agriculture and public works (for example, MGNREGA). The third section briefly outlines key concerns with women's engagement as service providers in some flagship programmes of the government of India. It highlights the excessive reliance on underpaid labour of women for implementation of these programmes.

Public Spending on Social Sectors and Implications for Women's Livelihoods

A discussion on the fiscal policy of the country is necessary, as the fiscal space available to the government determines the scope of its interventions both directly for women's livelihoods, as well as in critical social sectors such as education and health, which have a bearing on women's engagement in paid work as well as the unpaid work of women. The following section argues that women's dependence on public provisioning of essential services is higher than that of men. Hence, the low magnitudes of public investment in these sectors, an outcome of the low tax–GDP ratio, has implications not only for the overall wellbeing of women, but also specifically for their livelihood and employment.

Greater Dependence of Women on Public Provisioning of Essential Services

Women's dependence on publicly provided essential services, especially in social sectors, tends to be higher than that of men. Accordingly, deficiencies in these services, as a result of inadequate public spending, are likely to have a disproportionately adverse impact on women's labour. For instance, Agarwal (2001) observes that 'access to public health facilities, sanitation, safe drinking water are not only general issues, they also have a gender specificity in that women are affected not only by their own ill-health but also, as principal caregivers, by that of their families'. This becomes clearer on a closer examination of women's reliance on public provisioning of other services.

It is observed that the dependence of women on public provisioning of healthcare services is high. An underfunded, weak public health system has both direct and indirect implications for women. For instance, data from the Ministry of Health and Family Welfare et al. (2009) shows that even now, women depend more on government hospitals for deliveries. A weak public healthcare system also increases the dependence of households on private medical health facilities. Given the patriarchal nature of familial relations in most households, the higher costs associated with private healthcare are likely to restrict women's access to healthcare facilities. Moreover, women also have to bear the additional burden of caregiving in situations where a family member falls ill and requires additional care.

Similarly, in education—an important precondition to employment opportunities, especially in the formal sector—it has been observed that girls depend more on government institutions as compared to boys. This is reflected in the higher enrolment rates of girl children in government schools, as compared to boys. This, in part, is attributable to the preference by the families to send the boys to private schools, as they are perceived to be providing better education than government schools. According to *PROBE Revisited* (De et al. 2011), many parents are still unwilling to invest in girls' education due to patriarchal beliefs. Generally, parents prefer to send their sons to private schools, whereas the girl child is sent to government schools (Dubochet 2013; Prasad et al. 2013). Noting that, 'If a choice has to be made between sending a boy or a girl to school, the boy will usually be given precedence', UNICEF (2002) emphasises that 'most vulnerable children and girls are first to be affected when education budgets shrink'.

Even in the domain of livelihoods, it has been witnessed that the participation of women in government's employment-generation schemes has been higher than men. Two of the biggest flagship schemes of the government of India—MGNREGA (for providing wage employment in rural areas) and Ajeevika (for promoting self-employment through SHGs)—have seen high rates of participation by women. During 2013–14, a total of 2.9 crore households were provided employment under MGNREGA, with women making up 56 per cent of the beneficiaries (up to September 2013). The person-days employment for women is well above the stipulation of one-third as per the Act. Similarly, under Ajeevika, women constitute more than 50 per cent of beneficiaries.

As noted previously, social sectors like health and education are intricately linked with women's livelihoods and labour, both directly and indirectly. Not only do these sectors have a strong bearing on factors such as human capital and employment avenues, which enhance livelihood opportunities available to women, women's high dependence on them also calls for an analysis of the adequacy of public spending on social sectors. A close look at the quantum of government expenditure on these sectors reflects that the restricted fiscal policy followed in India since the 1980s has had an adverse effect on public investment in critical social sectors. The overall public investment in India has been low, both in absolute terms as well as in comparison to some other countries, owing mainly to the low tax–GPD ratio in India (see Figure 9.1, and Tables 9.1 and 9.2). This has resulted in low magnitude of resources available with the government for expenditure. Government expenditure in India, as a proportion of GDP, has remained almost stagnant at around 27 per cent, from 2001 till 2012 (see Table 9.1). This is much lower than the ratio for most countries such as Brazil, Russia, India, China, South Africa and Mexico (the BRICSAM countries), that is, 40 per cent for Brazil, 33 per cent for South Africa and 38 per cent for Russia during the same period. This, in turn, has resulted in low public investment

Figure 9.1: Tax–GDP Ratio and Total Government Spending to GDP Ratio: India, Brazil and OECD Average, 2010

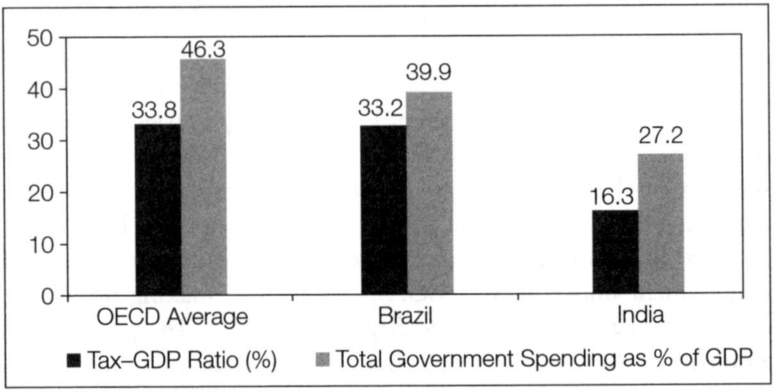

Note: Figures as of 2010.

Source: Compiled by Centre of Budget Governance and Accountability (CBGA) from International Monetary Fund (2014); Organisation for Economic Cooperation and Development (2014); Government of India (2013).

Table 9.1: Total Government Expenditure to GDP Ratio for BRICSAM Countries, 2001–12

Country/Year	2001	2006	2011	2012
Brazil	36.1	38.0	39.2	40.4
Russia	33.7	31.1	35.9	37.5
India	26.8	26.5	26.7	26.9
China	17.9	18.9	23.9	24.8
South Africa	25.9	28.2	31.9	32.6
Mexico	21.2	22.6	26.3	27.2

Source: Compiled by CBGA from International Monetary Fund (2014).

Table 9.2: Per Capita Government Expenditures: India, Other BRICS Countries and OECD Average, 2001–11

	General Government Expenditures Per Capita US$, at Current Prices and PPPs)	
	2001	**2011**
OECD average	10,716	16,548
Russia	3,395	7,917
Brazil	2,638	4,564
South Africa	1,784	3,537
China	469	2,004
India	422	997

Source: Compiled by CBGA from Organisation for Economic Cooperation and Development (2014).

in social sectors, adversely impacting both the quality and coverage of publicly provided essential services in the country.

Low Public Spending on Social Sectors

Both the Union government and state governments spend on social sectors, with states making up a major part of the public spending on these sectors. The spending of Union government on social services was merely 1.9 per cent of GDP in 2012–13, as per the budget estimate (BE), and has not crossed 2 per cent of the GDP in any year since 2004–05. However, spending by states on social sectors has also not been very substantial. Figure 9.2 shows the combined expenditure by the Centre and states on some of the critical social sectors, both in absolute terms and as a proportion of the GDP. Though in absolute terms there has been a consistent increase in government spending on these critical sectors, as a proportion of GDP, there has not been a significant increase. From 1989 to 2017–18 (BE), the combined expenditure by Centre and states on these has consistently remained below 5 per cent of GDP (see Figure 9.2 and Table 9.3).

Looking specifically at the education and health sectors, the analysis reveals that India's public spending on both health and education as a proportion of GDP is way below that of several developed and developing countries (in 2010) (see Figure 9.3).

Inadequate public spending on social sectors has constrained the effectiveness of government interventions in these sectors. This is

Figure 9.2: Combined Expenditure of the Centre and States on Education, Family Welfare, Medical and Public Health, and Water Supply and Sanitation, 1989–90 to 2017–18

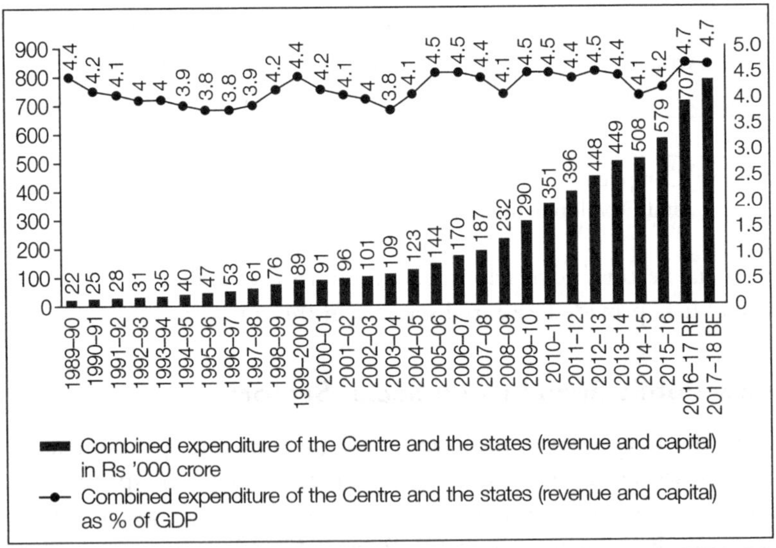

Note: GDP is at current prices and market prices, with base year 2004–05.
Source: Compiled by CBGA from Government of India, various years.

Table 9.3: Combined Expenditure of the Centre and States (Revenue and Capital) on Education, Family Welfare, Medical and Public Health, and Water Supply and Sanitation, 1989–90 to 2017–18

	1989–90	1990–91	1991–92	1992–93	1993–94	1994–95	1995–96	1996–97	1997–98	1998–99	1999–2000	2000–01	2001–02	2002–03	2003–04
Combined expenditure (Rs '000 crore)	22	25	28	31	35	40	47	53	61	76	89	91	96	101	109
Combined expenditure (as % of GDP)	4.4	4.2	4.1	4.0	4.0	3.9	3.8	3.8	3.9	4.2	4.4	4.2	4.1	4.0	3.8

	2004–05	2005–06	2006–07	2007–08	2008–09	2009–10	2010–11	2011–12	2012–13	2013–14	2014–15	2015–16	2016–17 RE	2017–18 BE
Combined expenditure (Rs '000 crore)	123	144	170	187	232	290	351	396	448	499	508	579	707	784
Combined expenditure (as % of GDP)	4.1	4.5	4.5	4.4	4.1	4.5	4.5	4.4	4.5	4.4	4.1	4.2	4.7	4.7

Source: Compiled by CBGA from Government of India, various years.

reflected in both the quality and coverage of services in these sectors (Centre of Budget Governance and Accountability 2012, 2013; Khan and Das 2014; Planning Commission 2013; Srinivasan 2015). When viewed from the perspective of women, this becomes even more critical. For example, cuts in public spending on education restrict access of women to quality education, in turn limiting their access to employment opportunities, particularly in the formal sector. As noted earlier, a cut in government's investment on health not only increases the out-of-pocket (OOP) expenditure of the family, resulting in shrinking of resources available within the household for

Figure 9.3: Comparison of Public Spending on Health and Education as a Proportion of the GDP for Select Countries, 2010

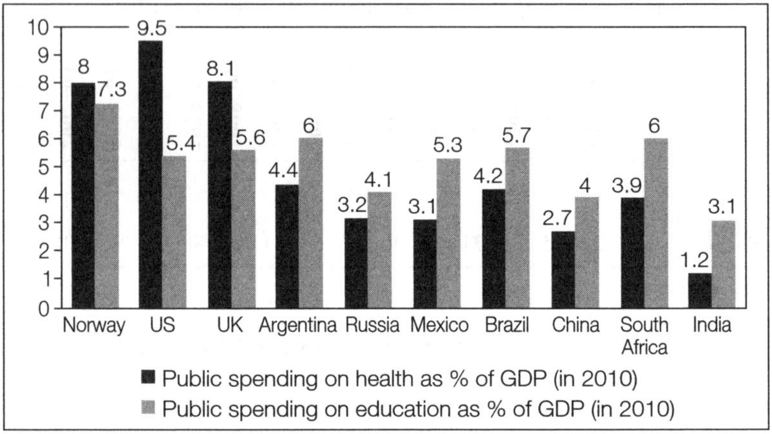

Note: The figure for China is based on UNESCO data and not the source cited below.

Source: Compiled by CBGA from United Nations Development Programme (2013).

women's needs, it also substantially increases the care burden of women in tending to the ill. Similarly, any cuts in budgets for improving water supply increase the labour of women in travelling long distances to fetch water for the need of the family, as fetching water for household needs is typically the responsibility of the women. Moreover, if the government were to scale down or withdraw the major livelihood programmes like MGNREGA or National Rural Livelihood Mission (NRLM), a large number of women, who are dependent on these programmes, would lose their livelihoods.

Apart from analysing the gender responsiveness of fiscal policy, another question that merits some discussion is the extent to which fiscal policy in general is responsive to the needs and demands emerging from the grass-roots. What is the space available for citizens to articulate their needs and concerns from government budgets? Are there institutional spaces available for people to participate in the planning and budgetary processes in the country?

The enactment of the 73rd and 74th Constitutional Amendments paved the way for establishing an institutional architecture and processes for decentralised planning in the country. Additionally, in several flagship programmes of the Union government such as the Sarva Shiksha Abhiyan (SSA) (Universal Education Campaign), National Rural Health Mission (NRHM) and MGNREGA that have a direct bearing on women's wellbeing, mechanisms have been created to enable a bottom-up process of planning. It follows, therefore, that the budgets formulated on the basis of such bottom-up planning would be more responsive to the felt needs emerging from grass-roots.

However, owing to limited fiscal decentralisation from states to local bodies and weak institutional capacity at the sub-state level, the process of decentralised planning has met with limited success. Barring a few exceptions, such as the People's Plan Campaign in Kerala—where an elaborate exercise of decentralised planning at the local level was undertaken, backed by a robust institutional architecture and processes—and a few other states like Karnataka and Maharashtra, experience points to limited efficacy of decentralised planning processes. Thus, the process of budgeting is by and large a centralised process where the scope for citizens to influence priority setting is fairly limited. It is, therefore, even more important that concerted efforts are made to make the government's plans and programmes more responsive to the challenges confronted by and needs of the disadvantaged: in this case, women.

GRB in Sectors Pertaining to Livelihoods of Women

An analysis of the fiscal policy being pursued in the country over the last decade or so reflects that it has not been very conducive to promoting social inclusion, particularly from a gender perspective. However, an analysis of the gender responsiveness of public policies and programmes also requires an examination of the implementation of GRB as an important policy strategy to address gender imbalances through government interventions.

Budgets are an important fiscal policy instrument for translating the government's priorities into outcomes. Though budgets are perceived to affect everyone in a uniform way, the manner in which governments raise and spend resources have marked gender implications. It is this recognition that has led to the adoption of GRB in the country in 2005–06. The strategy aims to incorporate a gender lens through the entire cycle of policy development, programme design, formulation of budgets as well as their implementation and monitoring. Though, even after a decade of its introduction, this policy strategy has not had a substantive impact, owing to a narrow interpretation of the strategy and its limited adoption, its proper implementation could lead to a substantive improvement in the outcomes of government schemes and programmes for women.

Against this backdrop, the following section analyses the implementation of GRB in two areas crucial to promoting livelihoods of women, that is, public works (MGNREGA) and agriculture.

GRB in MGNREGA

Public works programmes in India have traditionally offered a unique opportunity for women to earn cash incomes in a context where, too often, their ability to work outside the home is severely constrained by social norms (Narayan and Das 2014). Research in this field has also highlighted the potential of public employment programmes in promoting women's access to labour markets. In this context, the introduction of the National Rural Employment Guarantee Act (NREGA) in 2006 (renamed as MGNREGA in 2009) is an important development from a gender perspective. Though the primary objective of the programme is to guarantee 100 days of wage employment per year to rural households, it also has a number of provisions that seek to encourage women's participation in the programme.

The labour market in India is characterised by gender disparities in wages and participation. Not only are the market wages earned by women usually lower than the minimum wages, there is also a significant gender-wage gap in unskilled labour. While the average casual daily wage rate (in 2004–05), for men stood at Rs 101.5, the same for females was Rs 68.9 per day. Apart from wage disparities, women's work participation rates have also been low and declining. Data from the NSSO indicates a negative trend in women's work participation ratio in rural areas from 25 per cent in 2004–05 to 17 per cent in 2011–12.

A number of provisions under MGNREGA aim to address disadvantages faced by women in wage employment. This is reflected both in the earmarking of budgetary provisions for women under the scheme as well in the design of the scheme itself. The scheme guidelines mandate that a minimum of one-third of the beneficiaries under the programme, who have registered and requested for work, must be women. Accordingly, 33.3 per cent of the scheme's total allocations are reported in the Gender Budget Statement (GBS).[1] Though this stipulated benchmark has not been met in several states including Nagaland, Assam, Mizoram, Jammu and Kashmir and Uttar Pradesh, the participation of women in the programme, for the country as a whole, has been well above the mandated one-third, ranging from 40 per cent in 2006–07 to 53 per cent in 2013–14.

Besides the provision of one-third reservation for women, MGNREGA has several other wage and non-wage provisions that seek to strengthen women's participation in the programme. An important provision in this regard is the entitlement of equal wages to women and men under the programme. The Act also provides that work should be provided within 5 km of the residence of the workers, a provision which makes the scheme particularly attractive to women, who face a high burden of domestic responsibilities and restricted mobility. MGNREGA guidelines also provide childcare facilities at work sites, though reports from the field indicate that this provision is often not implemented. Equally important is the recognition of pregnant and lactating mothers as a special category for whom special work, which requires less effort and is close to their house, is required to be identified.

The MGNREGA guidelines also pay attention to women in special circumstances; widowed, deserted and destitute women are required to be identified by Gram Panchayats and covered under the programme. Besides this, several other sections of the population, in which women face double burdens of discrimination, are identified as vulnerable. These include persons with disabilities, Primitive Tribal Groups, Nomadic Tribal Groups, De-notified Tribes, senior citizens above 65 years of age, HIV-positive persons and internally displaced persons. The scheme guidelines require state governments to formulate specific plans to include these special categories in MGNREGA. This could entail specific works identified for these groups and provision within the management information system (MIS) for tracking their coverage.

Several observers have attempted to examine the outcome of the programme for women. Kelkar (2011) argues that relevant literature reveals only some anecdotal evidence on the impact of employment creation under MGNREGA on gender relations. However, credible evidence is available on women's participation in MGNREGA-generated employment. It has also been pointed that the design and implementation of MGNREGA should be strengthened to avoid exacerbating gender inequalities. In this regard, flexible working hours and broadening the scope of work to include such public works as to reduce women's time poverty have been discussed (Holmes et al. 2011).

Azam (2011) argues that there is a strong gender dimension to the impact of MGNREGA. Using NSSO data and analysing phase-wise implementation of the programme, the study found that the decline in LFPR has been slower in MGNREGA districts than in districts where the programme was not implemented. This effect is more pronounced in the case of female labour participation. The implementation of the programme has also had a positive impact on the wages of casual workers, with the real wages for female casual workers increasing 8 per cent more in MGNREGA districts compared to the other districts, as opposed to just 1 per cent for men (even though there is a marginal gender gap in wage rates for casual labour in MGNREGA).

On the issue of women's participation in MGNREGA, using data from the 2004–05 NSSO survey, Dasgupta and Sudarshan (2011) note that 'state-wise participation in the programme is positively correlated with women's participation in rural areas, though women's participation in NREGA is often higher than women's participation in other forms of recorded work'. They also find a negative correlation between women's participation in MGNREGA and the existing gender-wage gap in unskilled agricultural labour. Wherever women's actual wages as a share of men's are lower in the private sector, women turn to MGNREGA. This, they highlight, will increase women's bargaining power, and could potentially contribute to reduced gender disparities in the labour market.

Despite evidence of the potential that MGNREGA holds to reduce poverty and inequality in rural areas in general, and for women in particular, budgetary outlays for the scheme have been well below the estimated requirements. For the period of the Twelfth Five Year Plan (2012–17) alone, the Ministry of Rural Development had proposed an amount of Rs 3.6 lakh crore for the scheme. Against this, the amount approved was less than half, that is, of Rs 1.65 lakh crore. The allocations in the same period have not witnessed significant increases. Patnaik (2014) points out that MGNREGA being demand-driven, the allocations to the scheme should be flexible, subject to the demand for the programme. Though this is acknowledged in principle, in practice, allocations to the scheme do not get revised even when demand for work increases, resulting in delayed payments, and wage arrears. Consequently, there has been a rationing of wages which discourages workers from applying for work, leading to weakening of the programme. Given the demonstrated benefits of MGNREGA for women, the brunt of a weakening of the programme, which results from insufficient resources, is likely to be borne by women to a greater extent, impacting both the livelihoods and overall wellbeing of women.

GRB by the Department of Agriculture and Cooperation

Why Does the Agriculture Sector Matter for Livelihoods of Women?

The agriculture sector in India has seen increased participation of women due to growing rural-urban migration by the men, constituting an important source of livelihood for women. Women constitute around 40 per cent of the agricultural workforce, working in a variety of roles; from agricultural labourers, to cultivators and land managers

(Ramakrishnan and Nagar 2011). Kelkar (2009) points out that this increasing participation of women in agriculture is mainly due to increasing rural-urban migration by men, rise of women-headed households and growth in the production of cash crops which are labour-intensive in nature. Women perform significant tasks, both in farm as well as non-farm activities and their participation in the sector is increasing.

What are the Challenges Impacting Women's Livelihoods in the Agriculture Sector?

Women engaged in agricultural activities are confronted with a number of challenges. They face difficulties in using agricultural tools and technologies whose design is not women-friendly. Also, these are often more suited for larger irrigated land, whose ownership largely lies with men; women being poorer, often work on smaller pieces of land. Moreover, in the absence of ownership of productive assets, women's access to credit or government subsidies and schemes is restricted. Since, in most cases, women do not have ownership over land and other productive assets, they are unable to benefit from the programmes of the government, most of which are tied to ownership of these productive assets. Ramakrishnan and Nagar (2011) observe that 'among women-headed rural households, a lack of land titles reduces access to credit, inputs and information on new technologies'. In the period 2004–06, men received 94 per cent of the direct agricultural credit while they comprised around 67 per cent of the total cultivators. 'Women received on an average only 6 percent of the total direct agricultural credit in the same period' (Chavan 2008).

Moreover, there are also social taboos against women's participation in certain agricultural activities which are considered inappropriate for women. Within the sector, women are engaged in more labour-intensive tasks such as weeding, sowing, etc. A more fundamental problem is also linked with the fact that women's work on own family farms is treated as an extension of their household work, and adds a dual burden of domestic responsibilities.

A large proportion of women in agriculture are engaged as agricultural labourers. However, there is a marked difference in the wages being paid to men and women for same activities. Labour statistics (Labour Bureau 2015) show that for any given activity within the agriculture sector, wages being paid to women are lower than wages for men. Kelkar (2009) observes that 'employers and contractors offer simply lower wages to women, regardless of their performance on the job', implying that the wage differential is built on a pre-assumed gender character.

Given the multiple challenges that women face in the agriculture sector, the Department of Agriculture and Cooperation (DAC) under the Ministry of Agriculture has initiated several measures to mainstream the gender concerns in its programmes.

What are the Efforts Made by the DAC to Address these Challenges?

The department has been working to improve women's access to requisite inputs, technology and other resources, in addition to building their capacities and knowledge base through 'gender mainstreaming'. To pursue this, a National Gender Resource Centre for Agriculture (NGRCA) was set up in the department in 2004–05 for identifying and integrating gender concerns in the department's policies and programmes. Subsequently, a Gender Budget Cell was formed in 2009–10, with the objective of mainstreaming gender concerns in the policies of the department, engendering the design of programmes, and earmarking of funds for women farmers.

1. **Earmarking funds for women beneficiaries:** The department reported around eight schemes in the GBS till 2013–14 (BE). However, from the year 2014–15 (BE), the department reported only two programmes: the National Food Security Mission and National Mission on Oilseeds and Oil Palm (NMOOP), which are Centrally Sponsored Schemes (CSSs).[2] This change has primarily been due to the restructuring of some schemes within the department into larger mission-mode programmes. The department's efforts at addressing gender concerns through its schemes focus on both earmarking of specific proportions of funds under some schemes, as well as introducing specific measures for women. The department mandates that at least

30 per cent funds should be earmarked for women farmers under most beneficiary-oriented schemes of the department. Correspondingly, the department has reported 30 per cent of the total allocations under these schemes, in Part B of the GBS.

2. **Making the schemes' design gender-responsive:** In addition, there are other schemes where, though specific earmarking of benefits for women is not done, certain other provisions have been instituted. One such example is the Integrated Scheme of Oilseeds, Pulses, Maize and Oilpalm (ISOPOM), which provides a higher subsidy component for women and other disadvantaged groups. Similarly, the scheme on Support for Extension Services stipulates involvement of women as 'Farmer Friends' and their representation in Farmers Advisory Committees set up at block/district and state levels (Department of Agriculture and Cooperation 2014).

The department has also been working to develop gender-friendly tools and implements with Indian Council of Agricultural Research (ICAR), in order to reduce the drudgery of women. Also, the MIS of all beneficiary-oriented schemes are being revised to generate sex-disaggregated data, to enable an accurate assessment of benefits accruing to women farmers through the department's schemes. Such sex-disaggregated data would also help the department plan its policies better and make the requisite revisions to make its schemes more accessible to women. The department has also taken steps for gender sensitisation of extension functionaries at all levels within the department.

Are these Interventions Adequate?

Despite the significant efforts by the DAC to address some of the gender concerns in the agriculture sector, there are some additional factors that continue to restrict women's access to the schemes and programmes of the department. As has been pointed out previously, one major factor is the lack of ownership of productive assets, especially land. Women carry out substantial activities both in cultivation as well as non-farm activities; yet, 'women continue to have limited access to productive resources and services, markets and marketing facilities' (Ramakrishnan and Nagar 2011), which hinders their effective participation in the sector. At the same time, the differential wage rates prevalent in the labour market in the agriculture sector are also an issue. At another level, the whole approach which treats women's labour in own farms as an extension of domestic household chore, is also a concern.

While these are some issues that cannot be addressed by DAC alone and require some changes in overall socio-cultural norms and also the larger policy framework, the department could work towards bringing in some flexibility in the norms of its own schemes and programmes. One such step could be to de-link the schemes with the ownership of the productive assets and give recognition to 'user rights'. Nevertheless, the efforts by DAC are encouraging and need to be expanded and replicated by other departments as well.

Are Allocations Enough to Ensure Better Outcomes?

An important point that emerges from the foregoing discussion is that effective implementation of GRB is contingent equally on both gender-responsive scheme designs and adequate budgetary allocations for such schemes. It follows, thus, that departments need to simultaneously focus on engendering their respective schemes and at the same time ensure that they are adequately funded for the desired outcomes to be achieved. While a poorly designed scheme fails to address the specific challenges restricting women's access to livelihood in these sectors, a poorly funded scheme, no matter how gender-responsive in design, would not succeed in achieving the objective of promoting women's livelihoods. For example, if under MGNREGA, adequate funds are not allocated for construction and maintenance of crèches at work sites or if the Department of Agriculture does not budget adequately to support development of women-friendly agricultural implements, these gender-responsive measures would fail to encourage women's livelihoods. Similarly, if these schemes do not have provisions to address factors restricting women's access, even if well budgeted for, they would fail to promote women's livelihoods.

Also, it would be pertinent to reiterate that, as mentioned previously, the strategy of GRB is concerned with incorporating a gender perspective in each stage of the budgetary process, including programme implementation. Hence, for GRB to be meaningful and achieve desired outcomes for women's livelihoods, it is important that need-based planning and adequate budgeting are supplemented by effective scheme implementation. Often, well-designed and well-budgeted schemes fail to get implemented properly owing to a host of factors constraining their efficacy on the ground. Unless the schemes promoting women's livelihoods reach the intended beneficiaries, their impact would remain limited. For example, as has been discussed earlier, poor implementation of MGNREGA due to delays in wage payments restricts women's access to wage employment under the scheme. As Ghosh (2015) notes, when wage payments get delayed due to budget cuts, 'workers get disheartened and reduce their demand for work even when they need it; in other cases, the state and local authorities try to dissuade them or do not register their demand because they do not have the funds to provide the required work'.

Restricted access of women and under-valuation of their labour is not confined to specific sectors. The way women's work outside the home is being conceptualised has largely been marred by pre-conceived notions with regard to the 'caregiving' role of women and underlying assumptions that their labour is worth less than that of men; this is the case even in the government. The following section discusses the role of women as service providers in government schemes and brings to fore some issues in women's engagement as service providers in some flagship schemes of the government of India.

Women as Service Providers in Government Schemes

An important dimension of women in public employment pertains to their engagement as frontline service providers in various flagship schemes of the Union government. Public employment is often thought of as a better option for women as it provides better wages, working conditions and other benefits, such as paid maternity leave, often not provided by private employers and almost never in the informal sector (Ghosh 2009). However, an analysis of the nature of employment, the workload, the outcomes that this cadre of workers are expected to deliver and the compensation in lieu of the services rendered raises some serious concerns.

The implementation of important flagship schemes of the government of India, including the Integrated Child Development Scheme (ICDS) and National Health Mission (NHM) relies upon the underpaid labour of a large cadre of women serving as grass-roots level functionaries. Over 20 lakh women in the country are engaged as Anganwadi Workers (AWWs) and Anganwadi Helpers (AWHs), while over 8 lakh women serve as ASHA workers under NHM in rural areas alone (Ministry of Health and Family Welfare 2014). Women frontline service providers under both programmes work on contractual employment, with no job and little income security.

ICDS is one of the world's largest community-based programmes aimed at addressing nutritional, health and other development needs of young children, and pregnant and lactating women implemented through 12.4 lakh Anganwadi Centres (AWCs) across the country. Each AWC is managed by an AWW and an AWH. Each AWC is responsible for an extensive range of activities including providing supplementary nutrition to children below six years, pregnant and lactating mothers, immunisation, nutrition and health education, basic health check-up, and non-formal pre-school education to children of three to five years. The roles and responsibilities envisaged for AWWs under ICDS include an extensive list of 21 functions. Additionally, AWWs and AWHs are also routinely assigned tasks such as duties during election and Census surveys. Besides this, several other schemes (currently in pilot phase), such as Indira Gandhi Matritva Sahyog Yojana (Maternity Benefit Programme) and Rajiv Gandhi Scheme for Empowerment of Adolescent Girls are also being implemented from the ICDS platform, the implementation of which adds to the existing workload of these functionaries.

Despite the responsibilities expected to be performed by these functionaries, the scheme treats the AWWs and AWHs as honorary workers rendering their services for 4–5 hours a day. Notwithstanding the fact that in practice they have to work longer hours, women workers under ICDS are not recognised as government employees. Collectives of AWWs have for long been fighting for regularisation of their work, payment of minimum wages of skilled workers to AWWs and unskilled workers for helpers, social security benefits, paid medical leave, among others.

However, these efforts have met with little success. It is, in fact, worth noting that a Supreme Court ruling in 2006 held that AWWs do not hold civil positions, and the Minimum Wages Act is not applicable to them. Accordingly, they are paid an honorarium instead of wages, and continue to be out of the ambit of the Minimum Wages Act. For the services rendered by them, the honorarium paid to AWWs was revised from Rs 1,500 to Rs 4,500 per month and that of AWHs from Rs 750 to Rs 2,250 per month in 2018. It is also a concern that though the honorarium paid to these workers has been revised periodically, there is no mechanism in place for such a revision to take place on a regular basis.

The compensation paid to AWWs and AWHs does get supplemented by additional honorarium provided by some states, though this amount varies significantly from state to state. For instance, while Bihar does not provide any additional honorarium to AWWs and AWHs, the additional honorarium paid by Goa to AWWs varies between Rs 2,752 and Rs 4,200 for AWWs, and Rs 1,700 and Rs 2,300 for AWHs (based on qualifications and experience) per month. It is interesting to note, however, that in the case of Goa, even with the additional honorarium, the amounts paid to an AWW and AWH at the starting level (that is, Rs 5,752 and Rs 3,200, respectively) is below the State minimum wages of Rs 6,450 per month (Indian Staffing Federation 2014). Additional benefits extended to them include insurance cover under Anganwadi Karyakartri Bima Yojana (an insurance scheme for Anganwadi workers) and paid maternity leave for 180 days. AWWs and AWHs are, however, not entitled to pension, with the exception of some states like Karnataka, Tamil Nadu, Andhra Pradesh and Kerala. A few states have also introduced welfare schemes for the benefit for AWWs and AWHs. The Parliamentary Standing Committee on Empowerment of Women in a report, 'Working Conditions of Anganwadi Workers' (2011), has made several recommendations to improve the working conditions of these functionaries. The Committee has pointed out the need to assess the workload of AWWs and the adequacy of incentives stipulated for their services, stating that it is 'humanly impossible to perform the expected jobs within the stipulated time of 4–5 hours a day' (ibid.). The Committee has also recommended a mechanism for a periodical review and revision of the honoraria, benefits like yearly increments and dearness allowance. On the issue of insurance coverage, a doubling of the coverage and extending of some health insurance scheme or Employees' State Insurance (ESI) benefits to AWWs/AWHs is recommended.

As is the case with ICDS, the implementation of NHM hinges upon the unpaid labour of ASHA workers, who are expected to be the first port of call for any health-related demand. Each ASHA is expected to serve a population of 1,000. Their responsibilities include a wide array of activities including universal immunisation, referral and escort services for reproductive and child health (RCH), construction of household toilets and other healthcare delivery programmes. They facilitate preparation of Village Health Plans along with AWWs, functionaries of other departments and SHG members. Anecdotal evidence suggests that in addition to the already existing workload, ASHAs are also expected to carry out activities assigned to them by states. The responsibilities of ASHAs may require them to often work odd hours and travel long distances, without the necessary infrastructure and facilities such as transport and overnight stay at hospitals while escorting pregnant women.

As envisaged under NHM, the work of ASHAs is to be tailored in such a manner that it does not interfere with her normal livelihood. Consequently, ASHA workers, too, are not recognised as full-time workers but as honorary workers. They are not entitled to wages or honorarium; instead, they receive performance-based compensation which varies from state to state. ASHAs have been ascribed different roles in different contexts; however, irrespective of the roles they perform, it deprives them from any other source of livelihood. In doing so, it treats women as supplementary earners, which is a highly gendered issue (Eapen 2012).

Being honorary workers, ASHAs are not provided social security benefits such as maternity benefits and pension by the Union government. Though a few states have a fixed honorarium to supplement performance-based incentives, the overall payment to them is poor. It is reported that if an ASHA works according to expected standards, she would earn approximately Rs 1,067 and Rs 1,300 per month in Rajasthan and West Bengal, respectively, in addition to performance-based incentives, which is lower than the state minimum wages (Indian Staffing Federation 2014).

The Parliamentary Standing Committee on Empowerment of Women has also taken cognisance of the need to improve the working conditions of ASHAs and has accordingly made important recommendations. It has been suggested that several functions of the ASHAs be removed and a systematic survey be conducted to assess the workload and incentives stipulated for their services. The Committee strongly favours ASHAs receiving a fixed remuneration in addition to the usual incentives received by them. The Committee has also highlighted concerns pertaining to the security of ASHAs, who often escort pregnant women at odd hours, and recommended construction of rest rooms at hospitals by states to ensure their safety.

The practice of relying on the underpaid labour of women for implementation of such critical programmes raises gender concerns in more ways than one. Not recognising this cadre of women functionaries as workers and withholding their basic entitlements raises obvious questions of justice for these functionaries. Moreover, such a human resource policy for some of the largest and most critical programmes also raises concerns about the quality of services delivered though these programmes, on which a majority of the population, especially women and girl children, depend to meet their basic health and nutritional requirements.

Conclusion

As has been argued in this essay, women's economic circumstances and the government's ability to institute substantive interventions to strengthen women's participation in the economy is heavily contingent upon the broader macroeconomic framework. It is important to recognise that macroeconomic policy formulation, often regarded as a technocratic process, has marked gender implications. Fiscal policy, an important element of the macroeconomic policy, is crucial in shaping up the development framework adopted in a country. The total quantum of resources available for expenditure, which in turn determines the robustness of interventions in social sectors in general, and interventions for women's livelihood specifically, are determined by the country's fiscal policy.

The low level of government expenditure in the country, particularly on social sectors, is primarily a consequence of the constrained fiscal policy being pursued for the last one-and-a-half decades (2000–2014). It is important to recognise the differential gender impact of such a policy, especially from the perspective of marginalised and vulnerable women, whose dependence on public provisioning of essential services is higher than the rest of the population.

Against this backdrop, the adoption of GRB is imperative to ensure that gender-based challenges are recognised and addressed through adequate budgetary outlays. However, if the overall public spending is inadequate to effectively implement the government programmes, the GRB is bound to be limited in its ability to bridge the stark developmental deficits confronting women. It is important to recognise that gender budgeting cannot be seen as a 'public policy plug' that can address these development deficits, when the overall fiscal policy itself is not conducive to promoting their inclusion.

In the domain of women's livelihoods, the implementation of gender budgeting in some of the key Union government interventions, that is, MGNREGA and programmes of the Department of Agriculture, has recognised and addressed important gender concerns in the policy and design of these programmes. However, while inadequate outlays have constrained the implementation of MGNREGA, women's access to the schemes of DAC has been restricted, owing to various socio-cultural and economic factors (such as lack of ownership of productive assets, gender biases in labour markets, etc.).

Additionally, excessive reliance on women's underpaid labour in some of the flagship schemes of the Union government is a disquieting trend that has aggravated over the last few years (2005–2015). The responsibilities of at least some of these functionaries are proposed to increase even further with new schemes being launched from the platform of ICDS. In such a scenario, there is an urgent need to ensure minimum wages and review the working conditions of women workers engaged under ICDS and NHM.

In sum, a progressive fiscal policy made possible by a higher tax–GDP ratio and re-prioritisation of policies, budgets and the institutional framework to implement these in favour of women is essential to ensure better outcomes for women.

Notes

1. A GBS is presented as part of the Union budget each year since the adoption of gender budgeting in 2005–06. This statement presents information in two parts. Part A reports those schemes where the entire allocation is for women. Part B includes schemes where at least 30 per cent allocations, but not entire funds, are earmarked for women.
2. CSSs are the schemes and programmes which are operationalised by the central ministries, but implemented by the state governments or their designated agencies. The schemes have specific guidelines decided by the central ministries, and the budgetary outlays for these schemes are shared between the central ministry and the states in a pre-decided, fixed proportion. This sharing ratio varies across schemes.

References

Agarwal, Bina. 2001. 'Poverty in a Globalising World at Different Stages of Women's Life Cycle'. UN Expert Group Meeting on Gender and Poverty: Some Issues. New Delhi: United Nations Division for the Advancement of Women.

All-India Federation of Anganwadi Workers and Helpers. 2012. 'Charter of Demands Adopted at the Seventh Conference of AIFAWH held on 4–7 October 2012'. Available at http://aifawh.org/charter-of-demands (accessed 14 June 2014).

Azam, Mahtabul. 2011. 'The Impact of Indian Job Guarantee Scheme on Labor Market Outcomes: Evidence from a Natural Experiment'. IZA Discussion Paper No. 6548, Institute for the Study of Labor, Germany.

Centre for Budget and Governance Accountability. 2012. 'Unfulfilled Promises?: Response to Union Budget 2012–13'. Government of India, New Delhi.

———. 2013. 'How Has the Dice Rolled?: Response to Union Budget 2013–14'. Government of India, New Delhi.

Chavan, Pallavi. 2008. *Gender Inequality in Banking Services in India: A Note.* New Delhi: Macroscan.

Committee on Empowerment of Women. 2010. 'Working Conditions of ASHAs'. Lok Sabha, Parliament of India, New Delhi.

———. 2011. 'Working Conditions of Anganwadi Workers'. Lok Sabha, Parliament of India, New Delhi.

Dasgupta, Sukti and Ratna M. Sudarshan. 2011. 'Issues in Labour Market Inequality and Women's Participation in India's National Rural Employment Guarantee Programme'. *Working Paper No. 98*. Geneva: International Labour Office.

De, Anuradha, Reetika Khera, Meera Samson and A. K. Shiva Kumar. 2011. *PROBE Revisited: A Report on Elementary Education in India.* New Delhi: Oxford University Press.

Department of Agriculture and Cooperation. 2014. *Annual Report 2013–14.* New Delhi: Government of India.

Dubochet, Lucy. 2013. 'India: Moving Towards Equal Opportunities For All?' *Oxfam India*. Available at https://www.oxfam.org/en/research/india-moving-towards-equal-opportunities-all (accessed 5 April 2014).

Eapen, Mridul. 2012. *National Rural Health Mission: Identifying Critical Gender Concerns*. New Delhi: UN Women.

Ghosh, Jayati. 2007. 'Uncovering Women's Work'. *Infochange*. Available at https://www.infochangeindia.org/agenda-issues/women-work/6492-uncovering-womens-work (accessed 6 June 2014).

———. 2009. *Never Done and Poorly Paid.* New Delhi: Women Unlimited.

———. 2015. 'India's Rural Employment Programme is Dying a Death of Funding Cuts'. *The Guardian,* 5 February. Available at https://www.theguardian.com/global-development/2015/feb/05/india-rural-employment-funding-cuts-mgnrega (accessed 10 March 2015).

Government of India. 2013. *Indian Public Finance Statistics 2012–13*. New Delhi: Ministry of Finance.

———. (various years). *Indian Public Finance Statistics*. New Delhi: Ministry of Finance.

Holmes, Rebecca, Nidhi Sadana and Saswatee Rath. 2011. 'An Opportunity for Change?: Gender Analysis of the Mahatma Gandhi National Rural Employment Guarantee Act'. Project Briefing No. 53, Overseas Development Institute, London.

Indian Staffing Federation. 2014. *Indian Staffing Industry Research 2014: Flexi Staffing in Government and Public Sector*. New Delhi: Indian Staffing Federation.

International Monetary Fund. 2014. 'Recovery Strengthens, Remains Uneven'. *World Economic Outlook*. Washington, DC: IMF.

Kelkar, Govind. 2009. *Feminisation of Agriculture in Asia: Implications for Women's Agency and Productivity*. New Delhi: UNIFEM South Asia Regional Office.

———. 2011. 'MGNREGA: Change and Continuity in Gender Relations'. *Journal of Economic and Social Development* 7 (2): 11–24.

Khan, J. A., and S. Das. 2014. 'Exclusion in Planning and Budgetary Processes'. *India Exclusion Report 2013–2014* (first edition). New Delhi: Books for Change. Available at http://www.indianet.nl/pdf/IndiaExclusionReport2013-2014.pdf (accessed 6 June 2014).

Labour Bureau. 2015. 'Wage Rates in Rural India'. Labour Statistics, February. Labour Bureau, Government of India. Available at http://labourbureau.gov.in/schemes.html (accessed 19 January 2015).

Ministry of Health and Family Welfare (India), ORG Centre for Social Research, United Nations Children's Fund. 2009. *India Coverage Evaluation Survey 2009–2010*. New Delhi: Ministry of Health and Family Welfare.

Ministry of Health and Family Welfare. 2014. *Annual Report 2013–14*. New Delhi: Government of India.

Ministry of Women and Child Development. 2013. *Annual Report 2012–13*. New Delhi: Government of India.

Mitra, Sona. 2014. *Major Dimensions of Inequality of India: Gender*. New Delhi: Centre for Budget and Governance Accountability.

Narayan, Sudha and Upasak Das. 2014. 'Women Participation and Rationing in the Employment Guarantee Scheme'. *Economic and Political Weekly* 49 (46): 46–53.

Organisation for Economic Cooperation and Development. 2014. *OECD Factbook: Economic, Environmental and Social Statistics*. Paris: OECD Publishing.

Patnaik, Prabhat. 2014. 'Dangerous Withdrawal: Against the Scrapping of Employment Guarantee'. *The Telegraph*.

Planning Commission. 2013. 'Twelfth Five Year Plan (2012–17)'. New Delhi: Government of India.

Prasad, H. A. C., N. K. Sinha and Riyaz A. Khan. 2013. *Performance of Major Social Sector Schemes: A Sample Survey Report*. New Delhi: Government of India.

Ramakrishnan, Rajesh and Shailesh Nagar. 2011. 'Small-holder Women Farmers in India'. Discussion paper for Oxfam India, New Delhi.

Srinivasan, R. 2015. 'Why is India's Healthcare System in Such a Sorry State?'. *Money Control: Step Ahead*. Available at http://www.moneycontrol.com/gestepahead/curing/article/why-is-indias-healthcare-system-in-such-a-sorry-state-945447-1.html?classic=true.

UNICEF. 2002. *Barriers to Girls' Education, Strategies, and Interventions*. New York: UNICEF. Available at https://www.unicef.org/teachers/girls_ed/BarrierstoGE.pdf (accessed 14 June 2014).

United Nations Development Programme. 2013. *Human Development Report 2013—The Rise of the South: Human Progress in a Diverse World*. New York: UNDP.

10

Women and Common Property Resources

Towards Innovative Practice beyond 'Participation'

Sumi Krishna

> Rather than have only more women's participation, we wanted more women professionals. So, as part of the women's collective we trained women, like the widowed Hakima of Dador village in geology and water management. She has transformed lives around water more than I have. We participate in her programmes. It is important to have women at the policy making level, but women could also have patriarchal attitudes.
>
> —Sushma Iyengar, Kutch Mahila Vikas Sangathana (Shedde 2012: 61)

Since the early 1990s, landscapes and resources have been transformed by economic liberalisation, global trade and the mobility of capital. The accelerated corporate demand for resources has threatened ecological sustainability and the livelihoods of poor people. Public policy at the central and state levels has hastened the exploitation of resource-rich areas, which happen to be also the economically marginalised areas. The appropriation of land, water, biodiversity, minerals and other natural resources by big global and national players with the support of the State is being accomplished through the market, and by administrative and legal measures. Under the political hegemony of a globalised right pushing for speedier growth and productivity, the pace and quantum of extraction is likely to intensify thereby deepening conflicts and impoverishment.

When development is reckoned in terms of corporate growth and profits rather than the quality of life of the poorest, there is no barrier to the State taking over so-called wastelands, adapting land-use policies to favour high-market value crops, or to privatising water and bio-resources—all ostensibly for efficient use and conservation. The informed consent of the local people is mostly assumed; they are inadequately compensated, and the loss of food, livelihood and ecological security is glossed over. Because of the patriarchal division of labour and household provisioning responsibilities, women bear the brunt of the situation. In these circumstances, the theme of 'Women and Common Property Resources' takes on greater urgency.[1]

Dynamic Resource Landscapes

Resource landscapes are not static. They are made and remade through people's labour over time: this process involves dynamic relationships among groups of people; and between people and their environment.[2] For millennia, what we now understand as 'common property resources' (CPRs)—land, water, pastures, wetlands, forests, livestock, poultry, fish, food plants and herbs—was not an objective category but was taken for granted, enmeshed with the everyday lives and labour of people, especially of women, children and the elderly. CPRs are of various kinds. First, there are shared *landscape resources*, visible environmental spaces that may be open to all, even if 'owned' and regulated by the local community or the State: forests, grasslands, wetlands, water bodies, coastal seas and so on. Second, are *collectible resources* such as the non-timber forest produce (once called minor forest produce), fuel wood, pond fish, etc., that may be gathered from the shared landscapes to provide food, medicine and the resources to sustain livelihoods. Third, are *underground resources* like deep aquifers and mineral seams which are out of sight. Fourth, there are *bio-genetic resources* including rare and endemic plants, indigenous breeds of livestock and poultry that are a common heritage. And fifth, are the skills, information and knowledge related to *indigenous crafts*, which also constitute a special kind of CPR with natural resource linkages. All these different kinds of resources are critical both for people's livelihoods and the national economy.

In pre-Independence India, feudal rulers and the colonial State privatised CPRs often in the name of the people or the 'public good' but in effect to extract revenue. After Independence, the traditional CPR regimes that had survived over decades, if not centuries, were undermined by the nature and pace of development, new administrative and legal regulations and emerging market forces. CPRs are vital for livelihood and food security, especially in times of stress; when these pass into private hands, or are taken over by the State, usufruct rights have to be re-negotiated. When the traditional means of livelihood of marginalised groups (such as tribals/Adivasis, pastoralists and artisanal fishers) are threatened, this impinges on customary resource management practices and the position of women. In many parts of India, a cluster of factors (such as demographic trends, changes in land use and diversification of livelihoods) has increased women's livelihood responsibilities and labour even as their resource rights are being curtailed. Today, with the interrelated crises in food and energy security, and climate variation, we need to reclaim for women the resource spaces and livelihood opportunities that are being swiftly eroded.

Since the mid-1970s, women have increasingly figured in the global and national discourse around CPRs. Models of resource management and development have been extended by concerns for resource control and livelihoods; discussions on women's needs have been deepened by the concept of women's rights; and assumptions of an essential, natural identity shared by all women have been replaced by more nuanced gendered perspectives. This is reflected in the academic literature, in the documents of international agencies and in national public policy statements, but not necessarily in programme interventions. To what extent has our more complex understanding of the terms of discourse helped to change the lives and livelihoods of poor women? What are the factors and circumstances that enable women to organise around shared resources and to transform their lives in the male-dominated societies of which they are a part?[3]

India's mainstream community-based natural resource management programmes have mainly addressed landscapes (forests, watersheds) and biodiversity, with mixed results. For instance, the decentralisation of water management through Water User Associations in the former Andhra Pradesh excluded the landless and women because membership was based on land ownership and women did not own land in their names (Jairath 2000; Krishna 2004a). Elsewhere, watershed programmes have created new resources using public funds but the benefits have been appropriated by those who were already better-off (Datar and Prakash 2004). The Joint Forest Management (JFM) programmes aimed to enhance women's participation through representation in local committees. In the early years of JFM in Odisha, Neera Singh found that 'even in jointly managed forest lands, the people, who are supposedly co-managers, are treated as mere hired labourers whose earnings are based on the minimum wage rate and not related to the value of the produce' (Singh 2004: 312; Vasundhara 1998). More than a decade later, in many states, despite regulations that allow local people (mainly Adivasis and women) access to non-timber forest produce, the most profitable of these resources cannot be freely gathered but are sold by auction to private agents.

Clearly, new resource rights are not easily separated from the old resource regimes (Krishna 2004a). This may be because decentralisation of resource management does not necessarily translate into democratisation; especially among communities which are not homogenous, old forms of patriarchal and class/caste privileges are re-established in new settings. Indeed, women's traditional familial nurturing role is reinforced when household needs for water, fuel wood, fodder, seeds, etc., are viewed as 'women's needs'. The unequal power relation and gendered division of labour that makes women fill the role of nurturers and resource managers and gives them these 'needs' is not questioned. So, resource management and conservation programmes tend to use women's labour, skills and knowledge in an instrumental way to improve efficiency rather than to enable women to gain control of resources and management decisions (see Krishna 1998, 2007, 2009).

Movements which have brought broad coalitions together in ecological struggles (as against opening up forest lands for mining, or the conflicts over coastal zones and water) have side-stepped women's specific concerns. Some social and environmental activists argue that highlighting women's interests will 'fragment' the struggle for rights. As I have written elsewhere (Krishna 2010), this is in line

> with the approach to the women's question within larger political formations and civil society groups who argue that the state or some other "bigger" adversary must first be fought and overthrown before taking on the struggle against patriarchy. In the regional political movements too, although women may be up front in the picket lines, they have tended to return to their hearths after the immediate objectives have been achieved.

Side-stream Interventions and Sustainable Livelihoods

I now turn to what I have called the 'side-stream' interventions (Krishna 2012a) that have sought to build sustainable livelihood alternatives based on shared resources and women's collectivity. Such interventions have been made in and across all the CPR categories mentioned earlier (that is, landscape, collectible, underground and bio-genetic resources, and knowledge of indigenous crafts). Some interventions have been facilitated by non-government organisations (NGOs); others have evolved from wider struggles on the ground. Generally, the side-stream interventions are more mindful of the interconnections both between common lands, water, forests, biodiversity, and between resource management and the socio-political contexts, and they have a more nuanced gender perspective. This distinguishes them from the mainstream natural resource management programmes. The struggles and achievements of side-stream interventions help to ground the debate on gendered resource management and sustainability.

A swathe of CPR interventions (whether large national programmes or small NGO-led projects) reinforce rather than challenge the gendered division of labour and women's unpaid work in the household and community. So, women will participate in discussions on household and domestic water use but are not present in discussions on irrigation and other productive uses of water. As Sushma Iyengar (see epigraph, Shedde 2012) says, it is not enough to just have women's participation. This is especially so if participation is viewed as an extension of women's domestic roles. Women have to move into positions of leadership and policy-making. And yet, those positions may be merely symbolic or the women may share the men's patriarchal attitudes. The 'invisible' knowledge of the women of Bhuj, gained collectively through years of struggle for water, had to be channelled and developed creatively. Iyengar (ibid.: 61) says,

> . . . we had to address social and gender relations, complex geology and strategise how women could take leadership in water management, restoration, harvesting and revival. If women dealt with drinking water, it was seen as a woman's issue, but if they dealt with agricultural water, men felt threatened. When men realized the end result was that they were all getting water, they let the women have their say.

The integrated water management achieved by the women of Bhuj is unusual for the quality of the intervention during a desperate drought and within a deeply patriarchal society.

Consider some well-documented examples over the last two decades. The M. Venkatarangaiya (better known as MV) Foundation in Ranga Reddy district of Telangana has enabled poor Dalit women to negotiate with government officials and integrate gender concerns into various land-based development schemes: managing watersheds and soils, improving fallow lands, cultivating orchards, participating in the planning process and demanding gender-equitable wage rates (Swaminathan and Jeyranjan 2008). So, too, the Deccan Development Society (DDS) has enabled Dalit women in the Medak and Zaheerabad districts to reclaim their position in the community as seed-keepers and their decision-making role in food production, despite tremendous opposition at all levels (Rao, n.d.). In the hills of East Godavari district, the work of an NGO, Anthra, with women forest-dwellers has helped to stabilise the Aseel strain of backyard poultry, which had rapidly declined in the 1990s due to changes in the cropping pattern and problems with the government veterinary system (Anthra 2008). Together with their communities, the women's *gottis* (groups) first increased the land under food crops and then used the crop residues as nutrition for their backyard poultry. They learnt to vaccinate their birds and to prepare and use herbal remedies. More birds were consumed at home and birds were sold at an older age earning a higher price. A decade after the intervention, household incomes have improved and the women have begun to rebuild what used to be a diverse food and farming system (Ramdas and Ghotge 2007). Such side-stream initiatives reflect that it is possible to safeguard and develop a traditional resource management system and create alternative livelihood opportunities while strengthening women's collective position in their communities.

Not all side-stream interventions, however, survive over the longer term. Smita Tewari-Jassal (2004) has drawn attention to the case of low-caste Mallahin agricultural labourers and pond-fishers in northern Bihar. With the help of Aditi, an NGO, the women negotiated a 10-year lease from the State Forest Department for cooperative rights to fish in their village pond. The women had to struggle to overcome the hostility of their own families, upper-caste men and Muslim fishermen in the village. Their hard-won collective rights to a productive resource opened up opportunities within the agrarian economy. But when the lease expired because of a government policy that sets a 10-year limit for such leases, the women's only option was to revert to their earlier occupation as wage labourers on the upper-caste farmers' fields. Bhulia Devi, a member of the Mallahin women's pond fisheries cooperative in Madhubani, Bihar, told Tewari-Jassal:

> Then we were veiled. Now that our *ghunghats* (veils) are off, and we have seen courts, *katcheri* (collectorate), attended meetings in Delhi, Calcutta, Orissa, Gujarat, Madhubani how can we go back to the hearth? ... Just to meet the collector to persuade him to give us the ponds, we made so many trips. Each trip cost at least Rs 100 and the collector says "Go". If they take away our livelihoods they will be guilty of *tiriya vadh* (murder of women, femicide). (Ibid.)

For these women, the loss of livelihood was akin to the loss of life.

As Tewari-Jassal (2004: 42) points out, for the poor Dalit fisher-women, their empowerment was 'ephemeral' against the combined power of the state, an unsympathetic bureaucracy and upper-caste/class adversaries. One might also surmise that to whatever extent the women gained the support of the community and the district authorities to claim a livelihood resource, the same support did not extend to the social sphere which continued to be as dominated by upper-caste/class males as before.

It is rare for a struggle around CPRs to simultaneously and deliberately address the inter-linkages of class/caste and patriarchy. One example is that of the Stree Mukti Sangharsh Chalwal (SMSC), the women's front of the Mukti Sangharsh Chalwal (Liberation Struggle) in southern Maharashtra, which has striven for the equitable distribution of water among other issues (see Kulkarni and Bhatt 2010; Kulkarni 2011). The struggle of thousands of *parityakta* or single women for homestead land rights included mainly upper-caste widows and deserted women. One group of 23 women succeeded in getting the government to legally transfer a plot of land (two *gunthas*—less than half an acre) to each of them for a nominal fee. The land had earlier been 'acquired' by the government to rehabilitate flood-displaced people but this did not happen, and the original owners (who continued to cultivate it) opposed the women's allotment in court. With the intervention of committed feminists and women's groups in Maharashtra and of the India Centre for Human Rights and the Law, Mumbai, after 13 years, the Mumbai High Court ruled in favour of the women. The women from the other villages, however, continued to struggle for homestead land. Seema Kulkarni (2011), who participated in the early phase of the SMSC struggle says, 'How far the demand gets an audience largely depends on the strength of the movements working on class, caste, tribe, ethnicity and gender issues in the state and their readiness to make alliances with each other to establish rights over resources'.

Craft Skills and Knowledge

A special kind of CPR (the fifth kind in my categorisation above) is a shared heritage of craft skills and knowledge. This case is from the Mithila region of northern Bihar where the women's routine painting on mud walls and floors was a customary, collective ritual activity (Krishna 2009).[4] Traditionally, a woman's caste determined the subjects and stylistic elements available to her. Upper-caste women painted mythological themes in a range of colour, while lower-caste women were restricted to nature, such as the tree of life against a background of bistre, the colour of pale burnt wood. Following a prolonged drought and crop failure during 1966–68, the All-India Handicrafts Board (a central government organisation) encouraged village women to supplement their income by painting on handmade paper for sale. This led to a burst of creativity around villages such as Jitwarpur and Madhubani and a new innovative idiom emerged. Lower-caste women broke free from their thematic and chromatic restrictions. A few women gained wider recognition as folk artists. Gender distinctions were eroded as some men, too, began to paint. Even as the majority of Mithila women continue to paint their homes in the customary manner, the now-famous Madhubani paintings on cloth or paper have become valuable commodities. Today, sons, brothers, husbands manage the women's artwork, marketing the paintings in metropolitan centres. Now, women are responsible for production; men control the trade.

Since the 1990s, the more lucrative sales of Madhubani art (like other folk arts and crafts) have been on the Internet. India succeeded in getting Madhubani paintings the international Geographical Indications or 'GI' status under the World Trade Organisation's (WTO) Geographical Indications of Goods (Registration and Protection) Act, 1999. But despite the geographical protection, urban middle-class women located far from north Bihar have been taking advantage of the commercialisation and de-contextualisation of Mithila art to produce Madhubani-style paintings of their own for sale on the Internet. There seems to be no mechanism to follow up on infringements under the GI notification; moreover, the GI tag applies to Madhubani paintings on cloth, not paper. Diversification of livelihoods opens up new spaces and contestations over resources. With the new information technology (IT), it is not easy to predict how interventions will play out; the outcomes may be positive in some ways and negative in others. New 'stakeholders' are always quick to take opportunistic advantage of new spaces; so, resource rights have to be continuously renegotiated.

Towards Egalitarian Practices

Side-stream interventions occupy an ambiguous space, situated amidst grass-roots struggles, different levels of government, NGO initiatives and donor/corporate agendas. Since the early 1990s, many autonomous struggles have become NGOs, dependent on various funding sources, individual donations, the government, national or international agencies. In the past, donors were just that; later, many donors wanted more engagement with their NGO partners; and now, donors are increasingly setting the agenda and micro-managing the partners' internal functioning. Donor interest is double-edged. This is sometimes beneficial, say, when it supports socially progressive and gendered perspectives, but donors also have their own constituencies who want to see successful outcomes within a 2–3 year timespan. The results that matter to external evaluators are those that can be objectively measured and demonstrated. The long-drawn subjective process that precedes success, coping with and overcoming obstacles, the energy and time required, the sheer drudgery—this is almost never documented. So, the impression that is conveyed is that such side-stream interventions are fairly easy to replicate and upscale; when replication does not yield comparable results, there is a feeling of being let down. No matter what the rhetoric, the focus veers towards the technical rather than the social. This makes it very difficult for interventions in a project mode to address the inter-linkages of CPRs with patriarchy and class/caste issues on the ground.

Furthermore, even the relatively more egalitarian societies (such as the tribal areas of northeastern India or the Adivasi belt of central India based on cooperation and collective labour) are becoming more stratified. As their linkages with the wider economy increase, women's autonomy and power to take decisions in the household and community are eroded. But traditional communities and systems of resource management are not always gender-equitable. Harking back to idealised communities elides over the hegemonic gender-power relations within them. Women are then caught in a cleft stick: on the one hand is the felt need to resist the appropriation of resources by the State and markets; on the other is the reluctance to fall back upon the inequities of tradition (see Krishna 1996a, 2004b).

There are other complex issues. Pradhan and Padhi (2013) comment that women have been active participants in the mass struggles in Odisha, non-violent struggles against the State's appropriation of resources (for example, forests, minerals, water) and armed struggles to overthrow the State. They suggest that besides the level of women's participation, the level of agricultural wages, rights to common resources and the extent of community support against sexual violence (whether in conflict situations or everyday domestic life) need to be addressed; individual assertion, 'heartening' though it is, does not necessarily reflect 'the collective taking a step forward'. They also raise the contentious issue of an 'ever widening chasm between the feminism of the privileged and that of the less privileged' and ask whether we are prepared to look at this 'widening rift'. In the context of single women's struggle for water and homesteads in southern Maharashtra, Kulkarni (2011) has raised a similar issue about the wider women's movement in India. The women's fronts of the political parties gave the autonomous women's movement 'its mass character', but with most autonomous women's groups making a transition to being NGOs, the 'boundaries' between funded NGOs and women's mass movements are 'becoming fuzzier'. This, she says, leaves 'the political nature of the women's question unanswered'.

There is no clear answer as to whether and how our more complex understanding of the terms of discourse, and the rich seam of progressive feminist theory and methodology, are helping to improve women's lives and livelihoods.[5] Poor women are innovative and pragmatic agents of change; without romanticising subsistence-based economies we need to learn how theory and struggle can come together in egalitarian practice. As Malti Mandi, a Santal peasant woman, told an international seminar in Manila, way back in 1990:

> What do you mean by mainstreaming? To make some room for us in all that is going on? But that is not what we want. We want no part in planting thousands of eucalyptus trees that rob our soil of water and other plants, leaving our children and cattle hungry. We want to *change* these processes. If we have our way, we will call the scientists to work with us, adding their knowledge to ours, and look for solutions that would be good for everybody. (Mazumdar 1998: 258)[6]

Interventions on the ground cover a wide range: evident in the varied responses of, for example, the Kutch Mahila Vikas Sanghatan, Bhulia Devi and Malti Mandi. It has become increasingly difficult for practitioners to move beyond interventions that simply seek to deliver services. Yet, context-specific 'side-stream' interventions do need to move beyond seeking women's participation to building bridges with grass-roots struggles in order to change entrenched social and gender perspectives. As I have written elsewhere (Krishna 2012c: 16), 'Women's experience of oppressive power is related to their sexual and economic subordination, but across the world women have also demonstrated their collective capacity to question and challenge gender ideologies, which is essential for transformation' (see also Krishna 2012a, 2014).

'If She Built a Country'

What if poor, marginalised rural women 'built a country'? Documentary film-maker Maheen Mirza and associate director Rinchin explore this question through the fraught lives and collective struggles of the Adivasi women of resource-rich Raigarh, in northern Chhatisgarh.[7] Their 2018 film *'Agar Wo Desh Banati'* shows how the coal mines, thermal powerplants and steel industry have destroyed the region's land, forests and rivers. The devastation has taken an unimaginable toll on human lives and livelihoods. The nexus of corporate entities and the State is powerful and repressive. And yet, the women fight their way through the labyrinth of the law and lead protests, *dharnas* and rallies to secure justice for their communities.

What if these poor rural women built a country? What if these women—who have nothing but their bodies and minds, and the dynamic energy of the *sanghathan* (collective organisation)—built a country? The women's vision of development is complex and nuanced, expressed metaphorically through stories, song and dance. Natural resources and people's lives are seen as one whole, where justice for the community and prosperity for the nation are not divisible, where the question 'what will future generations inherit?' is not a theoretical problem but a felt, living reality. Their resolute determination becomes a celebration of collective political strength and vision, and draws others to the movement.

Establishing alternatives is a long, difficult and fraught process. New egalitarian resource management regimes cannot be realised without addressing the wider socio-political and cultural contexts within which they are embedded. In order to challenge the institutional basis of marginalisation, we need to redefine terms like development, sustainable livelihoods, CPR, as *political* rather than descriptive concepts. It is only by traversing diverse paths of action, practice and research that we can begin to identify some of the factors and circumstances that enable women's collective transformative organisation around shared resources.

Notes

1. India's globalising economy presents many challenges to natural resource-based livelihoods. Development interventions that further the commercialisation of natural resources, often mediated by the State, change the way in which resource rights are perceived and exercised by different sections of society. Interventions to increase representation and community resource management at the local level are undermined by the fragmentation of rights (see Krishna 2004c, ed. 2004d, ed. 2007).
2. The environments in which people dwell and work are complex life-worlds. Tim Ingold (1993: 152) conceptualises a landscape as a bounded space 'constituted' by the activities of people. It is an 'enduring record of—and testimony to—the lives and works of past generations who have dwelt within it, and in so doing, have left there something of themselves'. The social imprint of generations, the 'taskscape' imbues landscapes with character; taskscapes and landscapes are transformed through time. See also Krishna (2012b).
3. See also Krishna (2009, 2012a, 2012c, 2015); Krishna and Kulkarni (2018); Krishna and De (2012).
4. For other examples, see Krishna 2003 (revised and included in Krishna 2009).
5. Krishna and Kulkarni (2018) point out that for four decades women have figured sometimes peripherally, at other times more centrally, in the discourse around water at the global, national and local levels. Over these decades, as the terms of discourse were changing—women to gender,

needs to rights, management to governance—alternative perspectives were being put forward and 'mainstreamed'. These shifts in discourse seem to reflect a deeper and more nuanced understanding of the issues. Yet, the tendency of policy-makers and even practitioners on the ground is to treat women as instruments to address a natural resource crisis. This throws up the question of whether and how altered perspectives actually impact the management of water in an equitable and sustainable way (see also Krishna 1996b for a detailed discussion on the 'appropriation of dissent'.)

6. Malti Mandi was speaking at a seminar on 'Gender Issues in Agriculture', convened by the Asian Development Bank in Manila in 1990. Her words were translated and recorded by Vina Mazumdar (1998), who was present as the interpreter.
7. I watched the film on 19 July 2019 at the Indian Institute for Human Settlements, Bengaluru. At the screening, Maheen Mirza spoke about the unusual process of making it along with the Adivasi women. For this and other such films, see Public Service Broadcasting Trust; and for conditions in Raigarh district, see Asher (2016); Lakshmi (2017); Purohit (2017).

References

Anthra. 2008. *Bridging the Knowledge Divide: Livestock, Livelihoods, Resources in the Emerging Context.* Hyderabad: Anthra.

Asher, Manshi 2016. 'The Coal Curse of Raigarh'. *The Wire.* Available at https://thewire.in/environment/raigarhs-coal-curse (accessed 26 April 2020).

Datar, Chaya and Aseem Prakash. 2004. 'Engendering Community Rights: Women's Access to Water and Wasteland in Gujarat, Maharashtra, Madhya Pradesh, Andhra Pradesh and Karnataka'. In *Livelihood and Gender: Equity in Community Resource Management*, ed. Sumi Krishna, 137–70. New Delhi: Sage.

Ingold, Tim. 1993. 'The Temporality of the Landscape'. *World Archaeology* 25 (2): 152–74.

Jairath, Jasveen. 2000. 'By-passing the Women: The Case of Participatory Irrigation Management Reforms in Andhra Pradesh'. Paper presented at the Indian Association for Women's Studies Conference, Hyderabad, 8–11 January.

Krishna, Sumi. 1996a. *Environmental Politics, People's Lives and Development Choices.* New Delhi: Sage.

Krishna, Sumi. 1996b. 'The Appropriation of Dissent: The State *vis-à-vis* People's Movements'. In *Class Formation and Political Transformation in Post-colonial India* (Vol. 4 of Series on Social Change and Political Discourse in India: Structures of Power, Movements of Resistance), ed. T. V. Sathyamurthi, 238–57. New Delhi: Oxford University Press.

———. 1998. 'Gender and Biodiversity Management'. In *Gender Dimensions in Biodiversity Management*, ed. M. S. Swaminathan, 23–26. New Delhi: Konark Publications Pvt. Ltd.

———. 2003. 'The Earth Mother Rides a Bicycle'. In *Empowering Women through Information and Knowledge: From Oral Traditions to ICT Vol. 1*, 197–202. Mumbai: SNDT and New Delhi: CWDS.

———. 2004a. 'A "Genderscape" of Community Rights in Natural Resource Management: Overview'. In *Livelihood and Gender: Equity in Community Resource Management*, ed. Sumi Krishna, 17–63. New Delhi: Sage.

———. 2004b. 'Gender, Tribe and Political Participation: Control of Natural Resources in North-eastern India'. In *Livelihood and Gender: Equity in Community Resource Management*, ed. Sumi Krishna, 375–94. New Delhi: Sage.

———. 2004c. *Globalisation and People's Development Choices*. Bangalore: Hivos, Netherlands, India Regional Office.

———, ed. 2004d. *Livelihood and Gender: Equity in Community Resource Management*. New Delhi: Sage

———, ed. 2007. *Women's Livelihood Rights: Recasting Citizenship for Development*. New Delhi: Sage.

———. 2009. *Genderscapes: Revisioning Natural Resource Management*. New Delhi: Zubaan.

———. 2010. Paper contributed to Two Decades of Impact and Learning: Regional Conference, Orissa Watershed Development Mission with DFID and N. R. International, UK, New Delhi, 21–23 April.

———. 2012a. 'Gender and Sustainable Livelihoods in India: Side stream/ Mainstream'. In *Women Reclaiming Sustainable Livelihoods: Spaces Lost, Spaces Gained*, ed. W. Harcourt, 125–41. UK: Palgrave Macmillan.

———. 2012b. 'Genderscapes: Understanding Why Gender Bias Persists in Natural Resource Management'. In *Mapping the Field: Gender Relations in Contemporary India, Vol. 2*, ed. Nirmala Banerjee, Samita Sen and Nandita Dhawan, 265–95. Kolkata: Stree.

———. 2012c. 'Redefining Sustainable Livelihoods'. In *Women Reclaiming Sustainable Livelihoods: Spaces Lost, Spaces Gained*, ed. W. Harcourt, 12–18. UK: Palgrave Macmillan.

Krishna, Sumi. 2014. 'Repoliticising the Gender and Livelihoods Agenda'. Keynote presentation at Workshop on 'Women, Labour and Livelihoods in the 21st Century: A Research and Policy Linkage Workshop', Tata Institute of Social Sciences, Mumbai, 11–12 December.

———. 2015. 'Women's Transformative Organising for Sustainable Livelihoods: Learning from Indian Experiences'. In *Oxford Handbook on Transnational Feminist Movements,* ed. Rawwida Baksh and Wendy Harcourt, 837–52. New York: Oxford University Press

Krishna, Sumi and Arpita De, eds. 2012. *Women Water Professionals: Inspiring Stories from South Asia.* New Delhi: Zubaan.

Krishna, Sumi and Seema Kulkarni. 2018. 'Gender and Water: Why We Need Alternatives to "Alternative Discourses"'. In *India's Water Futures: Emergent Ideas and Pathways,* ed. K. J. Joy and S. Janakarajan, 235–52. New Delhi: Routledge.

Kulkarni, Seema. 2011. Struggle of the Single and Widowed Women in Sangli District. *Poster Women.* Available at http://www.posterwomen.org/?p=5743 (accessed 24 April 2020).

Kulkarni, Seema and Sneha Bhat. 2010. 'Issues and Concerns of Deserted Women in Maharashtra'. *Economic and Political Weekly* 45 (38): 59–66.

Lakshmi, Supriya. 2017. 'Survey Reveals Pathetic Health Conditions around Raigarh Coal Mines, Plants'. *The Wire.* Available at https://thewire.in/environment/survey-reveals-pathetic-health-conditions-around-raigarh-coal-mines-plants (accessed 25 April 2020).

Mazumdar, Vina. 1998. 'Women from Equality to Empowerment'. In *Independent India: The First Fifty Years,* ed. Hiranmay Karlekar, 254–79. New Delhi: Oxford University Press.

Purohit, Makarand. 2017. 'Problems of Mine: When Coal Threatens Raigarh'. *India Waterportal.* Available at https://www.indiawaterportal.org/articles/problems-mine-when-coal-threatens-raigarh (accessed 25 April 2020).

Pradhan, Promodini and Ranjana Padhi. 2013. Paper presented at the National Conference on Women's Rights in Odisha: Culture, Politics and Development, Ravenshaw University, Cuttack, 22–23 January 2012, and reproduced in *Mainstream,* 3 August 2013.

Public Service Broadcasting Trust (PSBT). 2018. *Agar Wo Desh Banati* (If She Built A Country). Available at https://psbt.org/films/agar-wo-desh-banati-if-she-built-a-country/ (accessed 25 April 2020).

Ramdas, Sagari and Nitya Ghotge. 2007. 'Whose Rights? Women in Pastoralist and Shifting Cultivation Communities: A Continuing Struggle for Recognition and Rights to Livelihood Resources'. In *Women's Livelihood Rights: Recasting Citizenship for Development,* ed. Sumi Krishna, 41–61. New Delhi: Sage.

Rao, Rukmini. n.d. 'Backlash Against Dalit Women Creating Food Security in Rural India: Myopia or Another Chapter of Caste and Gender Discrimination?'. *Global Sisterhood Network.* Available at http://global-sisterhood-network.org/gsn/raoart.htm (accessed 24 April 2020).

Shedde, Meenakshi. 2012. 'Integrated Water Management Initiatives: Bhuj Women, India'. In *Women Water Professionals: Inspiring Stories from South Asia,* ed. Sumi Krishna and Arpita De, 55–65. New Delhi: Zubaan.

Singh, Neera M. 2004. 'Women and Community Forests in Orissa: Rights and Management'. In *Livelihood and Gender: Equity in Community Resource Management,* ed. Sumi Krishna, 306–24. New Delhi: Sage.

Swaminathan, Padmini and J. Jeyaranjan. 2008. 'Mainstreaming Gender, Engendering Development: Reflections on a Case Study'. *Economic and Political Weekly* 43 (17): 77–86.

Tewari-Jassal, Smita. 2004. 'Limits of Empowerment: Mallahin Fishponds in Madhubani, Bihar'. In *Livelihood and Gender: Equity in Community Resource Management,* ed. Sumi Krishna, 412–24. New Delhi: Sage.

Vasundhara. 1998. 'Non-timber Forest Products and Rural Livelihoods'. Mimeo, Vasundhara, Bhubaneswar.

11

Women and Land Rights in India

Towards a Democratic and Gendered Formulation of the Land Question

Smita Gupta

There is a tendency within the donor-driven developmental discourse to sanitise the question of women's land rights by reducing it to the narrow perspective of ownership of private property, held jointly with the spouse or independently. The notion of women's land rights (as well as women's work) is confined more and more to their homestead and family plot. This ignores a most important aspect of the patriarchal gender-based division of labour as well as survival strategies of poor households—the use, collection and processing of land-based resources (critical for household subsistence), an extension of women's unpaid household work. If these public or common property resources deplete or are fenced, women's burden increases. Therefore, though important, the question of women's land rights cannot be reduced to women's holding or inheritance of private property alone. Nor can the women's movement be solely or primarily concerned with inheritance, 'joint or individual titles' of private property in the name of women. Even though this is empowering, it is an extremely narrow, even elitist and market-oriented view of the women's land question in a situation of growing landlessness, inequality and diversion of land away from households.

This is for four reasons: first, because a vast section of poor working women are dependent on the use, collection and processing of land-based resources which are not primarily privately owned, bringing public and common land to the centre-stage. Second, land has moved away from households through land acquisition and takeover so that dispossession and displacement have undermined petty holdings, placing a huge burden on women responsible for family reproduction, bringing resistance to land grab on the women's land agenda. Third, widespread eco-degradation due to destructive technology and development policy has meant that women's drudgery has increased and productivity reduced, giving women a huge stake in environmental protection. Finally, high and growing landlessness is accompanied by dwindling availability of remunerative employment, underlining yet again the centrality of gender-sensitive redistribution of land to the tiller. If the land rights of a vast section of toiling women are to be addressed, the understanding of women's land rights has to be widened to include both the commons and ceiling surplus land locked up in large estates, public and private. The women's movement must widen the discourse and struggle for land rights by moving beyond titling and inheritance to stressing redistributive land reforms (in a consciously gendered manner) and also resisting the annexation and degradation of public and common land and land-based resources.

Viewed this way, the question is not of ownership or inheritance alone, it is most crucially of land-use policies and powers to manage lands of various kinds. Even as women from the working classes and oppressed sections fight to preserve, access and control the commons, they also struggle to hold on to or get a plot, a home, a roof. The women's land movement, therefore, has to negotiate this dialectic, combining resistance against containment to a family plot with a fight against evictions and displacement for redistributive land reforms and against the loss of the commons.

Another mistake that is often made is to view the land question as a rural or agrarian issue, but this is incorrect. In fact, even as urban populations increase and migration due to the agrarian distress rises, urban commons and public spaces shrink, with growing conflict and contestation. Once again, the State plays a key role in squeezing urban commons. Census 2011 (Government of India) reports a noticeable increase in urban population and urban units, with urban residents increasing from 27.81 per cent of total population in 2001 to 31.16 per cent in 2011. For the first time after Independence, the addition to urban population (by 90.99 million people) was larger than that of the rural population (90.47 million). The urban working class is increasingly stripped of all citizenship rights, with most spaces out of bounds for them, reducing their work and residence to illegal encroachment. The question of land is even more crucial for women, dependent as they are on shrinking commons for various items like residence, fuel and defecation.

Once the women's movement accepts these four cornerstones of a democratic women's land rights agenda in urban and rural areas—access to commons, gender-sensitive redistributive land reforms, environmental regeneration and determination of land-use policies—struggles for land rights will have to confront both patriarchy and neo-liberalism.

This is because, like colonialism, the current era of neo-liberalism, too, witnesses a huge demand by global capital for tropical biodiversity, land and land-based resources.[1] Along with other countries in the Global South, India is subject to plunder and loot of natural resources on an unprecedented scale, as the means to boost capitalist super-profits. This is accompanied by a massive dispossession[2] and displacement of petty producers from land and land-based resources. The growth model itself requires State power to unleash 'animal spirits' to create an 'investor-friendly environment'. This translates into an environmentally unsustainable and inequitable plunder of natural resources on the one hand, and the subjugation and disciplining of labour through labour law flexibility and regulation on the other, away from a Keynesian employment-intensive broad-based growth strategy.

In addition, the falling viability of cultivation and squeeze on off-farm employment on account of neo-liberal policies, with the consequent fragility of rural livelihoods have rendered rural workers extremely vulnerable to even the smallest of shocks, resulting in distress out-migration. Further, environmentally unsustainable technologies have caused huge ecological degradation, destroying the quality and productivity of land resources in agriculture, forestry and allied activities. These factors, namely, the plunder of land and land-based resources, agrarian distress and environmental degradation have together resulted in dispossession and displacement of large populations. The entire thrust of public policy in land since the mid-1990s has been to either privatise or statise land, taking away usufruct and ownership from peasants, slum-dwellers, and local communities in rural and urban settings. Since the neo-liberal State has abandoned dirigisme's conception of holding natural resources in public trust, statisation and privatisation have increasingly similar impacts on the livelihoods of the poor, and a great deal of the resistance is to protect these resources being handed over by the State to capital.

Loss of Commons

Common property resources or CPRs exist in three types of property relations: as the 'common property resources' of often differentiated communities (especially outside Adivasis or forest-dwelling communities) usually tended, collected/harvested by women and Adivasis; as 'state-owned resources' which are purportedly being held in public trust for their conservation but in fact are 'fenced' and 'enclosed' to dispossess primary producers and gatherers; and as private property. The entire thrust of public policy in land in the last couple of decades has been to either privatise or statise common property. The collapse and encroachment of the commons is accompanied by the strategy of containment to a small plot/home or dispossession.

Falling between the 'public' and the 'private' but not equivalent to either category, the natural commons encompass a broader concept of property, referring to social goods—lands, territories, forests, pastures and water bodies—which a community of people, not the State or a private entity, collectively owns, manages and controls (see Adhikari et al. 2004; Aggarwal 2001; Gaur et al. 2018; Jodha 1986). In contrast to the 'public', or State-owned resources which are increasingly enclosed and fenced, or private property administered by the State, the commons are owned as collective resources with a mind-boggling range of practices, rights and responsibilities. They are a crucial part of the means of subsistence of poorer communities, tended mostly by women from socioeconomically exploited and underprivileged communities and classes (see Mitra 2018; Naidu and Ossome 2016; Razavi 2007).

Women's relation with natural resources is a historical and social relation, deriving from the specific nature of the patriarchal gender-based division of labour (see Agarwal 1994, Braedley 2006). Eco-feminists are wrong when they insist that women have a special relationship with the environment as they have a 'natural predilection for conservation of natural resources', a biological essentialism. This romanticises what is primarily an outcome of women's exploitation under capitalism through the patriarchal division of labour.

Social cooperation and collective functioning for the commons is a crucial element, whose exact characteristic and underlying social relation is, of course, shaped historically. In postcolonial societies, an essential though often neglected part of the class struggle is the indigenous people's resistance to expropriation and enclosure of the commons, with women playing a very visible and sometimes decisive role. The peasant resistance against forcible land acquisition through farmers' struggles in India can be described as the complement to these struggles. Women's practical and strategic interests in biodiversity and food security often bring the women peasants into conflict with capitalist plunder and commercial exploitation.

Women, Work and Common Property

Women's work generally receives marginal treatment simply because much of it is 'invisible', in terms of market criteria or social perception. A considerable quantity of women's time is committed to unpaid labour, most of which remains invisible. The responsibility for social reproduction on women makes sure that a bulk of them is invariably engaged in some kind of productive and/or reproductive activity. Many of the activities associated with household maintenance, provisioning and reproduction are typically performed by women or female children. Many such women who are out of the purview of the definition of workers, but are engaged in domestic work which is economically gainful to the households, are considered as unpaid workers.

The NSS classifies those 'not in the labour force' into various activities—students, those attending domestic duties only, those attending domestic duties and also engaged in free collection of goods (vegetables, firewood, fodder for the cattle, etc.). Those attending domestic work and also engaged in free collection of goods (vegetables, firewood, fodder for the cattle, etc.), are considered non-workers. Basically, in developing countries with a significant component of non-market activities, boundaries between household work and economically gainful work are difficult to be drawn. NSS 2004–05 showed that of those involved in unpaid domestic work, 57 per cent of rural women and 19 per cent of urban women were engaged in the free collection of fuel wood for household consumption. Forestry and logging accounted for 12 per cent of the total rural unpaid workers.

The system of resource use in India is gendered such that environmental degradation affects women more than men. The annexation of natural resources and common property affects women disproportionately given their primary responsibility to collect and manage these CPRs. The dual processes of annexation and degradation (which have intensified under neo-liberal capitalism) have meant that women have to spend longer hours or pay more for what were once easily accessible

There are two ways in which households access CPRs: by using them in the commons or through collection. Use includes grazing within the commons in addition to collection of firewood, fodder and non-timber forest products (NTFP) for use outside the commons. Collection, a subset of use, includes the removal of CPR products. Use is clearly a superior marker of dependence than collection alone.

The gathering of CPRs is predominantly the work of women and children. The figures for women are lower, however, when the CPRs are used for commercial purposes. The dependence and drudgery is most pronounced for poor women. In tribal areas, the neglect in economic development has meant a greater dependence on CPRs.

CPRs provide the rural poor from 66 per cent to 84 per cent of their fuel requirements in the form of wood and dung. The corresponding figure for richer households is from 8 per cent to 13 per cent. The greater dependence of poor households on grazing land is because

(a) they have more livestock and (b) they do not have access to land for grazing. Poorer households had longer collection time (15–25 days' worth of work per household in three weeks) when compared to richer households (4–10 days' worth of work per household in three week). Poorer households spent more time (10–20 per cent of the total daily time of the poor) in a day doing CPR-related activity than better-off households. If not for CPR-based employment, the rural poor would have to spend a significantly larger number of days in a year being involuntarily unemployed. CPR provides 15–25 per cent of the total income from all other sources for poor households; the corresponding figure for the richer households is 1–3 per cent (Beck and Nesmith 2001).

Rawal and Saha (2015) show in Table 11.1 that for women aged 15–59 years, whose principal activity status is housework, if we examine the proportion of those who are engaged in particular unpaid activities, it is shocking to find that in rural areas, providing fuel for household use was the most important economic activity. In 2011–12, about 58 per cent women household workers provided fuel and fodder. Of them, about 42 per cent of rural household workers made dung cakes and about 44 per cent of rural household workers collected firewood, cow dung and fodder; 45 per cent obtained food for the household and 24 per cent tended kitchen gardens for household use. All development claims to the contrary, about 31 per cent of rural household worker women regularly fetched water from outside. Between 1999–2000 and 2011–12, the engagement of household unpaid workers increased in maintaining kitchen gardens and free collection of food, even as fewer women were engaged in animal care.

In urban areas, the most important economic activities were making or mending clothes with the involvement of 25 per cent of urban household worker women; 13 per cent of urban household worker women frequently worked in different activities for obtaining food.

Given the importance of CPRs in household sustenance and women's work, clearly the depletion and annexation of land resources is an integral part of the women's land question. The moment this is accepted, women's struggles for protection and expansion of land

Table 11.1: Proportion of Women Who Regularly Performed Various Activities of Economic Importance for Household Use among Women Who Were Principally Engaged in Household Work, 1999–2000 to 2011–12

S. No.	Activity	Rural		Urban	
		1999–2000	**2011–12**	**1999–2000**	**2011–12**
1	Various activities to obtain food	55.3	45.0	20.0	12.8
1.1	*Maintenance of kitchen garden*	14.1	24.2	3.4	7.9
1.2	*Maintenance of household animal resources*	32.7	22.2	4.5	2.5
1.3	*Free collection of food*	15.2	19.4	1.2	1.8
1.4	*Food processing for household use*	26.3	13.6	14.5	3.8
2	Various activities to obtain fuel and fodder	61.9	57.7	8.8	7.4
2.1	*Free collection of fuel and cattle feed*	39.6	44.1	5.4	5.3
2.2	*Preparation of cow dung cake*	48.8	41.8	5.8	4.8
3	Fetching water from outside	50.9	31.3	23.3	10.0
4	Making/mending clothing	28.6	29.6	28.4	25.1
5	Making baskets and mats	10.1	5.0	6.3	1.6
6	Tutoring own children or other children for free	6.2	7.6	13.9	13.3

Source: NSS, various rounds, from Rawal and Saha (2015).

rights comes in direct conflict with neo-liberal policies, as has been demonstrated by the struggles of the left and democratic women's movement in India.

Neo-liberal Reforms in India and Dispossession

Already, colonial intensification of private property regimes to maximise land revenue earnings (Bagchi 2010), based on titling and fencing of individual holdings, had undermined communal land systems. Under the British, lands were classified into revenue and forest, and all land that was uncultivated and uncultivable and could not be classified as a forest, was called 'waste', which were typically the village commons, pastures and the open scrublands on which nomadic communities subsisted. Grazing lands and unfarmed commons were considered un-remunerative and should be made to generate revenue through acquisition, privatisation and taxation. In rural Punjab, for example, the British decided to acquire 20 lakh acres of common grazing lands, expropriating pastoralists, for large settled agricultural colonies and canals for peasants, to form these oases of progress amidst the 'poverty, ignorance and oppression' of the arid pastoral regions (Bhattacharya 1995). Historians report similar enclosure of common pastureland from other parts of the country, like in Berar in central India.

The independent postcolonial State further undermined collective ownership and management of the commons and effectively made non-private land the property of the State, establishing its right to appropriate it for public projects. Large storage-based irrigated farming as the means to raise agricultural productivity resulted in an additional enclosure of the commons, with industrialisation, mining and infrastructure giving fresh impetus to this. According to NSSO (1999), land CPRs (open pastures, fallows or village forests) constitute about 15 per cent of the total geographical area of India, of which 23 per cent is community pasture and grazing lands and 16 per cent has been classified as village forests. The total area under such CPR has declined at 2 per cent every five years since the 1980s. As a result of these developments, landlessness in rural areas grew, as did class differentiation.

The restructuring of the Indian economy as it abandoned the post-Independence regulatory and protectionist framework and put in its place fiscal conservatism, deregulation, trade liberalisation, financial sector reforms and privatisation marks the beginning of yet another phase. The entire thrust for free trade and a simultaneous attack on agriculture has as its primary aim the re-opening of the 'lands of the global South to meet the increasing demands of the North, while direct acquisition of land in tropical areas is also being sought for the same' (Patnaik 2012). The priority given to attracting foreign investment generated an extraordinary 'race to the bottom' among the state governments, which competed with each other to offer land and resources at more and more attractive concessions to woo national and international corporate capital.

The policy to unleash 'animal spirits' by incentivising private investment in infrastructure, urbanisation and industries through tax and price concessions and handover of natural resources, with a consistent shift in the terms of trade against the peasantry, has impoverished both the land and its people.

The 'agrarian crisis' of the 1990s and 2000s and the liberalisation-privatisation policies initiated in the early 1990s were a defining moment with regard to common land as well, with the World Bank and other international capitalist institutions seizing this historic opportunity to put an end to community land systems, which in their view were the key impediments to the development of capitalist relations and penetration of global capital especially in mining and infrastructure development. All the open commons must be enclosed by the State, they argued, and traditional rights of use, access and grazing restricted, otherwise investors will have to negotiate with individual communities for their sacred groves, timber, fuel wood, food and fodder.

Processes of Dispossession

Not surprisingly, therefore, the process of annexation of CPRs through primitive accumulation, ever-present under capitalism, has accelerated and become more ruthless under neo-liberalism. Dispossession has been achieved through several routes, which, though logically separable, are simultaneous and mutually reinforcing with a proactive role of an aggressively interventionist State.

The post-Independence State fenced forests through the Forest Conservation Act (FCA) of 1980 and the Wildlife Protection Act (WLPA) of 1972, whose main intention is the establishment of exclusive protected zones with authoritative administration and is premised on the dubious view that local communities are inimical to the protection of forests and wildlife. The takeover of 23 per cent of India's geographical area by the government in 1980 through the FCA and the creation of national parks, protected areas and sanctuaries resulted in the closure of forests, depriving poor communities in and around these forests from exercising their forest rights, annexing them for private profit. Even as the forest-dwellers overnight became illegal 'encroachers' on their own land, large areas of forest land were diverted for cutting of forests for 'development' projects; since 1980, an average of about 40,000 hectares was diverted annually for non-forestry purposes, the pace of this increased rapidly to a 100,000 hectares a year between 2001 and 2006, and by 2014–15, the annual average was 90,000 hectares.

The expectation that the Forest Rights Act would recognise rights of forest-dwellers to use, protect and manage habitats, common resources and forests has been somewhat belied. While rejecting large numbers of applications for the recognition and vesting of forest rights on specious grounds, the Ministry of Environment and Forests continues to divert forest land for projects without bothering with people's rights, even recommending diversion where forest-dwellers have rights on the land (Gupta 2014).

Land alienation, a euphemism for land grab of Adivasis land by non-Adivasis, is widely prevalent despite several policies and laws for their restoration to Adivasis. The Panchayats (Extension to the Scheduled Areas) Act (PESAA) of 1996 has specific provisions dealing with the protection of resource rights of Adivasis. This Act has been completely subverted by the State and corporate sector. The Ministry of Rural Development of the government of India in its recent Annual Reports admits as much.

Chhattisgarh, Odisha and other Fifth Schedule States have found a novel way of undermining Adivasi land protection: by converting rural areas into urban ones. Since the protection is not extended to urban areas within the Fifth Schedule, the criteria for notifying areas as urban and rural are manipulated and the stringent provisions of PESAA are bypassed by merely re-classifying them as urban, so that land can be easily and forcibly alienated, encroached, acquired and diverted.

Forcible land acquisition has become a weapon with the State to deprive farmers of their land. Till 2013, the legal framework for land acquisition was provided by the archaic colonial Land Acquisition Act (LAA) of 1894, last amended in 1984. The main purpose of the LAA was to acquire land in a quick, cheap and easy manner with little concern for livelihoods and rehabilitation of landowners. One of the biggest weaknesses of the 1894 Act was that 'public purpose' was the sole and absolute prerogative of the executive, through opaque and authoritarian procedures not subject to democratic and judicial scrutiny. Land was often acquired in the guise of a more plausible purpose and then transferred to some other use.

The LAA kept acquisition costs low by an unfair and arbitrary method of evaluating the price of land and restrictive coverage of persons and assets, resulting in very low compensation. The procurer (the government) decided the price, and refused to transfer any part of the gains of the higher values accruing from the proposed change in land use to the affected persons, a system antithetical to a fair and democratic valuation. This was further achieved by basing the valuation on officially recorded sale deeds that are underreported in order to escape taxes and duties, and the payment of depreciated value for assets making it impossible to replace them.

The Right to Fair Compensation and Transparency in Land Acquisition, Rehabilitation and Resettlement Act, 2013, title notwithstanding, replaced a colonial Act with a neo-liberal one. The price for compensation is now linked to the stamp duty and circle rates rather than the highest actual market price as ordered by the Supreme Court, which are notoriously underreported. The acquirer, namely the State, continues to determine compensation, which is a conflict of interest. However, the most important failing is the vague definition of public purpose.

The new Act puts acquisition for the state and acquisition for companies on the same footing, against all previous legislative efforts.

Dispossession may not necessarily mean the formal loss of access and ownership of land, but would include destruction of its inherent productivity in a manner that compels owners to abandon cultivation and collection, and be forced to migrate out in search of work. The same would occur in the case of degradation and decrease in common land and associated livelihoods. Environmental degradation (broadly speaking, the twin processes of deforestation and land degradation) has an adverse impact on access to land and land-based resources, both in terms of quantity and quality.

According to the Indian Space Research Organisation's (ISRO) report on desertification in 2007 and its 'desertification status map', roughly 69 per cent or 228 million hectares of India's lands are dry, and extremely vulnerable. Worse, desertification threatens one-fourth of India's geographical area, or 81 million hectares, with rapid degradation of agricultural areas posing a grave threat to its productivity and peasantry. Resourcesat also shows that land degradation has already affected a third of the country's area at 105.48 million hectares.

One of the most important causes is the choice of unsustainable technologies in large development projects, with technologies chosen by the State having resulted in the destruction of the environment, the takeover of land and land-based resources and displacement of the local communities and windfall profits for private companies. Large-scale deforestation for mining and the subsequent production itself leaves the landscape scarred, hydroelectric projects and tunneling leave huge dumps scattered over the landscape and cause massive submergence, industries have polluted and poisoned of water, air and soil, etc.

The combination of three processes—reduction in public investment in employment-intensive environmental regeneration, the shrinking of the commons through large infrastructure, urbanisation and industrial projects and more draconian property regimes due to enclosing and fencing—increases 'degradation-pushed distress migration' from private and common lands.

Many large cities, too, have common lands used as a source of fuel, fodder, water, building material and food. Flood plains, tanks, lakes and other run-off based water bodies are used by the urban poor for floriculture, horticulture, pisciculture and traditional work. This land is highly sought after. A whole host of reasons—like large infrastructure and development projects, urban renewal and new urbanisation, city beautification; safety and security concerns, sports extravaganzas, industry, industrial corridors and SEZs—are uprooting individuals and communities from their homes and commons in cities.

The previous two decades have seen an unparalleled increase in forced slum evictions across the country in urban areas. The judiciary entered the arena of urban planning in a most draconian and anti-poor form (Bhan 2009). 'The Indian capital offers brutal confirmation of Jeremy Seabrook's contention that the word "infrastructure" is the new code word for the unceremonious clearance of the fragile shelters of the poor' (Davis 2006). The land freed through slum clearances is then used for high-value commercial enterprises like malls, complexes, office buildings or luxury housing colonies.

The government wants to move away from the present system of deeds and confer conclusive ownership titles to landholders through land titling. Every parcel of land will be assigned a unique identification number and land records will be maintained by a central land titling authority. This kind of consolidation and centralisation of land records is likely to facilitate even greater dispossession and land grab. It recognises only two categories of land, private and government, with the latter being a residual category. Community resource rights and common property are not recognised and will be recorded as 'government land', thus enclosing commons. It is ambiguous regarding the manner in which tenancy will be recorded, and is likely to result in becoming yet another reason for the concealment of unrecorded tenancy and eviction of poor tenants.

A large number of traditional forest-dwellers and other common property dependents have no formally vested and recognised rights. If the dual classification is to be followed without recognition of common property and rights, it might result in the enclosure of these commons and destruction of livelihoods on a massive scale.

'The draft Land Titling Bill is not about updating land records. It is not about the accuracy of land records, but about its finality for purposes of determining encumbrances and saleability. It is about deciding on a means by which land may be easily dealt with in the market' (Ramanathan 2011).

Cumulative Impact

The pursuit of fiscal conservatism and cutback in public expenditure on development and subsidies for the poor, the dismantling of protection of domestic economies and the push to privatisation of social and economic provisioning were the cornerstones of neo-liberalism in India. These policies in India resulted in huge numbers of people being evicted and displaced.

Financial liberalisation has played a central role in this, with the State assuring high rates of return on private investment, free financial movements across borders and pursuing deflationary policies with cut in public investment. The domination of finance capital results in policies which, on the one hand, cause stagnation in peasant agriculture and, on the other, result in the expropriation of land resources. These policies predate neo-liberal policies, but the strengthening and institutionalisation of encroachment achieved unprecedented heights in the current era. In times of crises, especially with demand deflation, weakening of peasant agriculture and the terms of trade turning against agriculture, encroachment became the more effective mechanism.

Thus, we see that the result of several laws and policies—for enclosures, exclusion, diversion, eviction, acquisition, alienation, titling, degradation and land-use zoning—governing vast tracts of land under different property regimes/ownership structures (like government land, public land, CPRs and private land) and uses (which was under agriculture, or under agro-silvi-pastoral systems, or under urban slums and forests, or considered wastelands and barrens where the poorest eke out their subsistence, etc.) has been to privatise or statise land and shift it to real estate, infrastructure, industry, etc.

Further, the fall in CPRs at an accelerated pace in terms of access, area and quality is undermining the livelihoods of CPR-dependent households as well as environmental sustainability. The twin processes of degradation and annexation results in lands where the poorest eke out their subsistence, and have been depleted, privatised or statised and shifted to real estate, infrastructure mega-projects, industry, etc.

Resistance and the Way Forward

Much of the resistance to this kind of land grab and eco-degradation comes from communitarian 'people's movements', with women, Dalits, and Adivasis forming their backbone. This proactive role of women in resistance is no surprise since the gender-based division of labour puts the burden of harvesting, collecting and preserving CPRs upon women.

While the communitarian people's movements have been effective in highlighting the annexation of the commons, they unfortunately suffer from extreme localism and their engagement with issue-based politics has resulted in a narrow approach and an inability to correctly identify the cause of encroachment of the commons and loss of resource rights as capitalist and primitive accumulation under finance capital. They fail to challenge the conservative macroeconomic policies that subsidise private profits through the windfalls from plunder of natural resources.

There is a tendency within communitarian movements—some of the people's movements—to romaniticise the community. They are thus often unable to raise demands and struggle for the democratisation of the community through gender equity, land reforms, anti-caste movements, etc. The localism impedes resistance to the government's neo-liberal natural resource policies, or to relate the fight for democratic ownership and control over the CPRs to the anti-imperialist movement.

While it is true that the State takes forward capitalist interests, the left and democratic women's movement demonstrates that the State is an important site of struggle, a weapon in the fight for women's rights over CPRs and the movement against dispossession. For the left and democratic women's movement, it is clear that it cannot romanticise customary tenure because of its patriarchy and discrimination against women.

Furthermore, CPRs are not pure ideals but themselves an object of struggle. There is little doubt that customary laws as presently defined discriminate against women, despite the fact that women are the bulk of Indian farmers, the main producers of food and perform the majority of agricultural tasks: sowing, weeding, harvesting, storing, processing and marketing, without having control over the land they farm nor security of access to it. As discussed, common property is tended and collected overwhelmingly by women, even though they exercise little control over its management.

Struggles against the gender-based division of labour and the patriarchal traditional/customary practices are, therefore, vital and there are worrying repercussions from a gender perspective in the recent uncritical endorsement of 'customary' systems of land tenure and decentralisation of land management (Esplen and Brody 2007; Hassim 2006). Women's organisations rightly fear that this can further the despotism and tyranny in traditional/'customary' practices. This is not to suggest that 'customary' practices are entirely adverse for women, or that statutory rights alone can further their interests. It is nevertheless difficult to insert gender equality concerns into processes where traditional institutions have a patriarchal character.

A huge number of donor-driven NGOs have mushroomed and are fairly visible in the media and on the policy 'high table'. They essentially address the issue of women's land rights from the perspective of the propertied classes and focus primarily on titles and inheritance, seldom questioning the unequal distribution of land or the capitalist degradation and plunder of CPRs.

There are two clear tendencies within the democratic movement for women's land rights, which are not necessarily contradictory or irreconcilable but often become sole preoccupations of different sections in the movement. On the one hand is the advocacy of laws that strengthen women's land rights under private ownership. While important, this has sometimes become an end in itself through the demand for joint *patta*s or titles, and adopted the language of international financial institutions to obliterate the question of land redistribution—the Indian left movements' most crucial demand since colonialism. The left and democratic women's movement in India fought for land reforms not merely with the limited agenda to attain the status of a landowner or petty producer, but to break from the oppressive shackles of landlordism. The demand is for more land rather than only for more gendered law; for redistribution of large estates holding ceiling surplus revenue land, for strengthening women's individual land property is of little use when marginalisation or landlessness is increasingly becoming the generalised condition of the land-dependent.

Redistribution of land is, therefore, critical; for women in particular, it is an important and crucial means of production and subsistence. As a 'social security system', it is sometimes more important than money and wages. Having some land at the village or the prospect of it at the end of a life of work away from it makes the difference for many between life and death or, increasingly, between life in the village and migration.

It is of course now widely recognised that the agrarian reforms under State-led redistributive efforts during the 'golden age' of land reform were largely gender-blind. These reforms were often based on an implicit assumption that assets allocated to households—typically to the male 'head'—would benefit all members equitably. Not only did such assumptions ignore the wellbeing of women and their dependents in the event of household dissolution (upon separation, divorce or widowhood), they were also blind to women's differing relationship to property and the fact that household ownership of land can more deeply exploit women's labour through heavier workloads in the form of unpaid family labour.

Conclusion

The women's movement has, for decades, fought for protecting land occupations and mobilisation against the destruction of natural resources. It is clear that a democratic struggle for women's land rights in a context of dispossession, degradation and agrarian distress has to demand policies that go beyond joint ownership. The current socioeconomic and macroeconomic situation, more than ever before, requires confrontation at both the local and global level, at both the sub-national and national level. Radical redistribution of ceiling surplus land is essential to break landlordism and generate greater equity, but has to be implemented in a consciously gender-sensitive manner. This has to accompany women's ownership and control over common property resources and public lands. The recognition of women as farmers has to come with access to adequate public investment and extension services; it has to accompany land titling and joint titles with the right to natal and marital property.

Traditional practices have several ecologically sound and exemplary democratic practices, but these unfortunately are often highly feudal and patriarchal. Women are excluded from decision-making institutions while bearing the burden of work. Democratisation and empowerment of women in 'state' and 'community' institutions is a fight that has to be fought. Ultimately, there is no escaping from contesting State policies and putting pressure on the State to regulate and discipline markets and capitalists to protect resource rights and prevent land and resource grab.

Notes

1. Land resources include soil, biomass and vegetative cover, water, etc.
2. Dispossession includes all forms of loss of access to and ownership of these resources—be it private, community or public rights.

References

Adhikari, Bhim, Salvatore di Falco and Jon C. Lovett. 2004. 'Household Characteristics and Forest Dependency: Evidence from Common Property Forest Management in Nepal'. *Ecological Economics* 48 (2): 245–57.

Agarwal, Bina. 1994. *A Field of One's Own: Gender and Land Rights in South Asia*. Cambridge: Cambridge University Press.

Aggarwal, Arun. 2001. 'Common Property Institutions and Sustainable Governance of Resources'. *World Development* 29 (10): 1649–72.

Bagchi, Amiya. 2010. *Colonialism and Indian Economy*. New Delhi: Oxford University Press.

Beck, T., and C. Nesmith. 2001. 'Building on Poor People's Capacity: The Case of Common Property Resources in India and West Africa'. *World Development* 29 (1): 119–33.

Bhan, Gautam. 2009. '"This is No Longer the City I Once Knew": Evictions, the Urban Poor and the Right to the City in Millennial Delhi'. *Environment and Urbanisation* 21 (1): 127–42.

Bhattacharya, N. 1995. 'Pastoralists in a Colonial World'. In *Nature, Culture, Imperialism: Essays on the Environmental History of South Asia*, ed. D. Arnold and R. Guha, 49–85. Delhi: Oxford University Press.

Braedley, Susan. 2006. 'Someone to Watch Over You: Gender, Class and Social Reproduction'. In *Social Reproduction: Feminist Political Economy Challenges Neo-liberalism*, ed. Kate Bezanson and Meg Luxton, 215–30. Montreal: McGill-Queens Press.

Davis, Mike. 2006. *Planet of Slums*. New York: Verso.

Esplen, E., and A. Brody. 2007. 'Putting Gender Back in the Picture: Rethinking Women's Economic Empowerment'. BRIDGE (Development-Gender) Institute of Development Studies, UK. Available at http://www.bridge.ids.ac.uk/sites/bridge.ids.ac.uk/files/reports/BB19_Economic_Empowerment.pdf (accessed 14 May 2020).

Gaur, Mahesh Kumar, R. K. Goyal, S. Kalappurakkal and C. B. Pandey. 2018. 'Common Property Resources in Drylands of India'. *International Journal of Sustainable Development and World Ecology* 25 (6): 491–99.

Government of India. 2011. *Census of India 2011: Provisional Population Totals*. New Delhi: Registrar General and Census Commissioner of India, Ministry of Home Affairs.

Gupta, Smita. 2014. 'Forest and Land Rights of Adivasis in the Current Conjuncture'. Paper presented at an international conference on 'The Return of the Land Question', Kolkata, 4–6 March.

Hassim, Shireen. 2006. *Gender and Social Policy in a Global Context: Uncovering the Gendered Structure of 'The Social'*. UK: Palgrave Macmillan.

Indian Space Research Organisation. 2007. 'Desertification and Land Degradation Atlas of India'. Government of India, Ahmedabad.

Jodha, N. S. 1986. 'Common Property Resources and Rural Poor in Dry Regions of India'. *Economic and Political Weekly* 21 (27): 1169–81.

Mitra, Manoshi. 2018. 'The Role of Women in Common Property Resource Management: Experiences from India'. Available at http://dlc.dlib.indiana.edu/dlc/bitstream/handle/10535/2388/The_Role_of_Women_in_Common_Property_Resource_Management_Experiences_From_India.pdf?sequence=1 (accessed 14 May 2020).

Naidu, Sirisha C., and Lyn Ossome. 2016. 'Social Reproduction and the Agrarian Question of Women's Labour in India'. *Agrarian South: Journal of Political Economy* 5 (1): 50–76.

National Sample Survey Office. 1999. *54th Round Common Property Resources in India*. New Delhi: NSSO.

Patnaik, Utsa. 2012. 'Some Aspects of the Contemporary Agrarian Question'. *Agrarian South: Journal of Political Economy* 1 (3): 233–54.

Ramanathan, Usha. 2011. 'Land Acquisition, Eminent Domain and the 2011 Bill'. *Economic and Political Weekly* 46 (44–45): 10–14.

Rawal, Vikas and Partha Saha. 2015. 'Women's Employment in India: What do Recent NSS Surveys of Employment and Unemployment Show?'. Society for Social and Economic Research Monograph 15/1, Society for Social and Economic Research, New Delhi.

Razavi, Shahra. 2007. 'Liberalisation and the Debates on Women's Access to Land'. *Third World Quarterly* 28 (8): 1479–1500.

12

New Cartographies of the Digital Commons

Going by Feminist Wisdom

Anita Gurumurthy

The Internet has heralded a new social context, disrupting life and work on a planetary scale. Even though it offers the material basis to rethink community and commoning on scales hitherto unprecedented, the promise of the Internet has been expropriated by contemporary capitalism. This essay emphasises the need for a historical-material analysis of informational imperialism that restores the central place of women's reproductive labour to understand motivations of capital in the network age and build an emancipatory politics adequate to current times.

The first section explores how the digital commons, especially the Internet, have been usurped by contemporary capitalism, vesting enormous power in the hands of a few. As control over information and data becomes key to extract rent, monopoly platforms in the network economy impose commodity relations on spheres of production hitherto overlooked. Myths about the 'sharing economy' establish the pro-capitalist digital commons as a new form of social control. In this open, networked world, the geographies of reproduction are enclosed, as capital, through its material-discursive force, takes away from labouring women and their communities the autonomy to reproduce themselves in relation to their local geography. Information technology (IT) intertwines with capitalism, fuelling the neo-liberal impulse for free choice, making entrepreneurial self-fashioning the norm.

The second section examines the silences around social reproduction in dominant information society theory, challenging the techno-utopic thesis of a new post-gender, post-race future. It argues the need for corporeal accounts of labour, showing how the new global gender-based division of labour in 'informational imperialism' exploits material and immaterial spheres of production, extracting surplus from the Global South and expropriating women's unpaid labour in the reproduction of everyday life.

Proceeding from the urgency to reclaim the anti-capitalist commons as a precondition for women's emancipation, the third section grapples with feminist visions of a 'sharing economy'. It suggests that a new ethics of affect and relationality, and of place, can lead us towards a counter-theory of commoning, bringing together the spatialities of the material and immaterial commons. This endeavour would also call for a governance framework for the Internet that can support global democracy.

The Structuring Conditions of Contemporary Capitalism

The Internet represents a radical technological paradigm that allows duplication and distribution of information, knowledge and cultural works, with near-zero marginal costs. The notion of the 'digital commons' emerged through such a paradigmatic shift articulated by three loosely aligned, networked social movements made possible by the Internet—the Free Software movement which focuses on software code; the Free Culture movement which focuses on cultural goods; and the Access to Knowledge movement that focuses on knowledge-intensive goods, such as scholarly publications and medicines (Stalder 2010). All three are founded on an understanding that the techno-social context of the Internet makes it plausible for information to be considered as a public, non-rival and non-excludable good that can be shared freely. Their communities adopt specific governance rules to organise production, access and maintenance (Morell 2010: 5).

The Internet itself is also seen as 'commons', a resource pivotal to non-hierarchical cooperation. The architecture of the Internet,

Internet protocols and technical norms, are hence seen as digital commons, developed by open communities of computer scientists, engineers and technicians, and coordinated by technical bodies,[1] so that all users can develop private and public activities (de Rosnay and Crosnier 2012).

Even though the digital commons, by virtue of the very nature of the Internet, incorporate characteristics of an inalienable public good, the 'unholy marriage between contemporary capitalism and the Internet' (Foster and McChesney 2011) usurps the Internet as a means of exploitation, vesting enormous power in the hands of a few.

Informational Capitalism

Powerful transnational corporations today wield inordinate power by monopolising information ownership. The takeover by Monsanto (an agricultural company) of Climate Corp (a weather data company) is a rather telling example of this. This deal gives Monsanto access to the information it needs for complete social control of agriculture.

Companies like Uber and Amazon—global 'platform' businesses—set and control the (considerably lower) standards upon which someone (preferably anyone) could become a supplier in the respective market (Olma 2014). Instead of cutting out the middleman, such digital platforms have the inherent tendency to become veritable monopolies, the new middlemen with unprecedented control over the markets they create.

Google and Facebook use the mundane labour of Internet users, creating value through user data and content. Patterns become central to Google's algorithms, crucially dependent on the mining of the 'collective wisdom' of Internet users (Bauwens 2014). The profit model of most of the free Internet, where access is free but participation is enclosed, is based on records of patterns of social activity that are packaged and sold to data brokers and advertisers. While enabling human cooperation, monopolies on the Internet exploit such cooperation for the benefit of private capital (Bauwens and Restakis 2015). This usurpation of pre-capitalist forms of social interaction includes a range of non-market and non-proprietary activities, such as production of open-source software, over networks.

The rise of forces that appropriate participation and collaboration in the networks marks the transformation of society into a 'social factory' that produces uncompensated value for platforms. Society is governed thus by an 'algorithmic ideology' that assimilates Internet users into a process of datafication in which 'capitalist ideology is inscribed in code and manifests in computational logics' (Mager 2014). Understandably, therefore, the protagonists of contemporary capitalism are rather vocal in their support for user participation in the Internet economy. Their survival depends on passionate appeals for users' 'free expression', but they are 'dangerous trustees of the commons-favorable protocols' (Bauwens 2014).

The transition to what has been called 'informational capitalism' is coextensive with a socioeconomic metamorphosis of information across a great (and still-undetermined) range, whereby commodity relations are imposed on previously overlooked spheres of production (Prodnik 2014). While Digital Rights Management systems 'lock' hardware and software to prevent intellectual property from being copied in the digital-informational realm, patents and Intellectual Property Rights (IPR) also extend capital's enclosures to people's histories, culture, creativity, genetic materials and more, in what may be labelled as a 'new feudalism' (Berry 2008) leading to the emergence of a rentier class. As we noted with Monsanto, information and data control is key to the workings of monopolies in the network economy. Foundational to contemporary capitalism, therefore, is the fact of the substitution of 'command over production' by 'command over markets'.

The 'seeping commodification' (Prodnik 2014) of everything through exploitation of the digital commons goes hand-in-hand with a contemporary consumer culture. Internet users buy into and stabilise informational capitalism and its advertising-based modes of production. Emancipated from its past instrumentality that used to draw its limits, consumption now justifies itself only by its own 'pleasurability'; consumption is its own purpose, an end in itself (Bauman 2001). A devastating consequence of this, inter alia, is that critique and efforts towards change become difficult.

Commons in Subversions of the Network Economy

Global informational capitalism is staunchly supported by highly influential mainstream theories espousing neo-liberalism. As has been pointed out by George Caffentzis (2010: 31), economic theories since the late 1990s introduced the notion of 'social capital' and the importance of 'community' and 'trust' at the very moment of the so-called triumph of the market. The wreckages of the capitalist crisis of 2008 required a creative response, a new strategy to save neo-liberalism from its own excesses. The notion of the commons has been a useful device to further what Caffentzis calls 'neoliberalism's Plan B'. Serving as the necessary intermediary between a stalled and successful neo-liberalism, the idea of commons and community loses its social-political content, and in an easy discursive slippage, is replaced with a pro-capitalist one. Caffentzis traces this slippage to the call by neo-liberal actors for the mobilisation of 'community' or 'civil society' as a key mechanism for saving the capitalist economy from its own demise (ibid.: 23). The pro-capitalist versions of 'sharing', 'collaboration' and 'cooperation' obscure the idea that common ownership contains resonances with social justice and can deliver greater economic equality.

In the 'sharing economy', economic justice is reduced to promoting entrepreneurial imaginaries of poverty alleviation, where the poor are responsible for working their way out of poverty. The czars of IT—Bill Gates, Steve Jobs, Larry Page, Mark Zuckerberg—leading technological innovation are elevated as iconic heroes offering 'models of behavior to be disseminated throughout society' (da Costa and Saraiva 2012). This myth is exported as information-age theory to developing countries that must emulate high-tech 'start-up' companies in their own path to economic growth. This new myth-making around the ideology of individualist entrepreneurialism is based on old masculinist ideals of nation-building and unencumbered creativity. It has emerged in tandem with the neo-liberal argument that excessive State regulation and the ways in which this curtails creativity are responsible for all economic and societal ills.

Adopt-a-woman portals represent a new commons in the entrepreneurial genre for competitive fundraising, connecting the deserving poor with willing patrons. Even political mobilisation and dissent follows a logic that aggrandises platforms. Online 'activist commons' such as Change.org—a corporation 'using the power of business for social good' (Change.org)—are a perfect example of how dissent is commodified. Using sponsored petitions from progressive groups willing to shell out dollars to promote their campaigns, the platform allows conservative, and even retrograde, campaigns, to use its resources, in the name of an 'open', free-for-all approach. Through its marketised version of protest, therefore, Change.org distorts and depoliticises collective action (Gurumurthy and Chami 2014).

In the network economy, we see a failed capitalist model seek validation for a growth theory compatible with social and environmental good. Even though the limits of ecological exploitation have been reached and the neo-liberal faith in markets has backfired, proponents of a brave-new-capitalist-world vehemently assert such compatibility. The 'carbon tax', for example, rationalises the perverse, pro-capitalist appropriation of the global commons as a mechanism to promote virtuous, sustainable growth (De Angelis 2009).

As much as they are based on the structures of contemporary social relations, adaptations of capitalism are also rooted in particular sets of representations that carry performative force. Processes of globalisation, for instance, are no longer merely a fact, but also a source of juridical definitions (Hardt and Negri 2000). As we saw with the notions of commons and community, this discursive turn de-essentialises and de-familiarises given ideas. Using a feminist lens to analyse a Canadian case in which the court accorded *de facto* property interest in a higher organism to Monsanto, Robertson (2005: 233) concludes that 'this is not simply another step in the commodification of farming', but reveals the changing 'lineaments of biopolitical sovereignty'. Bio-property is thus legitimated by representational practices of globalisation as opposed to parliamentary debate on economic growth, innovation, the environment, food security and the ethics of patenting higher life. The space for alternative conceptions of property and, consequently, opportunities for non-capitalist politics, is thus stymied.

In the historical material trajectory of capital, we are witness to an extraordinary flexibility in the adaptations of neo-liberal capitalism. In this management by flexibility, capitalism has found a new saviour in its old *bête noire*, the idea of the commons. Under the circumstances, participation in the (pro-capitalist) digital commons represents a new form of social control. Even though common-ownership regimes in the network society could, theoretically speaking, bring about a variety of desirable values—participatory production of diverse cultural artefacts and information; democratic and responsible management of natural resources; and efficient use of scarce resources (di Robilant 2012)—unfortunately, in current conjuncture, access to digital technologies is a political instrument of discipline.

Globalisation, Informational Capitalism and Dispossession

The processes of globalisation produce a growing fluidification of territory. They break down pre-existing boundaries to subsume the commons. But enclosure—or the subsumption of the commons—is not just a phenomenon happening across different scales. It is itself 'a rescaling agent' (Sevilla-Buitrago 2015: 7) that reorganises socio-spatial hierarchies to produce hegemonic structures of global political economy.

Information and communication technologies (ICT) that undergird the de-territorialisation of capital and financialisation of economic activities provide the technological architecture key to control new geographies of value. In this scheme of things, capitalism can effortlessly generate new scalar configurations of power 'subsuming the commons in broader value chains' (ibid.). Small retailers and women's traditional businesses lose out to global chains, while bottom-of-the-pyramid strategies target poor, labouring women in the Third World as disciplined and deserving subjects of trickle-down development. In this 'neo-liberalism from below', multinational corporations (MNCs) sell not only 'affordable' sachets of beauty products and junk food, but global goodies of micro-credit and micro-insurance, to mop up poor women's wages. Meanwhile, these solutions for poverty do not really bespeak any let up in the material conditions of poor women, who remain entrenched in conditions of exploitation: the case of M-money, propped up as an empowerment tool for women in Africa, being a stark illustration of the point (Diga and Mbarathi 2014). Cloaked in corporate imaginaries promising a technocratic ideal of flexible labour market optimisation, the new myth that has come to dominate discussions on the 'future of work' is gig work. Thoroughly embedded in forms of capitalist value production, gig work is characterised by gendered and racialised subordination of low-income workers, the unemployed, and the unemployable (van Doorn 2017). While a handful of platform companies—mostly from the Global North—mobilise workers on a planetary scale, wages of platformised labour in the gig economy are caught in a race to the bottom (Graham et al. 2017). Gig work arrangements are also almost always under the radar, tucked away in privatised spheres of policy and governance.

As Sevilla-Buitrago (2015: 5) submits, when space is mobilised to separate the commoners from the territorial basis of their autonomy, the socio-material links that allow a particular community to produce itself as a work of its own are severed. The dispossessed, of whom women make up a large majority, lose their place in the world, as their geographies of reproduction become enclosed. The local elite are co-opted into capital's logic, and become part of the global class, in these socio-spatial reconfigurations. The Smart Cities project in the developing world sells the dream of inclusive, world-class cities that partnerships with foreign capital will make real. But deals with high-tech foreign expertise to make Third World cities smart come with new gated townships for the elite, converting public land into real estate and gentrifying and segmenting the city (Moser 2015). The rhetoric of the Internet of Things offered by the Smart Cities project to power remote-controlled everything reveals the endless commodification of personal data and social time. Policy and regulatory techniques, such as surveys and digitisation of land records, become part of the tools of capitalist enclosure that facilitate land-grabbing by global forces, while also undermining women's rights to local resources by making men the default owners (Johnson 2014).

Big data represents another tyranny of scale, transferring control of people's destinies to corporations that have the capabilities for 'business analytics'. With mathematical aesthetics that 'are too powerful, too beautiful, and too seductive' (Faltesek 2013) to resist, big data allows big corporations to advance new argumentations that emerge as the science of the twenty-first century. Through these data sets, bodies, identities and interactions are removed from social contexts, as big data truths redraw lines of autonomy and bio-political sovereignty.

The 'open' digital commons symbolise emerging geographies of inequality, as extensions of older, historical forms. As Graham et al. (2014) observes in relation to Wikipedia:

> Many countries in the Global South have more articles in a non-local language (often the language of a former colonial power) than a commonly spoken local language ... (We) see a broad pattern of the Global North being represented in local languages while the South is largely being defined and described by others. (Ibid.)

The conclaves of presence and absence, participation and representation, generated by Wikipedia as a digital commons, mirror inequities in the informational or immaterial sphere of production. While they contain the potential for challenging hegemony through alternative knowledge or truths, their current modes of production reveal old hierarchies on new scales.

By creating new geographies of value, atomising labour and making the marginal perpetually vulnerable, informational capitalism expands its enclosures. Deploying the meme of openness in a networked world, it holds up free choice, competition and innovation as important values. As authentic choice evaporates from local communities, a new neo-liberal impulse for entrepreneurial selfhood is introduced. This emerging 'social entrepreneurship' project, however, may well end up treating the symptoms rather than the root causes of today's most virulent social and ecological problems (Edwards 2008). A starting point to challenge dispossession and loss of autonomy, therefore, is to unpack capital's cunning, its ever-evolving mechanics and tactics for exploitation.

Women's Labour in Informational Imperialism

As capitalism encloses the digital commons and network age platforms subvert 'collaboration' and 'sharing', articulations about what may be productive alternatives to re-politicise the commons discourse become important. A Third World feminist lens holds the potential to complicate critiques of contemporary capitalism and advance theories of an emancipatory politics of commons and community.

Making Social Reproduction Visible

Silvia Federici (2012) offers an engaging critique of Antonio Negri and Michael Hardt's post-Marxist theories of capital that hold wide appeal. Building on the contributions of Michel Foucault and Gilles Deleuze, Negri and Hardt invoke the notion of bio-power, as characteristic of the network society, in their celebrated work, *Empire* (2000). Bio-power, deployed through technics or technologies, is not aimed at prohibiting and punishing, but concerns the production of the real, as in, the totality of social life (Mapping the Commons 2011). 'Immaterial labour' (alternately, 'affective labour'), is central to 'biopolitical production', the direct production of subjectivity, knowledge and culture in the network society, wherein production and social reproduction are merged (Hardt and Negri 2000, 2004). Negri and Hardt offer the concept of 'multitude'[2]—a rhizomatic and diffuse network, which is the 'becoming *common* of labor'—that they argue is the new autonomous and revolutionary subject that will portend the destruction of Empire (Hardt and Negri 2004).

Negri and Hardt's conception of bio-political production, Federici avers, does not adequately capture the contemporary field of capitalist relations. She unpacks the limits of the concept's theoretical validity, arguing its inability to propose a regenerative and emancipatory politics:

> (Hardt and Negri's) ... picture of the common absolutizes the work of a minority possessing skills not available to most of the world population. It also ignores that this work produces commodities for the market, and it overlooks the fact that online communication/production depends on economic activities—mining, microchip and rare earth production—that, as presently

> organized, are extremely destructive, socially and ecologically. Moreover, with its emphasis on knowledge and information, this theory skirts the question of the reproduction of everyday life. (Federici 2011)

Relying on the multitude to resist dependence on wage labour and subordination to capitalist relations would, therefore, be tantamount to saying that capitalist development is capable of, and is already creating the conditions for, transcending exploitation. Such a thesis would obviously render illegible reproductive labour as a terrain of accumulation and exploitation. Such obscuring of reproduction, as Federici highlights, 'is true of the discourse on the commons as a whole, which is mostly concerned with the formal preconditions for the existence of commons and less with the material requirements for the construction of a commons-based economy' (ibid.).

In the platformising economy, Twitter and other social media sites benefit additionally from the labour of volunteer community managers whose efforts to moderate misogyny and sexism online are often unwanted, punished and viewed as censorship (Nakamura 2011). Working outside of the realm of 'the point of production', and 'outside the knot' of collective resistance, women of colour and sexual minorities spend hours of voluntary labour that adds value to these platforms. Just as reproductive labour has been feminised, devalued, ultimately offshored for pay, and borne by volunteers, this emerging category of workers online are the 'unpaid reproductive labour, producing social use values' (Huws 2014: 171).

Understanding informational capitalism and its predatory tendencies requires that we trouble dominant information society theory and its normalisation of the techno-utopic thesis of a new post-gender, post-race future, built on the marvels of the network. Capital's stalemate today comes from the devastation of systems of social reproduction through the flexibilisation and precarisation of work, the attack on the welfare State, and the complete inability of natural ecosystems to service capital in its endless greed for resource extraction and desperation to shift externalities.

This exploitation of bodies and the colonisation of peoples and nature is at the root of what Fuchs (2010) calls 'informational imperialism'. The history of Structural Adjustment Programmes

(SAPs) and the dismantling of the welfare State, and the consequent disinvestment by the State in the reproduction of the workforce, have pushed women's bodies to the brink, extending their work day and depleting their life force. Economic crisis has only increased male violence against women, forcing women into global circuits of prostitution. In India, for example, murder by male family members of widows for land-grabbing (Iaccino 2014), and for dowry (Press Trust of India 2015), reflect the rapaciousness of post-modern greed. The routine incidents of suicide by impoverished small farmers suggest extreme dispossession by accumulation (Biswas 2010). Feminist researchers have noted how the widows of small farmers are engaged by upper-caste landowners in these regions, as 'human scarecrows' (Dewan 2014; see also Chapter 7 in this volume). The dehumanisation of the material body and the evacuation of its dignity in these instances points to the need for a theoretical continuum that connects particular histories of development and economic policy with the conditions structuring contemporary capitalism.

Today, emboldened by the surveillance machinery, and in the name of cyber security, developing countries are spending hugely on a techno-development model in which digitally-enabled governance architecture becomes key to statecraft. Opening up access to the market for the poor, and shifting to panspectronic programmes in lieu of public institutional investment, the privatisation of social security, through cash transfers for instance, provides an exemplar of 'development as consumer choice'. The systematic negation of existing evidence of the disastrous impacts of such cash transfers on women's wellbeing and intra-household gender inequalities is matched only by the neo-liberal State's hyper-optimism about technology's ability to alleviate poverty. Ideologies of information society utopianism and privatisation disembed social and economic rights from their deeply social and gendered moorings, and de-socialise questions of wellbeing, care and support (Gurumurthy et al. 2016). This marks a complete departure from established theories and recognised notions of women's economic and political citizenship, shifting women's labour into the unidentifiable abyss of an ungovernable private sphere, bringing to nought the basic premises of gender justice in public policy. It would, therefore, hardly be an exaggeration to characterise dominant information society theory that collapses production and social reproduction into a hyperbolic misconception of 'affective labour' as patriarchal myth-making that has no patience for the social experience of women from the South, women of colour in the North and sexual minorities.

Global Division of Labour in Informational Imperialism

The network economy has reconstructed inequality 'as a pyramidal structure ... deepening the hierarchies that have historically characterized the sexual and international division of labor, which the anti-colonial and the women's liberation movements had undermined' (Federici 2012: 102). In fact, in this re-inscribing of race and gender in the workings of contemporary capital accumulation, both affective and physical labour is critical. Even though illustrative of a particular context in the Global North, Alison Hearn's case analysing women's labour in reality television is a striking argument about the limits of Hardt and Negri's immaterial labour thesis (Hearn 2010). As the promotional objects for the ostensibly labour-free world of the attention economy, these women (as indeed women in similar shows in the Global South would be) are the incarnation of hyper-socialised cyber-subjects. But, paradoxically, their performance no doubt drawing upon emotion, life energy and such, and seemingly autonomous, is nothing more than self-branding disciplined by the television industry and its logic of profit maximisation. As it mythologises and fetishises the end of labour and the hegemony of immaterial work in its narratives, the story of these women obscures the conditions of exploitation that tie their labour to below-the-line workers in the industry.

Perspectives on international migration are useful to understand the mobilisation and displacement of physical and affective labour from crisis-ridden regions to regions of wealth. Known as 'global care chains' (Hochschild 2000), these multi-directional transnational circuits of accumulation underscore the crises of reproduction and 'the intensified financialization of everyday life' (Lem 2014). They carry indelible marks of race, gender and class, revealing a global division of labour. The tale of the Rohingyas in Asia reveals the political economy of trade in bodies that enslaves the desperate community as indentured labour of the twenty-first century in deals struck between human traffickers, border authorities and the land-owning class (Hodal 2014).

Transnational pornographic business is yet another site of exploitation that speaks to the body politics of the virtual. The use of children and their physical bodies in producing virtualised affect, by organised cybersex activity in the Philippines, instantiates the expropriation of children's labour to 'service' human perversion (Murdoch 2014). It could also well be the most depraved frontier of enclosure—the subsumption of children who are society's future—into the logic of capital.

What becomes clear is that corporeal narratives in both material and immaterial spheres of the network economy need to be recovered in making legible the routes and rampages of capital. Framing informational capitalism thus in historical material terms is necessary to draw out the overrepresentations of hegemonic narratives that eclipse and erase others. As Caffentzis (2005) submits, 'the computer requires the sweatshop, the cyborg's existence is premised on the slave'. Hence, the surplus value from labour-intensive sectors of the economy underwrites those sectors marked by immaterial labour. Jakob Rigi echoes Caffentzis' thesis in his inference that the global division of labour in contemporary capitalism is gender-based, and reflective of an imperialist global order where the Global South transfers gigantic amounts of surplus value to the Global North:

> To the extent that their wages exceed the value that their labour time can potentially produce, (the) elite (class) exploits the surplus value producing working class ... This (rent extraction) creates a certain contradiction between privileged information workers who overwhelmingly work and reside in advanced capitalist countries, and are male by gender, and workers in service sectors (overwhelmingly women), and manufacturing and agricultural workers who overwhelmingly work and reside in the Third World. (Rigi 2014)

What we have also noted here is that the global division of labour in the present context is also gendered for the exploitation by the elite class of poorest women and their means of survival. The extraordinary duress that poor women in the developing world suffer in reproducing everyday life through their unpaid labour is central to the value generated by informational capitalism. Using its material-discursive apparatus, capitalism today encloses the commons necessary for Third World women to reproduce life and community, displacing them, delegitimising their rightful claims on the State, and dissipating their life force and social time. The project for Third World women's emancipation is thus linked inextricably to the restoration of the commons and community.

Towards the Commoning Configurations of Digital Space

Third World women have continuously held that gender justice and economic justice go hand-in-hand (Sen 2005). They have fought the usurpation of the commons, fighting regimes of exploitation and control, and reclaiming equity-based organisational principles that promote the rights of those who have been dependent on the commons for centuries. These highly embedded struggles have different histories, based on the histories of capital and colonisation. Notably, feminist readings of these movements trouble the unequivocalism of new movements theories (such as Manuel Castells' *Networks of Outrage and Hope* [2012]), which claim that social movements today arise through the autonomous communication networks supported by the Internet and wireless communication. Empirical evidence belies this assertion. As Federici (2012: 92) observes, the radical struggles in contemporary history are being fought by rural, indigenous, anti-colonial, anti-apartheid and feminist movements, and not by the intellectual or cognitive workers or by virtue of the Internet's common (the 'autonomous multitude'). The labouring women of remote villages of Rajasthan in India have led the struggle, demanding transparency from the state about their entitlements, that resulted in a bottom-up claim to what is now the 'right to information' law.

The debate here is not about whether the Internet and digital technologies can play a potentially progressive role in radical struggle.

The question really is of how a radical practice of technology can claim reproduction as the site of struggle. The livelihood struggles of women from the Global South provide alternative visions of a 'sharing economy' that is situated in a relational, interdependent ecosystem, where resource ownership and use are two mutually sustaining sides of social life. They show how freedom is inseparable from dignity, food, housing, livelihood and life, articulating thereby the indivisibility of rights.

As has been discussed in the earlier sections, capital is in a deadlock at this conjuncture, and must find a way to contain the costs associated with the crisis of social reproduction. It must limit the expenditures necessary to police and control the rebellions generated by the crisis. Capital needs a 'commons fix' (De Angelis, n.d.). Through its discursive power, capital today takes control over material and immaterial spheres of life, defying easy cognition of the specific workings of its power. Its expanding circuits envelop our life and sociality like a möbius band that has no other side.

And yet, the 'network condition' also confers the ability to connect and communicate with people globally, self-organise, share experiences, build solidarity and co-produce knowledge resources and commons at scales previously only possible through hierarchical and capital-intensive, command and control economies (Flanagan 2015). The project of emancipation in the network society must reclaim the anti-capitalist commons. This is not fetishism but an imperative, as there is no other way to sustain life, with freedom and dignity for all, than to common. Arguably, as De Angelis elaborates,

> … the commons are a vehicle for *claiming ownership* in the conditions needed for life and its reproduction … Within its realm, there lies the *possibility* that its labor activity, organization and patterns of social relations will not succumb to external pressures, but instead organize its own reproduction autonomously, following criteria of equity and justice as defined by the commoners themselves. This possibility depends on the *contingent* power relations within the commons; on the power of networked commons; and on forces *outside* the commons, such as capital. The commons therefore represents a field of *possibilities* in the struggle against capital … (and) this value

> struggle (emphasis added) is at the heart of the commons' potential as a social system and force that might overcome the hegemony of capital. (De Angelis, n.d.)

Internet as a Technology of Commoning and Community

The construction of common global interests with respect to the commons—the ecological commons, knowledge commons, the energy commons—is the centre of gravity of a new politics, the site where the class struggle of the twenty-first century will be played out (De Angelis 2009). The Internet is at the centre of this emergent politics. While its inherent qualities have been appropriated by capital for its enclosures, its promise for liberty and social justice represent the colonised Internet's emancipatory other. The future of the digital commons, therefore, depends on the governance regime of the Internet. Rifkin reminds us of Garrett Hardin's blindspot in his famous thesis, 'The Tragedy of the Commons' (1968):

> Hardin's description of the Commons ... omitted the most salient factors of the Commons model that allowed it to persevere over eons of history—that is, the self-regulating, self-enforcing protocols and accompanying punishments agreed to by its 125 members as a condition of participation ... In other words, Hardin left out governance. (Rifkin 2014)

Rifkin goes on to discuss the work of Carol Rose, 'The Comedy of the Commons', a rejoinder to Hardin's dystopic thesis. Rose's work—although it came before the worldwide web—speaks almost uncannily to the nature of the Internet as a common property. Asserting that the public's claim had to be superior to that of any private owner, because the (common) properties themselves were most valuable when used by indefinite and unlimited numbers of persons, Rose presented the thesis that the publicness of goods and services created the 'rent' of the property, and public-property doctrines protected that publicly created rent from capture through private holdout (Rifkin 2014: 127).

To rescue the digital commons from the repressive hegemony of what can be called the network-data complex, we would need to move towards a 'network-public' commons (Singh and Gurumurthy 2013). Examining common ownership regimes, Anna di Robilant suggests that such regimes should promote equality of autonomy—meaning, more equitable access to the material and relational means that allow individuals to be autonomous. The notion encompasses negative freedom, equality of access to basic material resources (or positive freedom), relational self-determination, and responsibility (di Robilant 2012: 294).

The 'openness' of the Internet and its commons nature has mostly been recognised for promoting freedoms, most notably, of speech. The communitarian rewards of the Internet are yet to be explored fully. Whether the Internet can generate the civic republican outcomes of participation, deliberation, knowledge production and responsibility will be a true test of its potential to advance equality of autonomy for all.

As a social system, the Internet represents the technological commons, but is also the means through which commoning itself can happen. By providing the material means for commoning, the Internet can sustain social reproduction that is outside of capital and its impulses. However, contrary to over-zealous and celebratory claims, connectivity is nowhere close to ubiquitous nor is it spreading as fast as many believe. Some 90 per cent of population in low-income countries and over 60 per cent globally are not online yet (Dutta et al. 2015). As a global community, we are indeed very far from the goal of equitable access. The Internet's information resources may be non-rivalrous, but as a physical material infrastructure, it is still excludable. As is well acknowledged, women's full participation in the information society is a distant dream.

Digital citizenship for all can only be obtained with an Internet that is a socio-cultural commons for communities and solidarities and an economic resource that can democratise the whole productive process. As we have seen, feminist struggles exhort us to visibilise the oft-buried narratives that signal the crisis of social reproduction. The privileged discourse of freedom cannot, in and of itself, foster a sociality of the network that allows everyone to become digital commoners. But this field of possibilities, as was discussed, is a value struggle; one that no doubt is intimately connected to the basic question of effective access to technology, but equally, to the affective-relational and spatio-scalar architectures of the Internet, which we will discuss now.

Reimagining the Internet

The social spaces of the digital realm are constituted in new assemblages, where encounters are temporary and provisional. Vacillating between choice and chance and between randomness and homophily, the affective content of these assemblages generate tensions (Molz 2014). William Davies (2015) observes how in the precarious social worlds mediated by connectivity, 'neo-liberal socialism' quietly brings in 'everything that was once external to economic logic, such as friendship'. Offering a thesis on the social condition of being networked, he posits that the relational conundrum confronting us today is a key ethical-institutional question:

> If people have become locked in themselves, gazing enviously at others, this poses questions that need institutional, political, collective answers. It cannot be alleviated simply with psychological appeals to the social, which can exacerbate the very problems they aim to alleviate, once combined with digital media and the egocentric model of connectivity those media facilitate. There is a crucial question of how businesses, markets, policies, laws and political participation might be designed differently to sustain meaningful social relationships, but it is virtually never confronted by the doyens of social capitalism. (Ibid.)

The subjectivities and inter-subjectivities that the Internet commons as an emancipatory space must foster require new imaginaries of the Internet. Property regimes of affect and relationality reflect a crisis of ethics, tied to the very social fabric of our shared lives.

This brings us to the second dimension of the value struggle, the spatio-scalar question. Unless the digital commons can generate a new 'technology of community', one that valorises a place-based commoning, the Internet dream cannot be realised. Global capital's undying instinct for abstracting the local into its value chains of exploitation, through scalar hierarchies that aggrandise some territories, raises deep questions about the ethics of globalisation. The possibility of community through various spatial and scalar choices has been Internet's gift to humanity. But the hegemonic model of production in the network economy has taken away from the majority of women on the planet and their communities their right to self-determination. An ethics of place in the network society must enable the socio-material links, the memories and connections, that give the marginalised 'a place of their own' in the networked world, while supporting new encounters and solidarities. These ethical explorations warrant a new 'counter-theory of commoning, fusing the spatialities of the material and immaterial commons' (Sevilla-Buitrago 2015: 18).

But much depends on the governance design of the Internet and how its unique nature and significance can be guided towards a digital citizenship for all. This would mean that the varying conceptions of the Internet—as markets, as the frontier of freedom, as a deliberative public, as a knowledge commons and more—are reconciled in a way that asserts the preponderance of a 'democratic society' rather than a 'capitalist economy' in governance arrangements of the Internet. The uniqueness of the Internet implicates myriad issues at the interstices of local, national and global scales, covering telecommunications, intellectual property, privacy, platform and intermediary regulation, and more. Given this complexity, conventional theories on commons ownership are rendered inadequate to address its commons nature and significance. Also, strong political economy considerations operate to prevent a transnational, global treaty on the Internet (Belli 2015).

A resolution of the question of 'global' Internet governance exhorts us to think metaphorically: do we seek bridges of mini-publics or do we seek a set of 'nested clubs' (Raymond 2012) for our collective futures? Or, to put it differently, what kind of an Internet can enrich our life worlds? Scholarly appeals to pragmatism, such as for a semi-commons theory, which 'usefully help us focus on the interdependence between the private and the commons' (Grimmelmann 2010) may be one road to take. But the charm of common property is not only in its location, in the in-betweenness of private property and State property. In fact, it may be the only solution to the crisis of privacy and trust confronting us today. Scholars like Morozov (2015) have urged that we think of a social ownership model for data. A data regime that is held in collective trust, is, perhaps, the only option that can redeem our datafied, proprietised cyborgism controlled by hyper-masculinist corporate greed. An important corollary here is that the world urgently needs another kind of datascape—data that is not for sale, is respectful of privacy and typifying a new imaginary of the digital, which values representations of the marginal and the plurality of communities.

As Barnes (n.d.) describes, the immaterial commons of the Internet can be managed by trusts rather than corporations:

> Such trusts would be separate from government ... its beneficiaries would be future generations and all living citizens more or less equally. Trustees would be legally bound to serve those beneficiaries, just as corporate directors are legally bound to serve stockholders. Each citizen's beneficial share would be a non-transferable birthright.

Concrete examples of feminist autonomous infrastructures include the Geek Feminism Wiki,[3] that has developed specific technologies to tackle gender-based online violence, such as bots against trolls, and building feminist online libraries and feminist servers, but also enabling offline safe spaces such as feminist hackerspaces which allow feminist, queer and trans hackers, makers and geeks to gather and learn with others (Toupin and Hache 2015). These community building attempts based on alternative governance models share in common a desire to proactively create the conditions for their autonomy while following an ethic of care, tackling actively all forms of violence, whether it be online violence or the violence that is intrinsic in resource extraction or the factory and assembly line work that is gendered and racialised (Nakamura 2014).

The collective wisdom to build a digital commons across multiple scales may not match capital's know-how to manage its empire on a planetary scale. But this would amount to jettisoning the project of emancipation of women, as capital's other. It would also mean the sacrifice of the life world at the altar of informational capitalism. Unlike modern capital, post-modern informational imperialism may not discern between the male master and his female slave. In a datafied universe, everyone is sold. The struggle ahead of us is both material and discursive. It is about bringing together a design of multiple mini-publics with an institutional framework of a global democracy and citizenship for all.

Notes

1. Such as the Internet Engineering Task Force (IETF) and the World Wide Web Consortium (W3C).
2. The concept of multitude was further developed in Hardt and Negri (2004).
3. See http://geekfeminism.wikia.com/wiki/Geek_Feminism_Wiki.

References

Barnes, Peter. n.d. Cited in 'Trusts'. *P2P Foundation [wiki]*, last modified 4 July 2015. Available at http://p2pfoundation.net/Trusts (accessed 31 July 2015).

Bauman, Z. 2001. 'Consuming Life'. *Journal of Consumer Culture* 1 (1): 9–29.

Bauwens, M. (last modified 1 November 2014). 'Netarchical Capitalism'. *P2Pfoundation* [wiki]. Available at http://p2pfoundation.net/Netarchical_Capitalism (accessed 24 July 2015).

Bauwens, M., and J. Restakis. 2015. 'Introduction to the Commons Transition Plan'. In *Commons Transition: Policy Proposals for an Open Knowledge Commons Society*, Foundation for Peer-to-Peer Alternatives, 7–12. Amesterdam. Available at http://commonstransition.org/wp-content/uploads/2015/03/Commons-Transition_-Policy-Proposals-for-a-P2P-Foundation.pdf (accessed 24 July 2015).

Belli, L. 2015. 'A Heterostakeholder Cooperation for Sustainable Internet Policymaking'. *Internet Policy Review* 4 (2).

Berry, D. 2008. *Copy, Rip, Burn: The Politics of Copyleft and Open Source*. London: Pluto Press.

Biswas, S. 2010. 'India's Micro-finance Suicide Epidemic'. *BBC*. Available at http://www.bbc.com/news/world-south-asia-11997571 (accessed 1 August 2015).

Caffentzis, G. 2005. 'The End of Work or the Renaissance of Slavery?: A Critique of Rifkin and Negri'. *Multitudes: Revue Politique, Artistique, Philosophique*. Available at https://fadingtheaesthetic.files.wordpress.

com/2013/05/george-caffentzis-the-end-of-work-or-the-rennalssance-of-slavery-common-sense-24.pdf (accessed 13 May 2020).

———. 2010. 'The Future of "The Commons": Neoliberalism's "Plan B" or the Original Disaccumulation of Capital?'. *New Formations* 69: 23–41.

Castells, M. 2012. *Networks of Outrage and Hope: Social Movements in the Internet Age*. Cambridge: Polity Press.

Change.org. n.d. 'Business Model: A Business Model for Social Good'. *Change.org*. Available at https://www.change.org/en-AU/about/business-model (accessed 9 February 2016).

da Costa, A., and L. A. Silva Saraiva. 2012. 'Hegemonic Discourses on Entrepreneurship as an Ideological Mechanism for the Reproduction of Capital'. *Organisation* 19 (5): 587–614. Cited in M. Ampuja and J. Koivisto. 2014. 'From "Post-Industrial" to "Network Society" and Beyond: The Political Conjunctures and Current Crisis of Information Society Theory'. *tripleC* 12 (2): 447–63.

Davies, W. 2015. 'How Friendship Became a Tool of the Powerful'. *The Guardian*. Available at http://www.theguardian.com/media/2015/may/07/how-friendship-became-tool-of-powerful (accessed 31 July 2015).

De Angelis, M. 2009. 'The Tragedy of the Capitalist Commons'. *Turbulence*. Available at http://turbulence.org.uk/turbulence-5/capitalist-commons (accessed 24 July 2015).

———. n.d. 'Crises, Capital and Co-optation: Does Capital Need a Commons Fix'. *The Wealth of the Commons: A World Beyond Market and State*. Available at http://wealthofthecommons.org/essay/crises-capital-and-co-optation-does-capital-need-commons-fix (accessed 31 July 2015).

de Rosnay, M. D., and H. Le Crosnier. 2012. 'An Introduction to the Digital Commons: From Common-pool Resources to Community Governance'. Paper presented at the First Thematic Conference on the Knowledge Commons, Governing Pooled Knowledge Resources: Building Institutions for Sustainable Scientific, Cultural and Genetic Resource Commons, International Association for the Study of the Commons, Louvain-la-Neuve, Belgium. Available at http://biogov.uclouvain.be/iasc/doc/full papers/Dulong-LeCrosnier.pdf (accessed 24 July 2015).

Dewan, R. 2014. Paper presented at the International Conference on Labouring Women: Some Concerns at the Current Juncture, Centre for Informal Sector and Labour Studies, School of Social Sciences, Jawaharlal Nehru University, New Delhi, 31 July–1 August.

Diga, K., and N. Mbarathi. 2014. 'Discontinuities in M-banking and Development Policy: A Case Study of Women in Kenya's Agricultural Sector'. Paper presented at the Round Table on Inclusion in the

Network Society: Mapping Development Alternatives, Forging Research Agendas, Bengaluru, 29 September–1 October.

di Robilant. A. 2012. 'Common Ownership and Equality of Autonomy'. *McGill Law Journal* 58 (2): 263–320.

Dutta, S., T. Geiger and B. Lanvin. 2015. 'Executive Summary'. *The Global Information Technology Report 2015: ICTs for Inclusive Growth*. World Economic Forum, Geneva, *xiii–xix*.

Edwards, M. 2008. *Just Another Emperor? The Myths and Realities of Philanthrocapitalism*. New York: Demos. Cited in P. Dey and C. Steyaert. 2012. 'Social Entrepreneurship: Critique and the Radical Enactment of the Social'. *Social Enterprise Journal* 8 (2): 90–107.

Faltesek, D. 2013. 'Big Argumentation?'. *tripleC* 11 (2): 402–11. Available at http://www.triple-c.at/index.php/tripleC/article/view/464 (accessed 9 February 2016).

Federici, S. 2011. 'Feminism and the Politics of the Commons'. *Uzbuna*. Available at http://uzbuna.org/en/journal/conversations-new-feminisam-and-art/feminism-and-politics-commons (accessed 31 July 2015).

———. 2012. 'The Reproduction of Labour Power in the Global Economy and the Unfinished Feminist Revolution (2008)'. In *Revolution at Point Zero: Housework, Reproduction and Feminist Struggle*, ed. S. Federici, 91–111. Brooklyn: PM Press.

Flanagan, K. 2015. 'P2P Summer School: The Art of Commoning'. *P2P Foundation*. Available at http://blog.p2pfoundation.net/p2p-summer-school-the-art-of-commoning/2015/02/19 (accessed 31 July 2015).

Foster, J. B., and R. W. McChesney. 2011. 'The Internet's Unholy Marriage to Capitalism'. *Monthly Review* 62 (10). Available at http://monthlyreview.org/2011/03/01/the-internets-unholy-marriage-to-capitalism (accessed 24 July 2015).

Fuchs, C. 2010. 'New Imperialism: Information and Media Imperialism?'. *Global Media and Communication* 61 (1): 33–60.

Geek Feminism Wiki. Available at http://geekfeminism.wikia.com/wiki/Geek_Feminism_Wiki (accessed 10 March 2019).

Graham, M., B. Hogan, R. K. Straumann and A. Medhat. 2014. 'Uneven Geographies of User-generated Information: Patterns of Increasing Informational Poverty'. *Annals of the Association of American Geographers* 104 (4): 746–64.

Graham, M., V. Lehdonvirta, A. Wood, H. Barnard, I. Hjorth and D. P. Simon. 2017. 'The Risks and Rewards of Online Gig Work at the Global Margins'. *Oxford Internet Institute*. Available at https://www.oii.ox.ac.uk/publications/gigwork.pdf (accessed 19 March 2018).

Grimmelmann, J. 2010. 'The Internet is a Semicommons'. *Fordham Law Review* 78 (6): 2799–2842.

Gurumurthy, A., and N. Chami. 2014. 'Network Morals, Development Ethics: Some Empirical Explorations'. Paper presented at the Round Table on Inclusion in the Network Society: Mapping Development Alternatives, Forging Research Agendas, Bengaluru, 29 September–1 October.

Gurumurthy, A., N. Chami and S. Thomas. 2016. 'Unpacking Digital India: A Feminist Commentary on Policy Agendas in the Digital Moment'. *Journal of Information Policy,* special issue on Gendering Global Media Policy: Critical Perspectives on 'Digital Agendas'.

Hardin, G. 1968. 'The Tragedy of the Commons'. *Science* 162 (3859): 1243–48.

Hardt, M., and A. Negri. 2000. *Empire*. Massachusetts: Harvard University Press.

———. 2004. *Multitude: War and Democracy in the Age of Empire*. New York: The Penguin Press.

Hearn, A. 2010. 'Reality Television, *The Hills*, and the Limits of the Immaterial Labour Thesis'. *tripleC* 8 (1): 60–76.

Hochschild, A. R. 2000. 'Global Care Chains and Emotional Surplus Value'. In *On the Edge: Living with Global Capitalism,* ed. W. Hutton and A. Giddens, 130–46. London: Jonathan Cape.

Hodal, K. 2014. 'US Penalises Malaysia for Shameful Human Trafficking Record'. *The Guardian*. Available at http://www.theguardian.com/global-development/2014/jun/20/malaysia-us-human-trafficking-persons-report (accessed 4 August 2015).

Huws, U. 2014. *Labor in the Global Digital Economy. The Cybertariat Comes of Age*. New York: Monthly Review Press.

Iaccino, L. 2014. 'Witch Hunting in India: Poor, Low Caste and Widows Main Targets'. *IB Times*. Available at http://www.ibtimes.co.uk/witch-hunting-india-poor-low-caste-widows-main-targets-1457809 (accessed 1 August 2015).

Johnson, J. A. 2014. 'From Open Data to Information Justice'. *Ethics and Information Technology* 16: 263–74.

Lem, W. 2014. 'Materialist Feminism, Migration, and "Affective" Labor: Mediations in Capitalist Reproduction'. *FocaalBlog*. Available at http://www.focaalblog.com/2014/07/23/materialist-feminism-migration-and-affective-labor-mediations-in-capitalist-reproduction-winnie-lem/ (accessed 9 February 2016).

Mager, A. 2014. 'Defining Algorithmic Ideology: Using Ideology Critique to Scrutinise Corporate Search Engines'. *tripleC* 12 (1): 28–39.

Mapping the Commons. 2011. 'On Biopower and Biopolitics'. *Mapping the Commons* [blog]. Available at https://mappingthecommons.wordpress.com/2011/01/28/on-biopower-and-biopolitics/ (accessed 31 July 2015).

Molz, J. G. 2014. 'Toward a Network Hospitality'. *First Monday* 19 (3). Available at http://firstmonday.org/ojs/index.php/fm/article/view/4824/3848 (accessed 31 July 2015).

Morell, M. F. 2010. 'Governance of Online Creation Communities: Provision of Infrastructure for the Building of Digital Commons'. Doctoral dissertation, European University Institute. Available at http://www.onlinecreation.info/?page_id=338 (accessed 24 July 2015).

Morozov, E. 2015. 'Socialise the Data Centres!'. *New Left Review* 91. Available at http://newleftreview.org/II/91/evgeny-morozov-socialize-the-data-centres (accessed 31 July 2015).

Moser, S. 2015. 'New Cities: Old Wine in New Bottles?'. *Dialogues in Human Geography* 5 (1): 31–35.

Murdoch, L. 2014. 'Philippine Children Exploited in Billion-dollar Webcam Paedophilia Industry'. *The Sydney Morning Herald*. Available at http://www.smh.com.au/world/philippine-children-exploited-in-billiondollar-webcam-paedophilia-industry-20140708-zszsd.html (accessed 4 August 2015).

Nakamura, L. 2011. 'The Unwanted Labour of Social Media: Women of Colour Call Out Culture as Venture Community Management'. *New Formations* 106–12. Available at https://lnakamur.files.wordpress.com/2011/01/unwanted-labor-of-social-media-nakamura1.pdf (accessed 19 March 2018).

———. 2014. 'Indigenous Circuits: Navajo Women and the Racialisation of Early Electronic Manufacture'. *American Quarterly* 66 (4): 919–941.

Olma, S. 2014. 'Never Mind the Sharing Economy: Here's Platform Capitalism'. *MyCreativity* [blog]. Institute of Network Cultures. Available at http://networkcultures.org/mycreativity/2014/10/16/never-mind-the-sharing-economy-heres-platform-capitalism (accessed 27 July 2015).

Press Trust of India. 2015. '24,771 Dowry Deaths Reported in Last 3 Years: Govt'. *The Indian Express*. Available at http://indianexpress.com/article/india/india-others/24771-dowry-deaths-reported-in-last-3-years-govt/ (accessed 1 August 2015).

Prodnik, J. A. 2014. 'A Seeping Commodification: The Long Revolution in the Proliferation of Communication Commodities'. *tripleC* 12 (1):

142–68. Available at http://www.triple-c.at/index.php/tripleC/article/viewFile/485/532 (accessed 9 February 2016).

Raymond, M. 2012. 'The Internet as a Global Commons'. *CIGI: Series on Governing the Internet: Chaos, Control or Consensus?*. Available at https://www.cigionline.org/publications/2012/10/internet-global-commons (accessed 31 July 2015).

Rifkin, J. 2014. *The Zero Marginal Cost Society: The Internet of Things, the Collaborative Commons, and the Eclipse of Capitalism*. New York: Palgrave Macmillan.

Rigi, J. 2014. 'Foundations of a Marxist Theory of the Political Economy of Information: Trade Secrets and Intellectual Property, and the Production of Relative Surplus Value and the Extraction of Rent-tribute'. *tripleC* 12 (2): 909–36. Available at http://www.triple-c.at/index.php/tripleC/article/view/487 (accessed 9 February 2016).

Robertson, S. 2005. 'Re-imagining Economic Alterity: A Feminist Critique of the Juridical Expansion of Bioproperty in the Monsanto Decision at the Supreme Court of Canada'. *University of Ottawa Law and Technology Journal* 2 (2): 227–53. Available at http://www.uoltj.ca/articles/vol2.2/2005.2.2.uoltj.Robertson.227-253.pdf (accessed 27 July 2015).

Sen, G. 2005. 'Neolibs, Neocons and Gender Justice: Lessons from Global Negotiations'. Geneva: United Nations Research Institute for Social Development. Available at http://www.unrisd.org/80256B3C005BCCF9/(httpAuxPages)/15E6EA635E8A955BC12570B500357029/$file/OP9pdf.pdf (accessed 31 July 2015).

Sevilla-Buitrago, A. 2015. 'Capitalist Formations of Enclosure: Space and the Extinction of the Commons'. *Antipode* 1–22. Available at http://www.urbantheorylab.net/site/assets/files/1143/capitalist_formations_of_enclosure_antipode.pdf (accessed 31 July 2015).

Singh, P. J., and A. Gurumurthy. 2013. 'Establishing Public-ness in the Network: New Moorings for Development—A Critique of the Concepts of Openness and Open Development'. In *Open Development: Networked Innovations in International Development*, ed. M. L. Smith and K. M. A. Reilly, 173–96. Massachusetts: The MIT Press. Available at http://www.idrc.ca/EN/Resources/Publications/openebooks/541-1/index.html#ch07 (accessed 31 July 2015).

Stalder, F. 2010. 'Digital Commons: A Dictionary Entry'. *Notes and Nodes* [blog]. Available at http://felix.openflows.com/node/137 (accessed 24 July 2015).

Toupin, S., and A. Hache. 2015. 'Feminist Autonomous Infrastructures'. *Global Information Society Watch: Sexual Rights and the Internet.* Available at https://www.giswatch.org/en/internet-rights/feminist-autonomous-infrastructures (accessed 19 March 2018).

van Doorn, N. 2017. 'Platform Labor: On the Gendered and Racialised Exploitation of Low-income Service Work in the "On-demand" Economy'. *Information, Communication and Society* 20 (6): 898–914.

Notes on the Editors and Contributors

Vinoj Abraham is Professor, Centre for Development Studies, Thiruvananthapuram, Kerala.

Anjor Bhaskar is Assistant Professor, Azim Premji University, Bengaluru.

Ritu Dewan is former Director and Professor, Department of Economics (Autonomous), University of Mumbai.

Jayati Ghosh is Professor, Centre for Economic Studies, School of Social Sciences, Jawaharlal Nehru University, New Delhi.

Chirashree Das Gupta is Associate Professor, Centre for the Study of Law and Governance, Jawaharlal Nehru University, New Delhi.

Mohit Gupta is a research scholar at Centre for the Study of Law and Governance, Jawaharlal Nehru University, New Delhi.

Smita Gupta is an economist and activist. She works with the Adivasi Adhikar Rashtriya Manch and Centre for Adivasi Research and Development.

Anita Gurumurthy is Executive Director, IT for Change, an NGO working on digital technology and social justice.

Praveen Jha is Professor, Centre for Economic Studies and Planning, and Adjunct Professor, Centre for Informal Sector and Labour Studies, School of Social Sciences, Jawaharlal Nehru University, New Delhi.

Mary E. John is Professor and Senior Fellow, Centre for Women's Development Studies, New Delhi.

Kanika Kaul works with The Hunger Project. She was formerly with Centre for Budget and Governance Accountability, New Delhi.

Sumi Krishna is an independent scholar on gender, environment and development, and former President, Indian Association for Women's Studies (2005–08).

S. Krithi is Assistant Professor, School of Livelihoods and Development, Tata Institute of Social Sciences, Hyderabad.

Avinash Kumar is Assistant Professor, Centre for Informal Sector and Labour Studies, School of Social Sciences, Jawaharlal Nehru University, New Delhi.

Yamini Mishra is Director, Global Issues, Amnesty International, London, United Kingdom.

Neetha N. is Professor and Acting Director, Centre for Women's Development Studies, New Delhi.

Archana Prasad is Professor, Centre for Informal Sector and Labour Studies, School of Social Sciences, Jawaharlal Nehru University, New Delhi.

Isha Ralli is a research scholar at Department of Humanities and Social Sciences, Indian Institute of Technology, Bombay.

Nisha Srivastava is former Professor of Economics, University of Allahabad, Allahabad, and Visiting Professor, Institute for Human Development, Delhi.

Saumya Shrivastava works with IPE Global. She was formerly working with Centre for Budget and Governance Accountability, New Delhi.

Index